A Celebration of State Capitols

State Capitols

RICHARD R. GIBSON

Published by
Richard Gibson, Author

CapitolCelebrations.com   author@CapitolCelebrations.com

Managing Graphics Director: Bryant Gregory
Associate Graphic Artists: Ted Slater, Karen Glazener, David Hanson

Managing Editor: Motte Brown
Associate Editors: Julie Devine, Tom Neven, Carol Rusk, Gina Gregory, Beth Brown

Photography: Richard Gibson, except where acknowledged.

Cover photo: State of Washington Capitol
American flag, istockphoto
Back Cover photo: State of Illinois Capitol

ISBN: 978-0-615-27072-2

Printed in China.

PLAN OF
PROJECTED CAPITO
WASHING

Acknowledgment of State Reviewers

The author wishes to gratefully acknowledge the assistance of the following individuals who served as reviewers of their state's draft of the text and provided corrections and/or made suggestions.

STATE REVIEWERS

AL	Robert S. Gamble	Senior Architectural Historian, Alabama Historical Commission
	Melanie Betz	Former Curator, Alabama Historical Commission
AK	Chris Wyatt	Administrative Assistant, Executive Director's Office
	Steve Henrikson	Curator of Collections, Alaska State Museum
AR	Dr. David Ware	Capitol Historian, Arkansas Secretary of State's Office
	Judi Dietz	Tours Director
AZ	Michael D. Carman	Arizona Capitol Museum Division Director
CA	Vito Sgromo	Curator, California State Capitol Museum
CO	Edna Pelzmann	Manager of Visitor Services, Colorado State Capitol
CT	Jill Cromwell	Director, Capitol Information and Tours
DE	Richard B. Carter	Chief Administrative Assistant, Delaware State Senate Majority Caucus
	Beverly Laing	Site Supervisor, Delaware State Museum
	James Stewart	Administrator, Delaware State Museum
FL	Andrew N. Edel	Exhibit Projects Manager
GA	Timothy Frilingos	Museum Services Manager, Georgia Capitol Museum
	Dorothy Olson	Former Capitol Museum Director
HI	"Uncle Joe" Tassill	Tour Coordinator, Governor's Office of Information
ID	Linda Morton-Keithley, CA	Administrator, Public Archives and Research Library
IL	Mark W. Sorensen	President, Illinois State Historical Society
IN	Jennifer Hodge	Coordinator, Capitol Tour Office
IA	Joan Arnett	Tour Guide Supervisor
KS	Andrea Burton, M.A.	Capitol Tour Coordinator, Kansas Historical Society
KY	David L. Buchta, MHP	Director and State Curator, Kentucky Division of Historic Properties
	Paul Gannoe	Former State Curator
LA	Faye Tillery	Supervisor, State Capitol Tours
ME	Earle G. Shettleworth, Jr.	State Historian
MD	Elaine Bachmann	Director of Artistic Property
MA	Mary Rinehart	Director, State House Tours and Government Education Division
MI	Kerry Chartkoff	Michigan State Capitol Historian
MN	Brian Pease	Site Manager, Minnesota Historical Society
MS	Brenda Davis	Architectural Historian, Mississippi State Capitol
MO	L.T. Shelton	Curator of Collections
MT	David A Walter	Research Historian
NE	Robert C. Ripley	Capitol Administrator
NV	Ronald M. James	State Historic Preservation Officer
NH	Virginia Drew	Director, The State House Visitor Center
	James Garvin	State Architectural Historian
	Kenneth E. Leidner	Director, State House Visitors Center
NJ	Philip A. Hayden	Tour Program Coordinator
	Penny Gardner	Programs Manager, New Jersey State Legislature Office of Legislative Services
NM	Dr. Estevan Rael-Gálvez	New Mexico State Historian, State Commission of Public Records
	Christal J. Benavidez	Legislative Information and Tours
NY	Stuart W. Lehman	Education Coordinator, New York State Capitol Tour Program, New York State Office of General Services
NC	Raymond Beck	Historian, North Carolina State Capitol
ND	Terry Medler	Capitol Tour Guide, North Dakota Facility Management
OH	Gregg Dodd	Deputy Director for Communications, Marketing and Events, Capitol Square Review and Advisory Board
	Mike Rupert	Communications Specialist, Capitol Square Review and Advisory Board
	Chris Matheny	Historic Site Manger, Capitol Square Review and Advisory Board
OK	Jolane Reimer	Manager, Capitol Information Center
	Edward H. Cook	Director of Development, Oklahoma Centennial Commission
OR	Layne Sawyer	Manager of Reference Services
PA	Jason L. Wilson	Historian, Pennsylvania Capitol Preservation Committee
RI	Thomas R. Evans	State Librarian, Rhode Island State Library
SC	Daniel Elswick	Senior Historic Architecture Consultant
	Andrew W. Chandler	Architectural Historian
SD	Harold H. Schuler	Author — *South Dakota Capitol in Pierre*
TN	James A. Hoobler	Curator of the Capitol, State of Tennessee
TX	Alice Turley	Curator of the Capitol
	Douglas Young	Design Manager
UT	Kent Powell, Ph.D.	Historian, Utah State Historical Society
VT	David Schütz	State Curator
VA	Mark Greenough	Capitol Historian and Tour Supervisor, Capitol Guided Tours, Commonwealth of Virginia
	Jim Wootton	Executive Director, Capitol Square Preservation Council
WA	Richard Emde	Tour Services Coordinator
WV	Debra Basham	Archivist, West Virginia Archives and History
WI	Claire Franz	Capitol Tour Manager
	James Schaff	Lead Tour Guide
	Jerilyn Schneider	Capitol Tour Leadworker
WY	Velma P. Sierra	Capitol Information Specialist
	Julia A. Sargent	Former Capitol Information Specialist

Other Credits and Identification of Photos

The author further wishes to thank and acknowledge the following individuals/agencies for their assistance or photos provided.

OTHER CREDITS

Use of images:
American Numismatic Association, ALPCA (American License Plate Collector's Association-Rocky Mountain Region), Affordable Flags & Fireworks, Inc., Fort Carson - The Mountain Post, Hallenbeck Coin Gallery, Inc., Jeff Richardson, NASA, John Cranor, T. H. Benton/VAGA, New York, NY, Oscar Mooneyham ("in character" Civil War uniformed soldiers), Howard Noble - Pikes Peak Trolley Museum

Consulting:
Cathy Ziegler, Appraisals by Ron Theisman

Use of article as basis for story:
Nashville Historical Newsletter/Ted Guillaum

PHOTOGRAPH CREDITS

All photographs © Richard Gibson except those provided by:

p. 23 - Arizona, Saguaro flower	Kathy Darrow
p. 112 - Montana, Glacier Park	Wayne Tobiasz
p. 175 - South Dakota, Pasque flower	Kathy Darrow
p. 183 - Texas, Bluebonnet flower	Michael A. Murphy/TxDOT
p. 211 - Wyoming, train	Wayne Tobiasz
p. 235 - Governor Mansions - TN	State of Tennesseee Photo Services
Timeline train photos	Wayne Tobiasz
Civil War re-enactments	Wayne Tobiasz
Timeline: 1750 revolver	Dr. David C. Andersen
Timeline: 1670 English lantern clock	Dr. David C. Andersen

PHOTO IDENTIFICATION

(Scene photo shown at bottom left corner of first page for each state)

AL	Shrimp boat on Gulf Coast
AK	Mendenhall Glacier
AZ	Grand Canyon
AR	Lake Conway
CA	Golden Gate Bridge
CO	Pikes Peak and Garden of the Gods
CT	Old Saybrook Lighthouse
DE	Countryside barn near Dover
FL	Cypress Gardens
GA	Atlanta skyline at dusk
HI	Nawiliwili Harbor in Kauai
ID	Shoshone Falls
IL	Farm scene with horse near Sylvan Lake
IN	Indy race car
IA	Roseman Covered Bridge of Madison County
KS	Pioneer wagon with sunflowers
KY	Kentucky Derby and horse farm
LA	Louisiana swamp
ME	Pemaquid Point Lighthouse in Bristol
MD	Annapolis harbor
MA	Old North Church and historic Boston
MI	Sunrise toward Mackinac Island
MN	Countryside pond and farm
MS	Paddle wheel boat
MO	St. Louis Arch and Mississippi River
MT	Glacier National Park
NE	Chimney Rock
NV	Las Vegas and casino
NH	Lake and boats
NJ	Sea Girt Beach
NM	Palace of Governors
NY	Niagara Falls
NC	Wright Brother's plane
ND	Buffalo at Teddy Roosevelt National Park
OH	Amish horse and buggy
OK	Oil well and oil derrick
OR	Mt. Hood
PA	Civil War Re-enactment
RI	Newport harbor
SC	Palmetto tree at the State House
SD	Mt. Rushmore
TN	Country music band and electric guitar
TX	Texas Longhorn
UT	Delicate Arch
VT	Covered bridge
VA	Williamsburg coach and Old State House
WA	Mt. Ranier Park waterfalls
WV	Glade Creek Grist Mill
WI	Geese over lake near Oconto Falls
WY	Devils Tower

"That the buildings and art of a people are the expression of their

Contents

religion, their morality, their national inspirations, and social habits."
John Ruskin (English writer and art critic — 1819 - 1900)

Foreword

Like Victorian ladies in fine dresses, state capitols are often adorned with the finest materials that their state could afford when they were built. They are the grand dames of democracy. Each one shows her beauty in distinct and inimitable ways. The state capitols and statehouses are the homes of the legislatures. They are "the people's house" and they belong to the citizens of their state. Inside their walls, citizens may not only observe, but also participate in the democratic process.

State capitols are beautiful structures that reflect the personality of the state and its founders. No two capitols are the same, even though some shared the same architects. But time is the enemy, and it has taken its toll on many statehouses and capitols across the country. Over the past 10 years, we have seen several states, such as Kansas, Nebraska, Utah and Virginia rally behind their renowned capitol buildings to make sure their unique natures, differences and history are preserved for future generations. That is why getting to know every capitol is such a treat.

I've been studying state legislatures for the National Conference of State Legislatures, and the capitols and statehouses where they work, for more than 20 years. I feel fortunate to have had the opportunity to visit nearly every capitol. Because I study how space in capitols is used, I have seen a side the public never sees. I've ventured into the attics above legislative chambers and peered down at the legislative members while workmen replaced ceiling lights. I've wandered through cavernous tunnels and seen the wires sagging like limp spaghetti as they wended their way beneath the floors. I've even swung out high atop a capitol building and touched a golden dome. Yet for all of the amazing opportunities I've had to see these buildings up close, I am very envious of Richard Gibson. He has traveled to every capitol and statehouse. He has walked the halls, talked to historians, and thumbed through archives to give us a sense of these amazing buildings. In these pages, he spreads out his scrapbook of state histories, postcards and photographs so we can all share in his journey.

Most of us don't have the opportunity to learn about each state's quest for statehood, yet these stories are remarkable. A brief description of that quest is presented for each state and paired with other short stories and anecdotes about the history and the quirks that make each state one-of-a-kind. Gibson explains how the capital city was selected and what the legislature's role was in choosing the location. Because each state and capitol are unique, the information collected here is varied and highlights the individuality of the people and the buildings.

Perusing these pages, you will discover that Richard Gibson has taken the time to learn each of these great ladies' stories, and he shares their secrets with us.

Kae M. Warnock
Policy Specialist
National Conference of State Legislatures

Dedication

This book has been a long and arduous journey from time of conception to publication. Through it all, I have seen my two daughters grow up and have kids of their own. Over the years, I have traveled thousands of miles, stayed in countless motels, and obtained resource materials from capitols, internet sources, libraries and antique shops. My cameras have been used to take several thousand photos and have migrated from film to the digital age. I have accumulated an enviable collection of vintage capitol postcards, photos and memorabilia. Hours and hours of writing and re-writing have gone into this project. I have endured one computer crash. There have been times of frustration, times of disappointment and times I wanted to give up. Yet, through persistence and much prayer, it has finally become a reality. Some familiar with the project have termed this book a "labor of love."

That being said, I wish to whole heartedly express my appreciation to the many capitol tour guides, managers and coordinators; curators, historians, archivists and museum directors as well as other titles not mentioned. I sincerely appreciate their assistance in providing resource materials and the giving of their time, expertise and input in reviewing portions of this book. Without their assistance and authoritative knowledge of details and truth from fiction, this book would not be what it is today. To those gifted individuals who have been instruments in carrying on the history and assuring stories reflect the truth about the capitols, I dedicate this book.

Additionally, there is one other person worthy of mention. That person has accompanied me on many a capitol trip — though there were many trips that I "struck out" on my own and for that she is probably thankful. My wife, Ella, has watched this project develop over a good part of our married life. I'm sure she had doubts that it would ever be finished. In 2001, after several years of mis-diagnosis, she was diagnosed with early onset of Alzheimer's disease. That too has been a long journey for both of us. Several years ago when she could still communicate, she told me she wanted to see the book finished before she died. As her mind withered away and my attention was drawn to her care, it became more and more challenging for me to focus on the book and keep "plugging away." There were times when I thought she was hanging on just to see it finished. Although she is now confined to an assisted living home, is under hospice care and doesn't always know who I am, I wish to thank her for sticking it out and believing in me. I think she would be honored and pleased to have this book dedicated to her. She deserves it!

CAPITOL AVE Timeline

1700

1705 - WILLIAMSBURG, VA

1713 - BOSTON, MA

1736 - PHILADELPHIA, PA

1762 - NEWPORT, RI

1876 - SALEM, OR

1871 - CARSON CITY, NV

1900

1899 - ALBANY, NY

1878 - LANSING, MI

1888 - AUSTIN, TX

1977 - TALLAHASSEE, FL

1969 - HONOLULU, HI

2000

1974 - PHOENIX, AZ

1966 - SANTA FE, NM

1778 - RICHMOND, VA

1792 - TRENTON, NJ

1779 - ANNAPOLIS, MD

1796 - HARTFORD, CT

1800

1857 - COLUMBUS, OH

1819 - CONCORD, NH

1845 - TALLAHASSEE, FL

1851 - NASHVIELE, TN

1825 - CORYDON, IN

1840 - RALEIGH, NC

VOTES FOR WOMEN June 5th

REPEAL PROHIBITION

NO 10-324

KEEP COOL WITH COOLIDGE

AL AND JOE LET'S GO

RE-ELECT HOOVER SPEED RECOVERY

BABE RUTH

WIN WITH TAFT

WIN WITH WILSON

1915 - LITTLE ROCK, AR

1904 - ST. PAUL, MN

PENNA 1915 117447

1932 - LINCOLN, NE

1935 - BISMARCK, ND

I LIKE IKE

STEVENSON

KENNEDY

U.S. AIR FORCE

U.S. MOURNS SLAIN PRESIDENT

EVERY BUDDY WILLKIE US

ROOSEVELT

U-784-R OHIO 38

NO THIRD TERM

1955 S DAK 1-1510

DEWEY

23-1369 KANSAS 42

1938 - SALEM, OR

11

ALABAMA
Montgomery

A CIVIL PLACE ...
A LANDMARK OF HISTORY
The Civil War and the Civil Rights Movement both trace their roots to this site.

"*We dare defend our rights.*"

BRUNI KAREN

★ Facts & Figures

Architectural style	Greek Revival
Architect	Daniel Pratt (attributed to)
Exterior material	Brick covered with stucco
Dome surface	Terne coated metal covered with an elastomeric coating
Building height (to tip of dome)	120'
Construction period	1850-1851
First occupied	1851
Capital population (Census 2000)	201,568
Census estimate 2007	204,086
Direction capitol faces	West
Original cost	$64,000

The Past Remembered

NEW PHILADELPHIA

Years before a capital was considered, Andrew Dexter, a town developer who moved to Alabama from Massachusetts, staked out an undeveloped area of land that he envisioned would be the seat of state government. In 1817, he persuaded investors to purchase this tract of land. It became known as New Philadelphia. The property included a high knoll which overlooked the Alabama River. While plotting sites for this tract of land, Dexter had the foresight to set aside this high knoll for a state house. As New Philadelphia grew, it was merged with a nearby village and together became known as Montgomery.

GOAT HILL

To this day, the capitol is often referred to as Goat Hill, especially among staff members.

However, the origin of the nickname is uncertain. Records from the early days do show that goats and other animals were allowed to graze the grounds. But when or what prompted the name Goat Hill is not known.

FULFILLING THE VISION

As noted, Dexter's vision was to see a state house built on the high knoll overlooking the Alabama River. Although Dexter did not live to see his dream fulfilled, an elegant Greek Revival style state house designed by Stephen D. Button was built upon the high knoll in 1847, a year after the state capital was relocated from Tuscaloosa to Montgomery. In 1850, this building was destroyed by fire. However, the state wasted no time in constructing a new state house, the one that stands today on the same site. Although the architectural style remained the same, the design is attributed to Daniel Pratt.

GREEK REVIVAL II

In 1852, a large box-shaped clock was given to the state. It was mounted on the roof of the capitol and placed in front of the dome even though the architectural style of the state house is Greek Revival. Although the clock is unique among capitols, it is not considered a welcome sight by all. It has been referred to by some as looking like a "big outhouse." A former Director of Archives and History once remarked, "Original Greek edifices do not commonly have clocks." But unique it is, and it certainly sets this capitol apart.

SPROUTING WINGS

Over the years the State has added annexes to the capitol in every direction except the west. Beginning in 1885 an East wing was added, followed by the South wing in 1906, then the North wing in 1912 and a second East wing in 1992.

A DOUBLE FUNERAL

The first White House of the Confederacy was located in Montgomery. At one time, Jefferson Davis, the President of the Confederacy, resided there. When Davis died, he was initially buried in New Orleans. Three years later, it was determined that his final resting place would more appropriately be in Richmond, the capitol of the Confederacy. Thus, Davis was given two funerals—three years apart. While en route to Richmond, the train carrying his body stopped in several cities including Montgomery to allow Alabamans to pay tribute to their fallen leader.

A nine-foot, bronze statue of Jefferson Davis stands in front of the capitol.

In February 1861, delegates from the Southern states met in this room, the Old Senate chamber, to draft the Confederate Constitution.

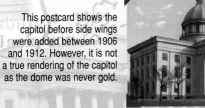

This postcard shows the capitol before side wings were added between 1906 and 1912. However, it is not a true rendering of the capitol as the dome was never gold.

Side view of the capitol shortly after completion of the south wing in 1907

A photo postcard c. 1920 shows an early view of the capitol.

Historical Happenings

1800 — 1900

1819	1849	1851	1861	1885
President Monroe grants statehood	Fire destroys first state house on site	Capitol completed (central portion)	Alabama seceeds from Union	East wing added

The top of the dome is 120' above the rotunda floor.

★ The Inside Story

THE MURALS STORY

Eight murals depicting Alabama history encircle the interior dome ceiling. The murals were painted by Scottish immigrant Roderick Mackenzie. He received $7,500 for his work, but most of the money was spent on materials. Completed in 1930, the artist is credited with establishing the color scheme present in the capitol.

SEEING DOUBLE

Immediately past the entryway are two beautiful, twin-spiral staircases. Each staircase ascends two flights to the third floor. From the first floor, they appear to be unsupported. However, a cantilever technique was used in which the staircase was nailed from underneath. This dramatic construction is attributed to Horace King, who also was an accomplished builder of covered bridges. Horace, an African-American, was born as a slave and learned his trade from his master who happened to be an engineer and bridge builder. Not only was Horace an accomplished engineer, he was also elected to the Alabama State Legislature in 1868.

Visitors are greeted by twin spiral staircases.

1912
North wing
completed

1965
Martin Luther King
declares: *"I have a dream!"*

1985
Legislature moves
to new building

1992
$60 million
renovation completed

2000

★ Claim to Fame

THE "AVENUE OF FLAGS"

Unique among state capitols, flags of the fifty states line the curved walkway leading to the capitol. At the base of each flagpole is a native stone from that state. In the late spring and summer, blooms of the crape myrtle trees add a special accent to this scenic walkway.

STANDING IN THE GAP

Two significant, historic events occurred on the steps of the Alabama capitol. The first was in 1861 when Jefferson Davis accepted the oath of office as President of the Confederacy. A century later, in 1965, the much acclaimed Civil Rights march led by Dr. Martin Luther King Jr. which began in Selma, Alabama, culminated on the steps of the capitol.

Crape-myrtle trees at the state house

This six-pointed brass star marks the spot where Jefferson Davis took the oath of office as President of the Confederate States of America in 1861.

The "Avenue of Flags."

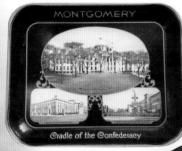

A serving tray declares the "Cradle of the Confederacy."

★ For What it's Worth

IT'S ABOUT TIME!

Etched on the wooden wall inside the clock on the roof is a hand written note with the date "Febr 9th 1852." It also states, "This clock was presented to Ala. by the City of Montgomery."

A snow globe depicts the state house.

Perched in front of the dome, this landmark clock provides a unique feature to the state house.

The hand-etched words inside the clock.

ALASKA
Juneau

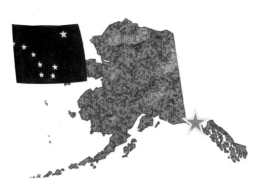

JEWEL OF ALASKA

Built as a territorial capitol in Southeast Alaska, the capital in Juneau has survived relocation efforts despite greater population growth in Alaska's interior.

"North to the future"

★ Facts & Figures

Architectural style	Modern
Architect	James A. Wetmore w/U.S. Treasury Dept.
Exterior material	Brick faced concrete and limestone
Dome surface	None
Building height	97'
Construction period	1929-31
First occupied	1931
Capital population (Census 2000)	30,711
Census estimate 2007	30,690
Direction capitol faces	South
Original cost	$1,000,000

★ The Past Remembered

TWO CENTS WORTH

The purchase of Alaska from Russia in 1867 — formally known as the "Treaty of Cession of Russian America to the United States" — was negotiated by William Seward, U.S. Secretary of State, for $7.2 million. This equates to less than two cents an acre. For several years, exploration was limited and skeptics considered the transaction a bad deal. The purchase became known as Seward's Folly.

However, that opinion drastically changed with the discovery of gold in 1880 in an area that became known as Juneau. Ultimately, Alaska turned out to be a land more vast and beautiful, and more rich in natural resources than the Russians or Americans had ever imagined.

BLACK GOLD

Upon hearing of the prospect of "gold in them thar hills," prospector Joe Juneau relocated his quest for gold to the area that would later bear his name. By the 1940s, the mines in the Juneau area alone had yielded over $150 million! However, this figure hardly compares with the wealth generated by the oil discovery in northern Alaska in the 1970s. During the oil boom, Alaska had the highest per capita income of any state.

WILLOW WEEP FOR ME

Juneau was the most populated city in 1900, replacing Sitka as the District Capital. As Alaska developed, the population center shifted toward its interior near Anchorage. This growing populous began pressuring the legislature to relocate the capital closer to the Alaskan interior.

In 1960, shortly after statehood, the issue first appeared on the ballot but was defeated. It was defeated again in 1962. Finally in 1974, the measure passed and two years later Alaskans selected a small town named Willow, about 70 miles north of Anchorage, for the location of the capital.

Although plans were drawn by a San Francisco firm, the price was more than Alaskans were willing to pay. The voters reversed their initial vote and Juneau remained the capital. Refusing to give up, proponents of a move propose motions to relocate in nearly every legislative session.

UNINTENDED CAPITOL

Alaska's capitol was constructed as a multi-purpose building. Never intended to be a state capitol, it has served as the library, post office, museum, archives, courtrooms, Alaska Communications System and the Alaska Territorial Building. When the building's construction was completed in 1931, the inscription on the front of the building read "Federal and Territorial Office Building." Today, the inscription reads, "Alaska State Capitol."

Although the building's appearance — a six story office building — does not rival most traditional capitol architecture, the city is wedged between a scenic mountain range and Gastineau Channel, part of the Inside Passage to Southeast Alaska. What the Alaska Capitol lacks in terms of architectural beauty, it makes up for in its unrivaled setting and background as evidenced by the influx of tourists each summer. In fact, summer tourism is so high that the city is studying the negative impact of this trend on its pristine, yet delicate, environment.

VANISHING HOPES

After years of dealing with the inadequacies of a make-shift capitol and in an attempt to solidify Juneau as the permanent capital, the City and Borough of Juneau held a design contest for a new capitol in 2005. The concept selected included a 150-foot glass dome but was generally not well received by Alaskans. Although the city acquired additional land as a site for the new capitol and has broken ground for a parking structure, there is no sight of a new capitol. Due to the lack of funding by the legislature, the plans stalled in 2008 and the City put the project on hold — at least for now.

A NORTHWEST MIGRATION

In recent years, the functional center of government has gradually migrated northwest of Juneau to Alaska's largest city — Anchorage. With the election of Sarah Palin as Governor in 2006 and without fanfare, Governor Palin is the first to choose not to live in the governor's mansion and the first to allow the cabinet to live outside of Juneau. In an effort to be more accessible to the bulk of Alaskans, Governor Palin maintains an office in Anchorage and most of her commissioners are located near the population center away from Juneau. However, the legislature continues to meet in Juneau during the ninety days they are in session. Whether Alaska ultimately decides to relocate its capital to the northwest or whether a new capitol in Juneau is built remains to be seen.

Across the street from the capitol is this life-size casting of a brown bear entitled "Windfall Fisherman" by Juneau sculptor R.T. "Skip" Wallen.

A "Get Out the Vote Campaign" during 1982, circulated "money" sponges and plastic-coated magnets to encourage voters to vote "no" on the capital relocation issue.

VOTE NO ☒ WILLOW

The four pillars in the portico are made of Tokeen marble, native to southeastern Alaska. It took two years to construct these pillars.

Pearls of Wisdom
"This Alaska is a great country. If they can just keep from being taken over by the U.S., they got a great future."

Will Rogers — August 13, 1935
On a visit to Alaska just two days before the fatal plane crash that took his life

Historical Happenings

1800

1900

1867
U.S. purchases
Alaska from Russia

1880
Gold discovered on
Gastineau Channel by Joe
Juneau; Juneau founded

1898
The Klondike/Yukon
Gold Rush

1911
Congress approves
funding for a capitol

1931
Capitol
completed

The original Senate chamber
has stenciled ceilings.

This
unique state
seal emblem
is on display.

A stone-fired clay mural,
c. 1930, features native
Alaskan hunters.

★ The Inside Story

MUSEUM QUALITY

Alaskans are proud of their history and have artistically transformed ordinary hallways into a museum atmosphere. Historic photographs, newspapers and artwork are on display throughout the halls of the capitol.

EUROPEAN INFLUENCE

As noted, the capitol was designed to house various governmental offices. Originally, the floors of the building were simply numbered one through six with the Post Office occupying the second floor. Because the building was built on a slope, the 2nd floor was street accessible.

A mandate from the U.S. Post Office noted that although the Post Office was street accessible, it needed to be located on the first floor. To comply, the floors were renumbered using the European method of counting floors. In this case, the lowest level became the "ground floor" followed by the first floor, second floor, etc.

LOBBY ART

The marble sculpture, "Two Alaskan Otters," greets visitors entering the capitol. These were sculptured in memory of the thousands of sea animals which were killed as a result of the Exxon Valdez oil spill in 1989. There is also a frieze (or wall painting) in the lobby area just below the ceiling featuring gold painted designs with a dark blue background. The designs include symbols of Alaskan life, forests and mining. Although igloos are also shown, native Alaskan Eskimos used these only as temporary shelters.

On each side of the lobby, stone fired clay murals that give the appearance of wood carvings depict Alaskan hunters and fishermen.

The lobby area features brass doors, marble sculptures and other works of art.

1959
newspapers
triumphantly
proclaim
statehood
for the
49th state.

BIRDS AND LEGISLATORS FLY SOUTH

Each January, as the legislature convenes, lawmakers migrate from the north — namely the Anchorage, Fairbanks and bush areas. Mostly arriving by air, they temporarily take up residence in Juneau to attend the legislative session which usually ends in May.

A unique
door handle

1941 Alaska attacked by the Japanese and becomes part of WWII Pacific Front

1959 President Eisenhower grants statehood

1974 Voters approve capital move initiative

1976 Voters select Willow as new capital site

1982 Voters repeal relocation of capital

2000

2005 Architect for a new capitol chosen

★ Claim to Fame

CAN'T GET THERE FROM HERE

Juneau is the only capital city, other than Honolulu, that is inaccessible by road. The east is bordered by water and the west hails mountains with no road access. At present, the main highway extends about five miles south and dead ends 35 miles north of the city. Thus, travel to Juneau is restricted to flying or taking the "marine highway," a ferry that accommodates vehicles. Some residents are advocating that the highway be extended, making it more accessible to all.

MILES AND MILES WITH NO PLACE TO GO

Despite its few roads, Juneau boasts the largest area of land of any capital in the United States. The City and Borough of Juneau encompasses over 3,100 square miles. In contrast, the city itself has only about 60 miles of paved road.

A corner view of the capitol highlights the unique "U-shape" of the building.

END ROAD 1000 FT

★ For What it's Worth

JUST FOR THE HALIBUT

One of the historic photos on display in the capitol is a picture of a 400 pound halibut — a record catch at the time. However, since then, larger catches have been recorded.

CHECK PLEASE

Once the check (Treasury Warrant), dated August 10, 1868, for the purchase of Alaska by the U.S. was returned as paid, it was placed in the National Archives in Washington, D.C. A copy resides at the Alaska State Museum in Juneau.

CAPITOL INVESTMENT

When Congress appropriated funds to purchase land for a future capitol building, only half the required funds were allotted. In response to the shortage, Juneau's citizens raised donations to make up the additional $23,000 necessary to acquire the land.

19

ARIZONA
Phoenix

WHERE COPPER IS KING

Built before statehood, Arizona's original capitol was modestly constructed. Years later, wings were added and the dome was upgraded to copper. Ultimately, the building was relegated to museum status, flanked by the new capitol.

"God enriches"

Facts & Figures

	Capitol Museum	Executive Tower
Architectural Style	Neo-classical	High rise
Architect	James R. Gordon	Varney, Sexton Sydnor & Associates
Exterior material	Tuff stone and gray granite	Pre-cast concrete panels
Dome surface	Copper	N/A
Building height (to tip of dome)	92'	136'
Construction period	1899-1901	1973-74
First occupied	1900	1974
Capital population (Census 2000)		1,321,045
Census estimate 2007		1,552,259
Direction capitol faces	East	West
Original cost	$135,774	$18,250,221

The Past Remembered

THANKS, BUT NO THANKS

When Arizona's first capitol was occupied in 1900, Arizona had not yet achieved statehood. At that time it was known as the Arizona Territory. Statehood was on the minds of legislators who hoped their newly completed capitol would present a more "stately" appearance.

An attempt in 1906 to ratify Arizona and New Mexico as one state failed to garner enough votes from Arizona citizens. Finally in 1912, statehood was granted and the already constructed building became the state capitol of the last of the original 48 states.

TOWER OF POWER

As many people flocked to the Sunbelt over the years, Arizona's population increased significantly. State government continued to grow as well, creating the need for more office space.

In 1960, Senate and House legislative buildings were added adjacent to the Old Capitol. Although visitors are naturally drawn to the Old Capitol, now serving as a "living museum," the Governor's office is located in the Executive Tower. The new capitol, completed 1974 is nine stories high and connects to the Old Capitol.

WE DEMAND A RECOUNT

Close elections and challenges by losing candidates have occurred many times throughout U.S. history. Arizona is no exception. In 1916, the vote was so close in a gubernatorial election (within 30 votes), the State faced a "no decision" when neither candidate would concede defeat. Although the challenger claimed victory, the incumbent governor, George Hunt, refused to admit defeat. Hunt was convinced that he was the victor and refused to surrender the governor's office.

Not to be denied, the "new governor," Tom Campbell, set up an office in his home. Each man carried on as though he were the winner. To make matters more confusing, the State held two inaugurations and two State of the State addresses!

Wax figure of Governor Hunt

Later, a judge ruled that Campbell had won. But in 1917, the ruling was overturned by the State Supreme Court, giving the governorship back to Hunt. In all, Governor Hunt eventually served seven, two-year terms. The admiration for Governor Hunt is acknowledged at the capitol with a wax figure in his likeness, displayed in the Capitol Museum.

Although the original ceilings were stenciled, a description or drawings of the stencil detail were never found. At the time the capitol was converted to a museum, the artist who painted these stencils used his imagination in creating a "jackalope" (a fictitious cross between a jack rabbit and an antelope). Deer and other animals are also depicted on the ornate ceiling. Today, these colorful insets are considered a spoof of the original stenciling as the original details are only conjectured.

"Jackalope"

State Capitol, Phoenix, Arizona.

A tiny palm tree, just in front of the capitol and barely noticeable, was said to have been planted when the building was first completed.

State Capitol, Arizona

An early postcard showing a tin dome before it was painted a reddish copper color. In 1976, the dome was covered with copper.

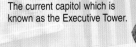

The current capitol which is known as the Executive Tower.

Pearls of Wisdom

"In purely State affairs the State is supreme, and the people of the State should have the absolute right to determine just how they wish their judicial system conducted."

Theodore Roosevelt —1910
In a speech made at the capitol

Historical Happenings

1800

1863
Congress creates
Territory of Arizona

1881
Gunfight at
Tombstone's
O.K. Corral

1900
Old capitol
completed

1900

1903
Capitol sustains
fire damage

The inner dome.

★ The Inside Story

THE FIVE "C's"

There is a mosaic of the Great Seal of the State in the rotunda. Although picturesque, the mosaic is missing a portion of official state symbolism. The seal shows three of the five "C's" which represent Arizona. Depicted are a <u>c</u>opper miner, a blue sky symbolizing the <u>c</u>limate and <u>c</u>otton rows indicating the importance of this crop to Arizonians. Missing from the official state seal is <u>c</u>attle and <u>c</u>itrus. Although this seal is incomplete, most other representations correctly portray the official seal.

CAN'T TAKE THE HEAT?

A unique feature of the House and Senate galleries is the use of "bull's eye" windows. The architect, obviously aware of the unforgiving heat of the Arizona sun, designed round windows – similar to portholes – that can be opened to allow cooler air to enter while hot air escapes through a large skylight.

Note the porthole windows.

A 1991 photo shows decorative bunting draped from the balconies on each floor of the rotunda area, creating somewhat of a kaleidoscope effect. The bunting was later removed due to safety concerns.

A beautiful, yet incomplete, mosaic portrays the state seal (see story).

DITAT DEUS

GREAT SEAL OF THE STATE OF ARIZONA

1912

1906 — Joint statehood with New Mexico rejected by Arizona

1912 — President Taft grants statehood to Arizona

1924 — Citizenship granted to Native Americans

1960 — House & Senate move to new buildings

1974 — Executive Tower completed

1981 — Old capitol restored as a museum; dome fully coppered

2000

★ Claim to Fame

CACTUS GARDEN

A unique cactus garden with many native cacti is featured on the grounds of the capitol. Most notable is the Saguaro, often referred to as a giant cactus. It is native only to the Sonoran Desert and is the largest species of cactus in the U.S. With a 200 year life-span, the tree-like cactus can grow to be over fifty feet tall and weigh over five tons. No other capitol rivals such a unique display of cacti. The saguaro blossom, which blooms for less than twenty-four hours, is the state flower.

COPPERTONE

The Old Capitol has the only copper-colored dome among current state capitols. In 1976, an initiative to cover the dome with native copper culminated with miners from Arizona donating enough copper to cover the dome. Although other capitols also have copper domes, Arizona is the only one that has a true copper color. In addition to the dry climate helping to prevent the copper from turning green, the polyurethane sealant is the primary reason the dome has held its color.

THE WINDS OF CHANGE

At the crest of the egg-shaped copper dome stands a sixteen-foot, pure white winged statue. Known as the "Victory Lady" or "Winged Victory," she holds a wreath in one hand symbolizing victory and in the other hand is a torch symbolizing liberty. The statue is more than just ornamental, it is also a wind vane that turns as the wind changes direction.

★ For What it's Worth

THE ARID ZONE

It is commonly thought that the name Arizona means "arid zone." This, however, is a myth. The name Arizona came from "arizonac," a Papago Indian name meaning "where the small springs come together." However, the actual location of the Arizonac spring was a silver mine in Sonora, Mexico.

ANNIE GET YOUR GUN

During the restoration process it was discovered that the Victory Lady sculpture was perforated with bullet holes. The Wild West legend is that during the capitol's formative days, some settlers did not hold the symbolism of the Victory Lady in high regard. Although no one has ever admitted to taking shots at the statue, it is surmised that the bullet lacing is the result of some desperadoes' target practice.

The figure perched atop the copper dome is known as *Victory Lady*.

An elevated view of the Capitol complex.

The Great Seal attached to the front of the tower.

ARKANSAS
Little Rock

A SORDID BEGINNING

Resembling the design of the national capitol, construction of the Arkansas capitol was riddled with corruption and a shaky start.

STATE MOTTO

"The people rule"

★ Facts & Figures

Architectural style	Neo-classical
Architect	George R. Mann & Cass Gilbert
Exterior material	Batesville limestone and Arkansas granite
Dome surface	Indiana limestone
Building height (to tip of dome)	213'
Construction period	1899-1915
First occupied	1911
Capital population (Census 2000)	183,133
Census estimate 2007	187,452
Direction capitol faces	East
Original cost	$2,205,779

The Past Remembered

PRISON BREAK

Construction of the present capitol displaced the state penitentiary which formerly occupied this site. Not only did the State use the prison site to construct the capitol, it also took advantage of "convict labor" to assist in the construction. Inmates continued to occupy the prison until the first floor of the capitol was in progress. It took sixteen years and nearly two and a half times the original budget appropriation to complete.

RAINING IN

By the end of the 19th century, the government had outgrown the old capitol which had been used for nearly sixty years. However, it took more of a direct "hint" to convince the legislature that a new capitol was necessary. During a legislative session in 1899, a heavy rainstorm erupted resulting in plaster falling from the ceiling in the Senate chamber. Upon the senators' arrival, they found a big mess. That same day, the Senate chamber fell onto some of the senators' desks and reportedly landed on some senators. That same day, the Senate passed legislation for a new capitol. Later that year, a groundbreaking ceremony was held.

AROUND THE CORNERSTONE

Although the cornerstone was laid in November 1900, major construction did not begin until three and a half years later. This was principally due to former Attorney General-turned-Governor Jeff Davis's ongoing opposition to the project on legal and budgetary pretexts. Ultimately this led to a court action to cease its construction.

IN DISPUTE

After resuming construction on the new capitol in 1904, other problems developed. Disputes erupted between the quarry owners and the Capitol Commission over delays in limestone shipments and the quality of materials and workmanship. To make matters worse, six state senators were charged with bribery, although only one was convicted

TESTED BY FIRE

Beginning in 1906, tests to determine the soundness and safety of the building were conducted. In 1909, one of the tests involved setting a fire in the building, which was allowed to burn for two weeks. Although the capitol performed well under the tests, the project was halted once again when the contractor, architect and entire Commission were discharged because the building was deemed unsafe. To

The Monument to Confederate Women.

The State seal is highlighted in stained glass.

make matters worse, the contractor sealed off the building in an effort to claim ownership.

A CAPITOL REPO

In 1909, Governor Donaghey led a successful effort to regain control of the building. State officials resorted to breaking in the front door and dismissing the contractor's guards. A fence surrounding the capitol was erected, watchtowers complete with guards were installed and the state militia was put on stand-by. Noted architect Cass Gilbert was hired and a new contractor was put in charge to reconstruct and complete the building. Some design features were changed to incorporate improvements. In 1911, the legislature was able to occupy the building though still unfinished. Additional funds were appropriated in 1913 and the capitol was finally completed in 1915.

An early photo, dated 1923, shows the capitol. Note the vintage automobiles.

A linen-era postcard depicts the capitol. Postmarked January 1918, it reads "This is a nice town of 69,000 pop. They have some fine buildings here. The snow is melting fast as it is warm here."

Pearls of Wisdom

"This project was conceived in sin ... it will prove to be the most infamous steal ever perpetrated against the people of Arkansas."

Governor Jefferson Davis
c. 1900

Historical Happenings

1800   1900

1803   **1836**   **1842**   **1899**

Arkansas acquired from   President Andrew Jackson   First State House   Groundbreaking
France as part of the   grants statehood   completed   ceremony
Lousiana Purchase

★ The Inside Story

CURTAIN CALL

Both the House and Senate legislative chambers are in the shape of a circle. To enhance this circular effect, a round, stained-glass skylight was designed for each chamber. Giant chandeliers purchased from the Mitchell-Vance Company of New York were added around 1913. From the beginning, legislators complained about the acoustics. In an effort to reduce glare and to improve the acoustics, curtains were added. However, the curtains had little effect on the acoustical problem.

BRONZED AT TIFFANY'S

As you enter the building, big bronze doors line the front entryway. These massive doors, six in all, are ten feet tall and four inches thick. They were purchased from Tiffany's of New York for $10,000 in 1910 but their current value far exceeds the original cost. Keeping them sparkling and free of fingerprints is quite a challenge for the capitol maintenance crew.

THE FAMILY TREE

In honor of the Arkansas Centenary in 1936, former Governor George Donaghey ordered an ancient walnut tree, which was on the family farm, be cut down. The wood from the tree was then made into a table which was presented to the State. It is currently on display in the Governor's Reception Room.

A huge chandelier is suspended from the rotunda dome.

Curtains are hung between the sections of stained glass in the Senate and House chambers.

One of two grand marble staircases.

A model of the capitol, made by a student, is on display.

1901 Construction ceases
1904 Construction resumes
1913 Monument to Confederate women erected
1915 Capitol completed
1957 Little Rock segregation incident – Federal troops intervene
2000

Claim to Fame

HOLLYWOOD DOUBLE
Hollywood producers have filmed movies at the Arkansas capitol and used it as a "stand-in" for the U.S. capitol. Among the movie titles featuring the Arkansas capitol are *Under Siege* and *Stone Cold*.

IN VICTORY AND DEFEAT
Former President Bill Clinton served as governor for twelve years in this building. He holds the distinction of being the only Arkansas governor who was elected, then defeated and later re-elected.

GROUNDS FOR AN AWARD
Another similarity to the U.S. Capitol is the countless floral and rose gardens throughout its grounds. Arkansas takes great pride in its spectacular landscaping.

Pink roses, from one of the many gardens decorating the grounds, frame the capitol.

For What it's Worth

IF THIS BE LITTLE ROCK, WHERE IS BIG ROCK?
Legend has it that in 1722, a French explorer named Bernard De La Harpe sighted a stone outcropping – the first on his journey – along the Arkansas River and named it "Little Rock." Although not much is left of the famous "Little Rock" due to the weathering process and human causes, it is still visible beneath a railroad bridge in downtown Little Rock. For the record, a larger rock formation that juts out from the land and is further up the river is said to be called "Big Rock."

AR • KAN • SAW
In 1881, in reference to a controversy over the spelling and pronunciation of the state's name, the General Assembly passed a resolution which stated the name is to be spelled "Arkansas" but pronounced "Arkansaw." For the record, the origin of the name is "Akansa," an alternate name for a Native nation known as the Ugakhpa or, more usually, the Quapaw. It is said to mean "people of the south wind."

CALIFORNIA
Sacramento

A "CAPITAL ON WHEELS"
Going for the gold prompts a rush to secure the capital.

"Eureka"

⭐ *Facts & Figures*

Architectural style .... Renaissance Revival
(Mid 19th Century)

Architect (Original) .... Miner Frederick Butler
(Others) ..... Reuben Clark, Gordon P. Cummings
and A.A. Bennett

Exterior material .... California granite with plaster
on brick and cast iron

Dome surface .... Copper

Building height (to tip of dome) .... 242'

Construction period 1860-74

First occupied 1869

Capital population (Census 2000) 407,018
Census estimate 2007 460,242

Direction capitol faces .... West

Original cost $2,972,925

28

The Past Remembered

"CAPITAL ON WHEELS"

Once statehood was achieved in 1850, several towns vied for the honor of becoming the capital, including San Francisco. During the period of 1849–54, the capital repeatedly switched locations. The legislators were on the road so much that it literally became known as the "Capital on Wheels." Beginning in San Jose, then Vallejo, then Sacramento, back to Vallejo, on to Benicia, and finally back to Sacramento again.

THE BRIBE OF BENICIA

Becoming the capital of the state was an honor and a benefit highly sought by rivaling communities. Bribes and enticements to persuade lawmakers to choose their town were common. In an effort to lure the hearts of legislators over to their side, the town of Benicia made a rather enticing and unusual offer — to "deliver" 20-30 eligible young ladies as potential wives for the unmarried legislators.

SACRAMENTO — NO, SAN JOSE — NO IT'S SACRAMENTO

In 1849, the California Gold Rush brought an influx of people into the region. The gold fields located in close proximity to Sacramento caused its population to flourish and by 1854, Sacramento became one of the largest cities in California. Thus, it was no surprise when the legislature declared Sacramento City as the permanent capital. This declaration, however, had its dissenters.

When supporters of San Jose challenged the ruling, a Supreme Court battle ensued. The judges decided that San Jose was indeed entitled to be the capital. However, the decision was reversed upon the death of one of the ruling judges and subsequent gubernatorial appointment of his successor. Even after the capitol was built in Sacramento, attempts to lure the capital away by San Jose and Berkeley continued.

THE LONG FORGOTTEN APSE

The capitol was constructed in the shape of an "E." At the rear of the capitol, at the center of the "E," was a fifty-four foot semicircular structure known as the apse. The apse was considered by many to be the most beautiful part of the capitol. But in 1949, as the need for office space grew, the apse was torn down and replaced with a six-floor East Annex.

The State Capitol of California

A cast-pewter souvenir cup, made in Germany c. 1900, features the capitol and reads "Souvenir of Sacramento."

A postcard with a 1909 postmark sends greetings across the country to a friend in Maine.

A rare leather postcard, postmarked 1906, and a photo c. 1930 show the apse at the rear of the capitol. The aesthetic appeal of the apse was a popular point of interest.

SACRAMENTO

A celluloid button attached by a chain to a nameplate c. 1900 shows a photo of the capitol — possibly for a convention.

The capital grounds comprise 40 acres, most of which is a park. Established in 1869, there are 400 kinds of plants from around the world.

Pearls of Wisdom

"Give me men to match my mountains."

Sam Foss (poet & journalist) attributed — c. 1869
Etched on the front of the
Supreme Court/library building

An old glass slide depicts the capitol.

CAPITAL PAK

PRODUCE OF U.S.A.

CALIFORNIA BARTLETTS

LAMBERT MARKETING CO.

Labels, produced by the Lambert Marketing Company and picturing the California capitol, were affixed to fruit crates in the 1940s.

Historical Happenings

1800

1900

1849	1850	1854	1874	1928
California Gold Rush	President Fillmore grants statehood	Sacramento becomes permanent capital	Capitol completed	Second remodeling

A view of the inner dome gives the appearance of neon lights.

★ The Inside Story

CHECKERBOARD

The first floor and basement rotunda areas of the capitol are covered with black-and-white marble tile in a checkerboard pattern. Originally installed in 1872, the black tile was imported from Belgium while the white was mined in New York and Vermont. During the restoration, new tile was laid in most areas except the first and second floor west foyers. Although the source of the black tile was once again Belgium, the white in this area is from Alabama.

HALF & HALF

When the capitol was first completed, the state used gasolier (natural gas fueled) lighting fixtures. After the invention of the incandescent light in 1879, the state was not convinced that electricity would eventually replace gas and so opted to install combination fixtures which were half gas and half electric.

The state seal appears in this stained glass window.

A LIVING MUSEUM

The capitol was given a facelift in 1982 as part of a restoration process. Three of the nine museum rooms of the first floor were renovated to replicate the 1906 appearance of the Governor's Suite. The lower level also features a theater in addition to a display of artifacts and pictures commemorating the capitol's history. Restored with a Victorian flavor, the entire capitol now functions as a "living" museum of its past.

The rotunda

Presented to the State in 1883, this statuary depicts Columbus making his plea to Queen Isabella of Spain for the "new earth."

This marble mosaic floor features a poppy design.

Known as *Eureka*, meaning "I've found it," this ceramic tile creation celebrates the discovery of gold in California.

1949
Apse dismantled

1951
East annex
added

1972
Study determined
capitol might collapse
in an earthquake

1982
Reconstruction
completed

2000

★ Claim to Fame

BORN INTO STATEHOOD

The State of California claims to have a common heritage with one of its statues, Minerva, which is sculpted within the pediment over the entrance of the capitol. Unlike other states, California bypassed being part of a territory before it achieved statehood. Likewise, the Roman goddess Minerva was said to have been born into adulthood.

★ For What it's Worth

CAN'T LEAVE "WELL" ENOUGH ALONE

During the 1890s, the basement or cellar of the capitol housed an eating establishment which reportedly served more alcohol than food. It was referred to as "The Well." Although access was not a secret, the entrance was hidden under a stairway. Late one evening in 1893 as the legislative session was winding down, the noise and frolicking became so boisterous and distracting that the Sergeant-at-Arms was sent to quell the disturbance. Apparently, a legislator decided to celebrate a recent legislative victory by inviting some of the most beautiful women in Sacramento to join him in the "Well." The champagne flowed freely and the scene became what is now described as "R" rated. An investigation ensued and the "Well" was closed, but only temporarily. Finally, in 1899 it was closed for good and is currently used for offices.

LIKE ICING A CAKE

During the restoration of the ceilings, much of the plaster detail needed to be redone. Workers used cake decorating tubes to recreate the original texture and shades of plaster.

On a cloudy day, a cascading fountain and red roses blend softly into the stark white features of the capitol.

EARTHQUAKE INSURANCE

Potential earthquake damage to the California capitol from a severe earthquake has been a concern for many years. In 1975, extensive seismic protectors were installed to the building. The building is now reinforced and engineered to withstand a magnitude equal to the Great San Francisco earthquake of 1906. Although, it is considered to be earthquake "safe," it is not earthquake "proof." In other words, damage from an earthquake might be sustained but minimized.

ON THE BALL

Because the California Gold Rush was a significant part of California's history, one might expect the capitol dome to be gilded with gold. However, this is not the case. Instead, the dome is covered with copper. Only the ball atop the cupola is plated with a layer of gold. In 1871, citizens donated gold coins valued at $300 — a sizable donation for that time — to provide the gold covering for the ball. The coins were then melted down and plated on the ball. Now, when the gold on the ball needs to be replaced, a thin layer of gold is attached to the copper through a process called electroplating.

Although the ball atop the cupola is made of brass, it is gold-plated.

COLORADO
Denver

THE MILE HIGH CAPITOL
At one mile above sea level, all seasons are colorful for the Colorado capital.

STATE MOTTO

"Nothing without the Deity"

★ Facts & Figures

Architectural style	Corinthian
Architect	Elijah E. Myers
Exterior material	Colorado gray granite
Dome surface	24-carat gold leaf
Building height (to tip of dome)	272'
Construction period	1886-1908
First occupied	1894
Capital population (Census 2000)	554,636
Census estimate 2007	588,349
Direction capitol faces	West
Original cost	$2,704,875

★ The Past Remembered

PIKES PEAK OR BUST

Prior to statehood, the territorial capital was located at the foot of Pikes Peak in Colorado City, now part of Colorado Springs. However, in 1862, Colorado City did not have lodging available to house the legislators. After less than a week of meetings, the legislators did go "bust" and relocated to Denver. From 1862-67, the territorial legislature met in Golden and Denver.

BEYOND THE SUNSET

On the way to California in 1860, the Henry Brown family stopped in Denver for a respite. As the story goes, Mrs. Brown was so captivated by the awesome sight of the gorgeous sunset over the mountains, she promptly informed Mr. Brown that she was staying in Colorado. Mr. Brown acquiesced to his wife's insistence to stay. Years later in 1874, he bought property on what is now downtown Denver. He donated ten of these acres to the city for purposes of building a capitol.

MR. BROWN'S LOST CAUSE

Due to a lack of funding and uncertainty that Denver would remain the capital, years passed before the capitol was built on the land donated by Mr. Brown. Frustrated by what appeared to be "a lost cause," Mr. Brown launched an unsuccessful attempt to reclaim his gift of the capitol site. The legal battle lasted seven years. Had the land been deeded back to Mr. Brown, it is likely that Denver would not have remained Colorado's capital. While waiting for the capitol to be built, Mr. Brown constructed several buildings in what is now downtown Denver. Most notable of these are the Brown Palace Hotel and the Trinity Methodist Church.

KANSAS' GOVERNOR DENVER

Surprisingly, the city of Denver was named after the governor of the Kansas Territory, General James Denver. At that time, much of Colorado was part of the Kansas Territory. Though he visited Denver only twice, General Denver was instrumental in routing the Union Pacific Railroad through eastern Colorado, building a station in Denver. His portrait is featured as one of 16 historical pioneers in the Hall of Fame stained glass windows found in the upper interior of the dome.

CAPITOL QUILT SHOW

The Capitol Quilt Show is a special event held in the Colorado Capitol from time to time. Citizens from around the state are given the opportunity to display their colorful quilt creations. During the event, over 200 quilts, demonstrating exquisite craftsmanship, are displayed in the capitol throughout three floors.

An aluminum tray depicts the capitol, c. 1920.

An old tin features the capitol.

Colorado honors a well-known educator, Emily Griffith. This stained glass window is located outside the Old Supreme Court Chambers.

The Capitol Quilt Show

Mailed in 1906, this postcard shows both the old territorial capitol located in Colorado City (Colorado Springs) and the current capitol.

Postmarked 1915, this card shows a sprinkler system in use.

Pearls of Wisdom

"Mr. Brown, thou may press on to California if such be thy wish. I shall remain here!"

Mrs. Jane Brown — c. 1860
Preparing to depart Denver for California

Historical Happenings

1800

1861 · **1862** · **1867** · **1876** · **1881** · · · **1900**

Colorado City selected
as territorial capital

Golden selected
as capital

Denver selected
as capital

President Grant
grants statehood

Voters choose
Denver as capital

The inner dome showing the "Hall of Fame."

The Grand Staircase

Colorado onyx lines columns and wainscoting.

★ The Inside Story

Polished brass railings and marble stairways line the Grand Staircase and lead to the second floor where the House and Senate chambers are located. Elevator doors and exterior doors are bronzed. The bright metallic look inside the building complements the golden dome on the outside.

STAIRMASTER

At the top of the inner dome, there is an observation gallery overlooking the Hall of Fame portraits — stained glass portraits of 16 pioneers who helped shape Colorado's history. To reach the gallery, however, there are 99 narrow, winding stairs from bottom to top. Though no easy feat, there is a view that makes the climb worth it. There is a breathtaking view of the panorama of the Colorado Front Range of the Rockies — from Rocky Mountain National Park to Pikes Peak.

ONE OF A KIND

The interior columns and corridors of the capitol are lined with a rare, rose onyx. The onyx is so rare that it has only been found in Beulah, Colorado. The limited supply was exhausted during the capitol's construction. The quarry site has now become a housing development.

PORTRAITS IN GLASS

The Hall of Fame portraits of 16 Colorado pioneers were so popular that years later more stained glass portraits were added in both legislative chambers and in other parts of the capitol.

Railings and balusters of brass add an exquisite touch to the staircases and railings.

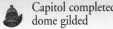

1894	1908	1909	1991	2000 2003
Executive offices occupied	Capitol completed; dome gilded	One Mile High marker placed	Dome re-gilded	New Mile High marker placed

★ Claim to Fame

A ROCKY MOUNTAIN HIGH

Denver is not the only state capital with an elevation exceeding one mile above sea level (Santa Fe, New Mexico being the highest at 7,199'). It is, however, the only capitol constructed at exactly the one-mile elevation of 5,280'.

THREE STEPS FORWARD, FIVE STEPS BACK

To commemorate the "mile high capitol," a brass plaque was placed on the 15th step. Since its placement in 1909, "souvenir seekers," otherwise known as thieves, repeatedly stole the plaque. To remedy the problem, in 1947 the words "One Mile Above Sea Level" was inscribed into the granite step where the plaque previously was set.

However in 1969, engineering students from Colorado State University conducted a study and determined that the one-mile mark was actually three steps higher than the inscription, the 18th step. A survey plug was placed there to indicate the new mile-high mark. But the story keeps going. During 2003, a survey team complete with the latest high-tech equipment, concluded that the correct spot is actually the 13th step. To make it official, former Governor Bill Owens was asked to place the new marker.

The Mile High Capitol has more than one marker to indicate the spot for one mile above sea level.

★ For What it's Worth

TUNNEL TALES

Several tunnels run beneath the capitol and cross underneath two streets, connecting to other state buildings. There are many tales regarding these tunnels. Until the late 1930s, a night watchman made his residence in one of the tunnels. Said to be a miser, he went to the bank each payday and exchanged his pay for silver dollars. After his death, the tunnels were searched in anticipation of finding a treasure. Reportedly, no silver dollars were ever found and what he did with his silver dollars remains a mystery.

HEADS OR TALES?

Another mystery involves a ghoulish discovery. In the 1920s, the governor instructed his staff to do a bit of cleaning. Boxes belonging to the 1880s territorial governor were found and inside, to their surprise, were two skulls! One theory is that the skulls belonged to members of the Espinoza gang who had been the subject of the governor's bounty offer. The governor had required proof that the villains were dead in order to collect the reward. When a bounty hunter produced the heads, the governor claimed there was no money in the Treasury to pay the reward. Although it was suspected the bounty hunter left the Espinoza heads at the capitol, history confirms this was not the case. So whose skulls were they? This mystery also remains unsolved.

NO GILDED GIRLS

Some capitols opted to top their dome with an allegorical statue and/or gild it. Colorado also considered a statue. For several months, the Board of Capitol Managers debated the best female model to grace the dome but could not reach an agreement. Instead, they chose a lighted glass globe to rest atop the golden dome.

FOUR SEASONS OF COLOR

CONNECTICUT
Hartford

MORE LIKE A CATHEDRAL
With statues surrounding the golden dome and spires pointing to the sky, this gothic structure resembles a cathedral.

"He who transplanted still sustains."

★ Facts & Figures

Architectural style	High Victorian Gothic
Architect	Richard M. Upjohn
Exterior material	New England marble and granite
Dome surface	Gold-leaf over copper, brick and marble
Building height (to tip of dome)	257'
Construction period	1872-79
First occupied	1878
Capital population (Census 2000)	121,578
Census estimate 2007	124,563
Direction capitol faces	North
Original cost	$2,532,524

The Past Remembered

DESIGN BY COMMITTEE

In 1872, legislators chose Richard Upjohn's design from among 13 architectural firms, though they still made significant changes to his plans. For instance, Upjohn's original design included a clocktower but public sentiment favored a traditional dome.

This point of contention halted work on the capitol until a compromise could be reached. The compromise that followed allowed for a dome but only by including other refinements. These included the addition of massive columns, an extension of the building, and detail work, which included carvings.

PROTECTOR OF THE PEOPLE

Prior to the capitol's completion, sculptor Randolph Rogers was commissioned to create a statue for the dome. Rogers, an American living in Rome at the time, sculpted a plaster model. He then sent the model to Germany where a bronze statue was made. He named the statue "The Angel of Resurrection." Its wings were said to represent "protection for the people of Connecticut."

When the building was almost finished in 1878, the 17-foot, 10-inch, 6,600 pound bronze statue of a winged figure was fastened atop the dome while the plaster model was placed inside the building. The statue was ultimately renamed "The Genius of Connecticut."

FALLEN ANGEL

After many years, the bronze statue became loose and was considered a safety hazard. In 1903, a heated battle in the legislature ensued over what to do with the statue. A local newspaper editor quipped, "The question facing Connecticut is whether it wants a loose woman on the roof or a fallen woman in the streets."

The legislature concluded that the statue could be secured by reinforcing the bolts. This proved to be a temporary fix as the Great Hurricane that struck Hartford in 1938 caused a "loose woman" once again. Fearing that the statue would continue to be a problem, it was taken down and placed in storage.

With the onset of World War II, the governor felt that it would be a patirotic gesture to have the statue melted down for its bronze content and used in the war effort. As a reminder that the statue once held a place of prominence atop the dome, the plaster model was given an extensive reconditioning, painted bronze and placed on a small gold-dome base in the north lobby.

The statue of Nathan Hale stands proudly in the East Atrium.

The plaster model replica of the *Genius of Connecticut.*

The Petersburg Express, a cannon mounted on a railroad car and moved from place to place by Connecticut troops in the Civil War at Petersburg, Virginia, is in the foreground of this early 1900 postcard and recent photo.

The Soldiers and Sailors Memorial Arch is prominent in this postcard. This winter scene postcard was sent in 1906.

An embroidered handkerchief features the Connecticut capitol.

A stereocard, c. 1880, shows a horse and buggy and an early view of the capitol grounds.

Pearls of Wisdom

"I only regret that I have but one life to lose for my country."

Nathan Hale — 1776
Inscribed on the base of his statue
Located inside the capitol

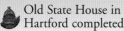

Historical Happenings

1800

1788
Fifth state to ratify the Constitution

1796
Old State House in Hartford completed

1830
Legislature begins meeting alternately between New Haven and Hartford

1879
Hartford becomes sole capital

Looking through the arms of the plaster model used to cast the *Genius of Connecticut* at the dome interior.

The interior dome

Colorful paint schemes enhance the stained glass skylights.

Stained glass windows in the House of Representatives resemble a church more than a capitol.

The atrium of the Legislative Office Building has a beauty of its own.

★ The Inside Story

STRESSED OUT

Amid concerns that capitol construction exceeded the budget, the contractor was advised to simplify the plans for the dome. In an effort to conserve costs, he reduced the supporting piers inside the building from solid granite blocks to a granite covering over bricks. He also used lime-based mortar instead of cement and as the mortar set, it shrank. As a result, the slack could not bear the weight of the dome and caused stress cracks in the supporting walls.

STRESS RELIEF

Realizing that there was now a more serious problem, the architect instructed workers to use molten lead (printer's lead) to shore up the slack and alleviate the stress. This corrected the problem and prevented future cracks. Some of the cracks, as well as the areas where lead was inserted, are still visible today. Although the contractor initially saved $6,000, repairing the damage caused by inferior materials cost an extra $47,000!

TATTLETALE COUSIN

Nathan Hale became a hero and martyr giving his life for his country. At the age of 21, he infiltrated the British lines as an undercover spy, but was betrayed by a cousin who sided with the British. Before he was hanged, his parting words, etched in the base of the statue, have been emulated by many American war heroes ever since.

★ Claim to Fame

GOTHIC CATHEDRAL

With Gothic spires, the capitol resembles a cathedral and has one of the most distinctive outward appearances of any capitol. The architect, Richard Upjohn, was noted for his design of churches and cathedrals, and incorporated the same High Victorian Gothic style into the capitol.

CHEAPER BY THE DOZEN

Original plans called for twelve unique statues to surround the dome. In an effort to reduce costs, the number was reduced to six different statues that were duplicated on the opposite side. In addition to the statues, twelve stained-glass windows and twelve pointed arches grace the dome. The twelve statues atop its dome are unequaled by any other capitol.

CIRCLE OF FRIENDS

The Senate chamber boasts a unique seating arrangement known as "The Circle." A ring is formed by 36 Senate desks and chairs. The circle is split in the middle at opposite sides to allow access to the center of the circle.

Twelve statues surrounding the dome symbolize six representations of humanity.

★ For What it's Worth

A STATE BY MANY NAMES

In past years, Connecticut license plates displayed the slogan "Constitution State." Connecticut is also known by other nicknames including the "Land of Steady Habits," "Nutmeg State," "Provisions State," "Blue Law State," and "Freestone State." The official name, however, is "Constitution State," as designated by the General Assembly in 1959.

HE WHO TRANSPLANTED STILL SUSTAINS

Although no one is certain of the state motto's origin, in 1889 the State Librarian attributed it to the 80th Psalm. The Psalm states "Thou hast brought a vine out of Egypt: thou has cast out the heathen, and planted it." (NKJV)

ORIGIN OF OUR CONSTITUTION

Long before the United States enacted its Constitution, Connecticut had already planted the seed in establishing a constitutional form of government. In 1638, Thomas Hooker, a Puritan preacher, gave a sermon espousing the idea of a democratic government declaring, "The foundation of authority is laid in the free consent of the people." The colony subsequently adopted his ideas and operated under this form of government known as the Fundamental Orders. It was the first written constitution in history and became the model for the U.S Constitution.

A close-up view of the High Victorian Gothic architecture.

DELAWARE

Dover

DELAWARE, A LANDMARK OF HISTORY

Delaware was the first state to ratify the Constitution. It was said that this small state sent "a first signal of a revolution."

STATE MOTTO

"Liberty and independence"

Facts & Figures

Architectural style	Georgian
Architect	E. William Martin
Exterior material	Handmade bricks
Dome surface (cupola)	Fiberglass-painted white
Building height (to tip of dome)	125'
Construction period	1932-33
First occupied	1933
Capital population (Census 2000)	32,135
Census estimate 2007	35,811
Direction capitol faces	West
Original cost	$749,306

The Past Remembered

The General Assembly originally met in New Castle. However in 1777, Dover was chosen as a more central location.

ON THE GREEN

In 1683, William Penn designated a public area known as "The Green" in his layout of the city of Dover. Today, it is anchored by the historic Old State House. It has served the city over the centuries and remains a gathering point for parades, concerts and other events.

COLONIAL REPRO

Legislative Hall, as the state capitol is known, was the first among several state office buildings in the Capitol Complex. The Georgian colonial style of architecture was designed to reflect the style popular in the mid to late 1700s. In order to closely mimic this style and that of the Old State House, the exterior walls are made exclusively of hand-made bricks. In addition to the red brick, white marble and white trim around the windows enhance the "authenticity" of the colonial theme. The roof is made of clay tiles to simulate the appearance of old wood.

HORSE BEHIND THE CART

At the cornerstone dedication in 1933, Delaware's Governor, C. Douglass Buck, noted that the cornerstone was being laid at the completion of the building rather than the start.

He humorously remarked, "We have placed the horse behind the cart." He went on to explain that modern construction methods had utilized steel beams, behind the brick and stone, to primarily support the building, making the cornerstone a strictly aesthetic and symbolic feature.

SMALL WONDER

Delaware, the second smallest state in area, designed the layout of its capitol in keeping with this theme. The primary government offices are intended to make legislators unusually accessible to the public in order to maintain this "small and intimate feeling."

WEATHER OR NOT

As buildings age, the weathering process often takes its toll. Delaware's cupola was no exception. During a remodeling, the cupola was rebuilt using a fiberglass material to replace the original wooden and metal structure.

The bell tower of The Old State House.

Close-in parking was not a problem in the early days of the capitol. Note the ivy growing up the walls.

A postcard, mailed in 1934, shows the capitol shortly after completion. Note the old car at the left of the capitol and the freshly-graded ground.

The Old State House, built in 1792, faces The Green and is also on the capitol grounds.

Pearls of Wisdom

"We learn, sir, that the general convention of the State of Delaware has unanimously ratified the new Constitution which I had the honor of sending you. This small state has the advantage of having given the first signal of a revolution in the general government of the United States, and its example can produce a good effect in the other conventions."

Louis-Guillaume Otto to Comte de Montmorin
December 15, 1787
New York

Historical Happenings
1800

1777
Capitol moves from
New Castle to Dover

1787
First state to ratify
the Constitution

1792
Old State House
completed

★ The Inside Story

Due to its Georgian colonial style, Delaware's capitol does not have a formal rotunda. Upon entering the building from either side, it is only a short distance to the foyer. In a sense, the building takes on the appearance of a mansion rather than a capitol. The colonial foyer is further accented by a black-and-white, checkered floor. A skylight in the center of the ceiling is illuminated by artificial light as it does not extend to the tower of this quaint capitol.

COLONIALISTS

A colonial staircase leads to the second floor where the colonnade — a series of equally spaced columns — adds to the architectural theme of Colonialism. Many of the furniture pieces used in the building are reproductions from Colonial times. The colonial color scheme and furnishings continue in the House and Senate. Paintings depicting the colonial period are mounted in both chambers.

A FULL HOUSE

Although the governor continues to maintain an office in Legislative Hall, the governor and his or her staff are primarily housed in a different building. Others housed in the capitol include the lieutenant governor, legislative chambers, offices of 62 legislators, the Legislative Council as well as additional offices.

Colonial staircases dominate the center portion of Legislative Hall.

Paintings of military heroes by Delaware artist Jack Lewis are prominently hung in both the House and the Senate. Note the cove in the center of the ceiling.

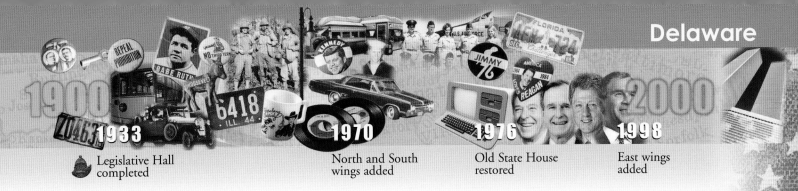

1900

1933 Legislative Hall completed

1970 North and South wings added

1976 Old State House restored

1998 East wings added

2000

★ Claim to Fame

SETTING THE PACE

Considering that Delaware was and is one of the smallest states, its boldness in becoming the first state to ratify the U.S. Constitution is a remarkable achievement that is significant in United States history.

DOUBLE DUTY

Until 1875, the Old State House was not only the capitol but also served as the Kent County Court House. This sharing of space by state and local government was not always amiable. As the building belonged to the court, the county refused to share its space in 1792. This forced the state to meet in temporary locations, including a Presbyterian church, until the dispute was settled. In 1875, the county sold the building to the state, thus ending the cohabitation.

THE PRESIDENT OF DELAWARE

During the Revolutionary period, the Assembly met in various locations. In 1776, the two governing bodies of Delaware were known as the Legislative Council (upper house) and the House of Assembly (lower house). Initially, the chief executive was elected by the legislature and was known as the president. In 1791, this position which was changed to governor became elected by the people.

A view of the remodeled east side in which two wings were added.

★ For What it's Worth

EAST SIDE, WEST SIDE

Which direction does the capitol face? In Delaware, it depends on who you ask. Historically, the front of the building faced west. But after the east side addition and renovation, the architect intended for this new addition to become the front entrance. Additionally, a matching brick wall was added in front of the building.

Traditionalists, who favor the original front on the west because it faces the Legislative Mall, appear to be in the majority.

OLD BUT NOT FORGOTTEN

The Old State House which served as the capitol for over 140 years is across the Mall from Legislative Hall. Because of its historical significance and its representation of Delaware's past, it attracts many tourists who may choose to visit this interesting site rather than the present capitol.

Delaware's Liberty Bell replica

Fall foliage accents the Mall in front of Legislative Hall.

FLORIDA
Tallahassee

OUT WITH THE OLD
IN WITH THE NEW

Like the decorative awnings that outlived their usefulness, the new capitol towers over the old which now serves as a museum.

"In God we trust"

★ Facts & Figures

	Historic Capitol	Capitol Tower
Architectural style	Greek Revival	New Classicism
Architect	Cary Butt and Frank Milburn	Edward Stone
Exterior material	Brick/stucco	Concrete
Dome surface	Copper	No dome
Building height (to tip of dome)	161'	307'
Construction period	1839-45; 1902	1973-77
First occupied	1845	1977
Capital population (Census 2000)		150,624
Census estimate 2007		168,979
Direction capitol faces	East	West
Original cost	$55,000, $75,000 (1902 addition)	$43,070,741

★ The Past Remembered

GOING THE DISTANCE

Prior to locating in Tallahassee, the territorial legislature alternated meeting in Pensacola and St. Augustine — nearly 400 miles apart. In time, the legislature became weary of traveling to these distant sites and thus appointed two men to search out a more central location.

The area they selected had rolling hills and was located near a stream and waterfall. Also nearby were the remains of the Old Spanish trail. It was determined that the site would make a good location for the permanent seat of government. The site was named Tallahassee after the nearby village of Seminole Indians.

PUTTING DOWN ROOTS

In 1824, a log cabin capitol was built on a site near the present capitol. In 1845, at the time of statehood, the legislature moved into the first section of the Historic Capitol which replaced the log cabin version.

Over the years, efforts were made to relocate or remove the capital. In 1900, the relocation question was put before the voters. Although three other towns were on the ballot, Tallahassee was reaffirmed with the majority of the votes. Ocala, Jacksonville and St. Augustine were also in the running.

PRESERVING THE PAST

In the 1970s, the State faced a decision to either abandon or restore the Historic Capitol. After considerable debate, a new capitol with a tower design was approved. The architect, Edwin Stone, recommended that the Historic Capitol be completely demolished and a replica circa 1845 be constructed in its place.

Concerted efforts by a group called "Save the Old Capitol" fought the recommendation, focusing their efforts on preserving the past. As a temporary solution, the legislature voted to defer a decision until the new capitol was completed. In the interim, a study was conducted to research the Historic Capitol's features, current condition and previous expansions. In a compromise, it was determined to restore the Historic Capitol to its 1902 appearance. This meant that the later additions of 1923, 1936, and 1947 would be demolished. Most were satisfied with this decision as it included the capitol's most nostalgic feature — the dome.

A COOL IDEA

From the time the Historic Capitol was completed, the heat from the Florida sun was a problem. In order to reduce solar gain, red-and-white striped awnings were installed during the 1890s on all the windows except for the north side of the building.

By the late 1930s with the advent of air-conditioning, the awnings were removed. This appearance remained until the Historic Capitol was renovated in the late 1970s. With the intent to replicate the appearance of the building to earlier years, the awnings were restored to the windows. More than nostalgic, the awnings do assist the air conditioning in cooling the building.

A ROOM WITH A VIEW

The observation deck on the 22nd floor offers an outstanding view of the city of Tallahassee. Looking almost straight down is a view of the Old State House dome. In addition to a great view, the East wing is an art gallery featuring works of Florida artists and also the Florida Artists Hall of Fame.

Red-and-white striped flowerbeds accentuate the entrance to the Historic Capitol while red-and-white awnings accent the façade. The flowers add depth and beauty to the building while the awnings help to supplement the cooling process of air conditioning.

A postcard with a 1908 copyright features the capitol with a poem and a picture of the state flower.

Awnings also accent the backside of the capitol.

The reverse of this postcard, mailed in 1909, includes a statement which indicates the capitol was "selected principally on account of its advantageous location from a geographical standpoint." That is to say it was located equidistant from Pensacola and St. Augustine. Today, Tallahassee is located far from the geographic population center of Florida, reflecting a notable population shift in the state.

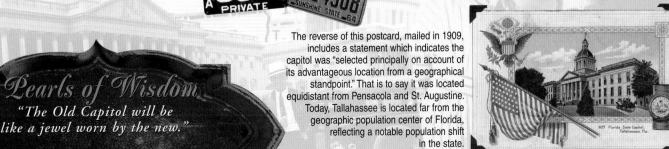

Pearls of Wisdom

"The Old Capitol will be like a jewel worn by the new."

Herschel E. Shepard — c. 1978
architect for the restoration of the Historic Capitol

Historical Happenings

1800

1900

1823
Tallahassee chosen
as seat of government

1845
President Tyler grants
statehood; First phase of
Historic Capitol completed

1891-92
Red and white awnings
replace shutters;
Cupola added

1900
Voters reaffirm
Tallahassee as capital

★ The Inside Story

ORANGE "A-PEEL"

The interior dome has a unique color combination. White panels and orangey-peach colored walls surround pink, blue and yellow pastels of colored glass. Prior to restoration, these brilliant hues of glass had long since disappeared. However, fragments of the original glass were discovered during the restoration process. From these pieces of glass, artisans were able to recreate the original colors of the dome. The interior dome is trimmed with a white wooden border and a painted ceiling.

The inner dome

A PATRIOTIC THEME

The floors in the rotunda of the Historic Capitol have also been restored. Known as Battleship linoleum, the color was a US Naval standard beginning in 1899. The walls have been refinished in plaster and painted light shades of red, white and blue in keeping with the original patriotic theme of colors.

NEW AND IMPROVED

The interior of the 22-story tower capitol has its own aesthetic charm. Elliptical shaped banister walls, leading to the 2nd and 3rd floors, border the entryway plaza. In the center of the terrazzo floor is a bronze state seal. The five medallions around the seal's perimeter are encased in Italian marble. Each medallion represents one of the five countries that have ruled over Florida.

The Senate chamber in the Historic Capitol, restored to its 1902 appearance.

The state seal in brass is surrounded by inlaid marble and is the centerpiece of the new capitol's rotunda.

KEEPING THE FAITH

Recognizing a history deeply rooted in religious principles, government officials decided to perpetuate the faith of their founding fathers. In 1976, a resolution was passed authorizing a room in the new capitol set aside for worship and meditation. Florida's Religious Heritage Chapel is one of only six states that have dedicated a room within the capitol for state officials, public employees and visitors to exercise their religious freedom of worship in a governmental setting.

The Senate chamber in the present Capitol.

1902
North & south wings and dome added

1923
East and west wings added; Dome painted silver

1936 & 47
Two more wings added to the Historic Capitol

1977
Tower capitol completed

1982
"1902" capitol restored and re-opened as a museum

2000

★ Claim to Fame

SOMETHING OLD, SOMETHING NEW

Completed in 1977, the Florida capitol is the most recently completed. (Note that Alaska is in the planning stages for a new capitol). The 22-story capitol was completed while the old one awaited the results of a petition to save it from destruction. The Historic Capitol, restored to its 1902 appearance, now serves as a museum. Although the new capitol has a beauty of its own, visitors are naturally drawn to the Historic Capitol with its dome and colorful awnings.

GOT 'YA COVERED

Florida is not the only capitol that once covered its windows with awnings during earlier years. Early photographs of capitols such as Arizona and Massachusetts also show awnings over their windows. However, Florida is unique in that awnings have been restored to its Historic Capitol.

WAY DOWN SOUTH

The capital city of Tallahassee also holds a distinction that occurred during the Civil War. Although it was occupied by Union forces after the war, it was the only Confederate capital east of the Mississippi River that was not captured by Union forces.

Overlooking the Historic Capitol, the 22-story capitol is flanked by the House and Senate's domes.

★ For What it's Worth

SAY IT WITH FLOWERS

Ponce de León is said to have named Florida, a Spanish word meaning full of flowers. The meaning of Florida is punctuated by a tradition that began in 1903 by the Women's Club of Tallahassee. At the start of each legislative session, a bouquet of flowers is placed on each legislator's desk. This gesture of good will continues to this day.

TAKING SIDES

Florida, officially a Confederate state during the Civil War, sent 15,000 troops to fight for the Confederacy. However, 2,000 Floridians were also reported to have joined the Union Army.

ALL IS NOT LOST

Over the years, the architectural drawings for the Historic Capitol seemed to have disappeared. In the process of restoring the Historic Capitol to its 1902 appearance, the only architectural drawings found were those showing the pediments.

Two different perspectives of the capitol.

47

GEORGIA
Atlanta

THE RUSH FOR GOLD LEADS TO A GOLDEN FINISH

A gold dome, topped with a statue of Miss Freedom, puts the crowning touch on the capitol of the state with the first gold rush.

STATE MOTTO

"Wisdom, justice and moderation"

★ Facts & Figures

Architectural style	Classical Renaissance
Architect	Edbrooke and Burnham
Exterior material	Indiana oolitic limestone
Dome surface	23 karat gold
Building height (to tip of dome)	271'
Construction period	1884-89
First occupied	1889
Capital population (Census 2000)	416,474
Census estimate 2007	519,145
Direction capitol faces	West
Original cost	$999,882

The Past Remembered

Atlanta is the fifth location to serve as Georgia's capital. Other locations included Savannah, Augusta, Louisville and Milledgeville. Only the last three capitals actually constructed capitol buildings.

GEORGIA'S ROYALTY

Georgia was named after King George II of England. In 1733, the King consented for James Oglethorpe to settle the area between Florida and South Carolina and to repel the Spaniards from Florida who were considered a threat. Oglethorpe was successful in this plan and remained in Georgia for nearly ten years. His likeness is prominently displayed on a sculpture in the capitol.

The bust of James Edward Oglethorpe, the state's founder, is at the top of a grand staircase.

UNDER BUDGET

Construction of a capitol in Atlanta began in 1884. The budget for the capitol construction was $1,000,000, one half of the state's annual budget. Upon its completion, a balance of $118.43 was returned to the treasury, marking the extraordinary event of a government project being completed under budget.

GIVING UP THE GOLD

The original surface of the dome was covered with tin. Remodeling plans in the 1950s called for the dome to be gilded with gold to commemorate the nation's first gold rush, taking place in the Georgia hills in 1828 — more than twenty years before the California Gold Rush.

Although the state could have sought monetary donations to fund the gold for the dome, citizens from the gold rush counties generously offered their own gold. These contributions were from their private collections of actual gold specimens mined during the gold rush era and new gold unearthed or panned for this purpose.

In a few months, 43 ounces of gold had been donated for the gilding. Adding to the campaign's nostalgia, a caravan of covered wagons pulled by a "seven mule team" transported the gold to Atlanta, taking three days for delivery.

A SHINING EXAMPLE

Just 19 years later in 1977, the weathering process had taken its toll on the dome and it was time for re-gilding. This time a new campaign was undertaken with the slogan "Make Georgia a Shining Example." A wagon train went on a six week trip across the state making stops at all the former Georgia capitals.

Later that year, when enough gold had been collected, 75 wagons made the final leg of the trip to the capitol. The last regilding occurred in 1998 with 85 ounces of gold from outside Georgia.

A stereoview card, c. 1900, shows an early view of the capitol.

A miniature Statue of Liberty is in the foreground while *Miss Freedom*, on top of the cupola, clasps a torch and sword representing liberty.

A grocery list, made of wood with red pegs, c. 1950s, features the capitol.

This "Litho-chrome" postcard was published by the Georgia News Company. Although postmarked 1908, authorities date the card sometime before 1904. Historical records indicate that the true color of the dome was gray. The finish was terne, a lead/tin alloy painted a gray color to blend with the stone. Not until 1958 was the dome gilded with gold.

Bright red flowers line the entryway in this 1992 photo.

Pearls of Wisdom
"Built upon the crowning hill of her capital city, whose transformation from desolation and ashes to life, thrift and beauty so aptly symbolized the state's restoration."

Governor John Brown Gordon — July 4, 1889
Capitol dedication address

Historical Happenings

1800

1788
Fourth state to ratify the Constitution

1828
Gold Rush in Georgia — first in the nation

1864
Federal troops occupied capitol grounds

1868
Atlanta approved as capital

1886
Coca-Cola first produced in Georgia

★ *The Inside Story*

MORE THAN JUST A CAPITOL

The capitol was never intended to house a museum, but after an International Exposition in 1896, several exhibits were given to the state for display at the capitol. To utilize extra space, displays of rocks and minerals were showcased to exhibit the state's rich natural resources. The concept was so well received that other exhibits were added. In 1955, the fourth floor was officially declared the "State Museum of Science and Industry."

During the recent restoration, the exhibits were scaled back and the museum is now known simply as the "The Georgia Capitol Museum." Prior to this restoration, a hall of flags also lined the railings overlooking the stairways. However, the flags were removed since the restoration committee's goal was to restore the capitol to its original appearance.

IN CHERRY CONDITION

In 1889, cherry wood desks were purchased for the House of Representatives. These desks, still in use today, have served the state representatives continuously for more than 100 years. The Senator's desks are made of oak.

ROOM FOR RENT

When the capitol was first completed, some areas were not used for offices. The adjutant general, also referred to as the "Keeper of the Building," resided with his family on the top floor. Until recently, visitors could climb to an observation ledge that circled around the dome for a "bird's eye view" of Atlanta.

The interior dome — as restored to its original color.

The House chamber has a cove ceiling instead of a dome which rises above the roof.

A flag display, previously part of the museum, was removed during a restoration.

A glass grid in the rotunda, installed prior to the installation of electric lighting, allows light to pass through to the lower level.

The rotunda walls are lined with Georgia marble.

1900

1889
Capitol
completed

1958
Dome gilded

1965
Miss Freedom statue
struck by lightning

2000

2001
Renovation
completed

★ Claim to Fame

GET OUT OF TOWN

During the Civil War in 1864, Federal troops occupied the grounds where the capitol was to be built. The takeover of Atlanta was so hostile that the civilian population was given written notice to register their presence and then be evicted from the city.

MISS FREEDOM'S MYSTERY

The origin and cost of the fifteen-foot statue Miss Freedom, mounted on top of the dome, remains a mystery today. It is believed to have come from Ohio, but a fire in the early 1900s destroyed documents relating to its purchase.

LIGHTNING STRIKES

Miss Freedom holds a torch with a frame in her hand — a 175 watt, metal-halide, light bulb — that burns 24 hours a day. Normally, the bulb is changed once a year by extending a bulb in a tube via a 30-foot pole. In 1965, lightning struck the torch of the statue and the flame structure was shattered and fell to the ground. While repairing the damage, workers noticed the hollow statue had been pierced with bullets. Like the Arizona capitol, the culprits apparently were taking target practice.

The Atlanta skyline dwarfs the golden dome of the state's capitol as seen in the foreground.

★ For What it's Worth

TURNING BACK THE CLOCK

On the night of February 21, 1964, in an attempt to allow more time to vote, Rep. Denmark Groover reached over the balcony of the House at the stroke of midnight in a futile attempt to turn back the clock. Instead, the clock crashed to the floor. At midnight, it ended the deadline for approving the re-apportioning of legislative districts to allow for more representatives.

CAPTURE THE FLAG

Although most states have kept the design of their original flag, Georgia continues to make changes. As with some other Southern states, Georgia elected to de-emphasize the Confederate theme of its flag which flies over the statehouse. In early 2001, legislators agreed to show five historic flags at the bottom of the state flag, thereby reducing the size of the Confederate emblem. In May 2003, Georgia raised its third different state flag in just 27 months. This one is said to resemble the first national flag of the Confederacy often referred to as the "Stars and Bars."

FIGHTING NOT PROHIBITED

In the early 1900s, Prohibition was a major issue in government. Tempers often flared as both sides were unwilling to give. During one of these heated arguments in the Georgia House of Representatives, a fistfight erupted. The debate continued on to the national level where it gave birth to a Constitutional amendment.

Pretty pink petunias add a pleasing foreground to the capitol.

HAWAII
Honolulu

KINGS AND QUEENS NO MORE!

Surrounded by pools of water, this open air capitol simulates the ocean from which the Hawaiian Islands emerged. Governed by kings and queens for centuries, this tropical paradise is now governed by a bicameral legislature.

"The life of the land is perpetuated in righteousness."

★ Facts & Figures

Architectural style	Modern
Architect	Belt, Lemmon & Lo and John Warnecke & Assoc.
Exterior material	Concrete
Dome surface	Open to the sky
Building height	100'
Construction period	1965-69
First occupied	1969
Capital population (Census 2000)	371,657
Census estimate 2007	375,571
Direction capitol faces	North
Original cost	$24,576,900

The Past Remembered

TREASURED ISLAND

In 1893, the United States Minister to Hawaii usurped control of the islands of Hawaii by overthrowing the monarchy and setting up a provisional government. Queen Lili'uokalani, Hawaii's last queen, made several unsuccessful efforts to maintain Hawaii's sovereignty, but with U.S. Naval forces anchored in the harbor, the Queen was forced to surrender her throne.

Perhaps the Queen said it best in her final protest: "Now, to avoid any collision of armed forces and perhaps the loss of life, I do under this protest, and impelled by said force, yield my authority until such time as the Government of the United States shall, upon the facts being presented to it, undo the action of its representatives and reinstate me in the authority which I claim as the constitutional sovereign of the Hawaiian Islands."

Though she appealed to President Harrison, her request fell on deaf ears. Soon after her plea, an Executive Council, composed entirely of Americans, replaced her. Living in Washington Palace, the Queen's personal residence until her death in 1917, the Queen was never restored to her monarchy. Few Americans are aware of Hawaii's sad story to statehood.

PARADISE LOST

In 1993, the U.S. Congress passed Public Law 103-150 which acknowledged the "100th Anniversary of the overthrow of the Kingdom of Hawaii." The resolution went on to offer an apology to the Native Hawaiians for the illegal overthrow. Hawaii was annexed five years later. In an effort to rectify the "past injustice," a bill

known as the Akaka bill was introduced before Congress in 2004 to grant special rights to ethnic Hawaiians. However, many citizens advocate unity with the U.S. and equality of its people. A third faction want more than what is being offered and (at the date of this printing) want the Kingdom restored, thereby removing the 50th star from the flag, in an effort to regain their "paradise."

REFLECTING REALITY

As with Iolani Palace, the designers of the capitol incorporated explicit symbolism depicting the state's origins of which the Hawaiians are also proud. The capitol, constructed in the late 1960s, is surrounded by two reflecting pools, symbolizing the seas which surround the islands. It has eight pillars shaped like royal palms representing the eight islands. The open dome represents a volcano while the building represents the island. An unknown author stated that the building is "a wonderful synthesis of pleasing art and forthright function."

Queen Lili'uokalani, whose statue is pictured here, boldly stated "Hawaii for Hawaiians." This statement was said to have cost her the throne.

A memento from the capitol dedication in 1969 is made from lava rock.

Iolani Palace, completed in 1882, once a prominent dwelling for kings and queens, stands in the shadows, but is not forgotten.

The Hawaiian crest is affixed to the Palace gate.

Pearls of Wisdom

"We are going to get into a war some day either over Honolulu or the Philippines.... If war was declared with some Pacific nation we would lose the Philippines before lunch, but if we lost these here, it would be our own fault."

Will Rogers — August, 1934
Seven years prior to the attack on Pearl Harbor

Historical Happenings

1800

1900

1778
Captain James
Cook visits Hawaii

1791
King Kamehameha
conquers Oahu

1810
All islands are under
the King's control

1893
Queen Lili'uokalani overthrown;
Hawaii becomes a republic; Sanford
Ballard Dole becomes President

★ The Inside Story

GOING TOPLESS

Absent a traditional capitol dome, or any ceiling for that matter, the center of the building is open to the sky. When it rains, rain falls into the center courtyard. Shortly after the completion of the capitol, it became apparent that the structure had a drainage problem. Although there were drains in the courtyard, the rainwater flowed away from the drains and toward the House chambers. It was reported that during one rainstorm, water cascaded down an elevator shaft.

PARTISAN POLITICS

As the building was being completed, it was reported that the Democratic senators had a sauna installed in the caucus room of the capitol. Questions were raised about its appropriateness. But the governor responded that it was the legislators' prerogative as to how they spend their construction funds. One Democratic senator remarked that it could be "greatly refreshing for weary senators" and that the Republicans were also welcome to use it.

ISLAND SYMBOLISM

As noted earlier, the Hawaiian capitol is rich in symbolism. The twenty-four concrete columns symbolize coconut palm trees, each cone-shaped legislative chamber symbolizes a volcano and the two reflecting pools which surround the building symbolize the ocean from which the islands emerged. Each pool is 18 inches deep and is supplied by three underground brackish wells.

NATIVE WOODS

The interior furnishings of the capitol, such as paneling, bookcases and high doors, are made of native koa wood — trees innate to the Island of Hawaii. Concerted efforts were made to use materials strictly native to the Islands.

THE SUN AND THE MOON

The House and Senate chambers, both cone-shaped and symbolizing volcanoes, reflect themes that complement each other. The Senate, adorned in ocean and sky tones, has a chandelier that symbolizes the moon and is made of 630 chambered nautical shells. The House utilizes earth tones, while its chandelier symbolizes the sun.

Open to the sky, Hawaii's "dome" appearance is forever changing.

In the center of the courtyard is a mosaic tile floor with shades of blue and green. Named *Aquarius*, it simulates the changing colors of the ocean.

A gold-plated copper and brass chandelier, symbolizing the sun, is suspended from the ceiling of the House chamber. The Senate chamber has a chandelier which symbolizes the moon.

1900

1959

1969

1995

2000

Hawaii becomes
a U.S. Territory

President Eisenhower
grants statehood
to the 50th state

Capitol
completed

Renovation
completed

While the Hawaiian state flower is the yellow hibiscus blossom, each island was assigned a different color of this flower. The red hibiscus, pictured here, is actually the color for the Island of Hawaii rather than Oahu where Honolulu is located.

★ Claim to Fame

THE ROYAL TREATMENT

Hawaii is the only state that was once a kingdom ruled by native royalty. Gone are the days of this monarchy. However, Hawaiians still cling to the memory of this whimsical monarchy. Statues of the past monarchy are placed in prominent places around the capitol.

ALWAYS OPEN

Unique among state capitols, the building has two grand entrances, but no doors. Thus, it is open to the public 365 days a year. Because of Hawaii's culture, the side facing the island's interior is dedicated to the farmers while the side facing the ocean is dedicated to the fishermen.

★ For What it's Worth

STREAKER OF THE HOUSE

In March 1974, a male hairstylist from San Francisco attempted to run naked through a legislative session in the House of Representatives. As he was being escorted out by police, he announced "I am the Streaker of the House!" He was arrested and charged accordingly.

MUSIC FIT FOR A QUEEN

Queen Lili'uokalani was especially noted for her musical compositions. Most notable was her song "Aloha Oe" (Farewell to Thee) which has been described as "immortal." It has been said that audiences often stand in respect to its captivating melody as though it were Hawaii's national anthem.

Palm trees blowing in the breeze with a rainbow over the mountains imply that all is well in "Paradise."

"The Eternal Flame," a War Memorial commemorates Hawaiians who have served and died in the Armed Forces.

IDAHO
Boise

HIGH ENERGY CAPITOL

Geothermal energy is used to bring warmth to this impressive and classy marble interior.

STATE MOTTO

"Let it be perpetual"

★ Facts & Figures

Architectural style	Neoclassical
Architect	J. E. Tourtelloutte & Charles Hummel (remodel)
Exterior material	Boise sandstone and Vermont granite
Dome surface	Terra cotta
Building height (to tip of dome)	208'
Construction period	1905–20
First occupied	1912
Capital population (Census 2000)	185,787
Census estimate 2007	202,832
Direction capitol faces	South
Original cost	$2,098,455

The Past Remembered

LOSING GROUND

In 1863, the Idaho Territory included Montana and most of Wyoming. When separate territories were created in 1864 and 1868 respectively, Idaho was reduced in size to what it is today.

TERRITORY DAYS

Prior to deciding on a permanent capital, the legislature met in Lewiston in northern Idaho Territory. During 1863-64, an attempt to establish a new territory composed of northern Idaho and eastern Washington was unsuccessful. It was to be named Columbia. As more people had settled in Southern Idaho, Boise was selected as the new capital.

HOUSE ARREST

After Boise was selected as the new capital, the citizens of Lewiston argued that it should remain the capital and challenged the decision. A bitter court battle ensued and confusion reigned over which town was the capital. When Boise proponents attempted to confiscate the records for relocation to Boise, the Lewiston legislators placed the records under armed guard.

In 1865, a new territorial governor was appointed and federal troops were called in to enforce the order. The governor gathered what records from the House sessions he could find as well as the state seal and left for Boise. In response to having the capital removed, Lewiston officials took the remaining records and tossed them in a jail cell!

HAILEY'S OBJECTION

Once the capital relocated to Boise, and Lewiston was out of the picture, the building of a territorial capitol was authorized in 1885. A town called Hailey objected to the action and obtained an injunction to cease the construction as it too sought the capital. Despite the delay, a red brick building was completed the following year and continued to serve after statehood was achieved — a total of 26 years.

MAKING ENDS MEET

In 1905, the legislature authorized its first state capitol to be built. They selected the local architectural firm of J.E. Tourtellotte over other entrants. The project was funded by the sale of public lands along with an amount from an endowment fund. The central portion was completed in 1912 which allowed staff to occupy the building. The former red brick capitol was still used until 1919 when it was necessary to demolish the building to allow for expansion. At each end of the building, wings were added.

NEW YEAR'S FIREWORKS

On New Year's Day 1992, a fire broke out in the capitol. Most of the fire was confined to the Attorney General's office. However, nearly two years were required to repair the damage and restore the capitol to its former condition.

A Tucks' "Oilette," a postcard resembling an oil painting, shows the former red brick capitol.

Miners, from the Empire State mine in Wardner, near Coeur d' Alene, pose for a picture in 1903. Mining was a big population draw in northern Idaho prior to 1900.

A postcard mailed in 1911 shows an artist's rendering of the capitol.

A tiny, milk-glass pitcher, c. 1915, shows the capitol.

B2280E5 Federal Bldg. and State Capitol Bldg. under construction, Boise, Idaho.

A vintage postcard, postmarked 1909, shows the capitol under construction. Note the start of the dome.

Pearls of Wisdom

"Idaho's Capitol on the interior is flooded with light. Its rotunda, corridors and interior as a whole is nearer perfect in this respect than any other building of its kind perhaps in the world."

J. E. Tourtelloutte — 1913

A souvenir pennant, c. 1950, illustrates the capitol.

Historical Happenings

1800

1900

1863
President Lincoln creates
Idaho Territory

1865
Capital relocates from
Lewiston to Boise

1869
Equestrian statue of
George Washington completed

★ The Inside Story

ON THE ROCKS

Idaho is known as the Gem State and the capitol represents that name well. The rotunda floor is covered with marble that forms a pattern known as "compass rose." At the center of this pattern is a sundial inlaid with minerals native to Idaho. There are also display cases filled with a wide assortment of rocks and minerals found in the state.

STARGAZING

In the center of the dome is a painted sky with forty-three stars. The stars symbolize that Idaho was the 43rd state. Thirteen of the stars are larger than the others. These represent the original thirteen states.

SHOW OFF

Pillars, columns and balustrades (railings) are covered in shades of white scagliola. Natural lighting shines in through skylights and windows to brighten the whitish color. In addition, balconies on each floor form rings around the rotunda that are lined with hundreds of fluorescent lights to further enhance the scagliola. Accenting the white color was no accident as the architect intended to emulate a bright and ashen color for the interior.

The inner dome.

This pattern is known as "compass rose."

Pillars are covered in scagliola veneer, an artificial marble.

Fluorescent lighting, forming rings around the rotunda, outline the dome.

1890 — President Harrison grants statehood

1920 — Capitol completed

1934 — Washington statue moves indoors

1982 — Heating system converted to geothermal energy

1992 — Fire damages 2nd and 3rd floors

2000 2002 — Renovation started

Claim to Fame

SOME LIKE IT HOT

Idaho has the only capitol heated entirely by geothermal energy. The system provides energy efficient hot water to the entire capitol complex which includes seven adjacent buildings.

Although the city of Boise has used the underground reservoir for similar purposes since the early 1900s, the state converted to this energy efficient source of thermal heating much later in 1982. Wells were drilled underneath the capitol to tap into this artesian water source. Water at a temperature of 164 degrees Fahrenheit is piped to the surface and circulated through the buildings. The state is able to save a considerable sum of heating costs by using this thermal energy source.

This drawing illustrates the natural geothermal heating of the capitol.

An overview of the capitol shows the mountains at its back door.

"SEALING" HER FATE

In 1890, Emma Edwards Green, an art student, was returning from art school in New York when she stopped in Boise. Attracted to the pioneer community, she decided to stay and offer art classes.

A contest to design the state seal offered a $100 prize to the winning design. Emma entered the contest and sought input from legislators as well as others in designing a seal representative of Idaho. Her efforts paid off as she was the unanimous selection of the committee. She holds the distinction of the only woman to have designed a state seal.

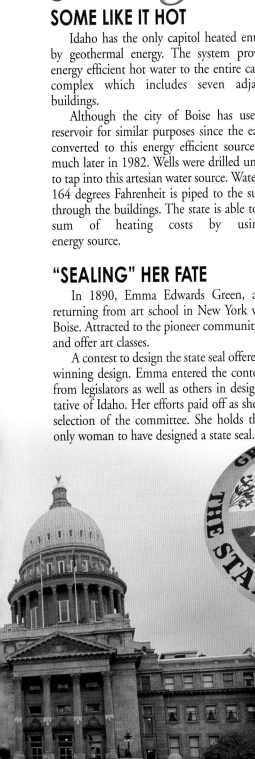

For What it's Worth

POSTAGE DUE

In the 1840s, Charles Ostner, an Austrian artist, immigrated to America. In 1864, he moved to the Garden Valley of Idaho. Ostner was especially grateful for his new citizenship and offered to show his appreciation by carving a statue of George Washington out of a huge chunk of yellow pine that he had found near a creek. Despite the fact that the only picture he had of Washington was on a postage stamp, Ostner was able to carve a close likeness. The sculpture depicts Washington astride a horse. Taking five years to complete, much of his carving was done at night over the light of a pitch pine torch held by his son.

He finished the sculpture in 1869 and donated it to the state where it was bronzed and displayed on the capitol grounds. However, in 1934 it was gilded with gold leaf and moved inside the capitol where it is displayed in a glass case.

A carving of George Washington on horseback

NO SMALL POTATOES

Until recently, Idaho had been one of six states that did not have a governor's mansion. However, in December 2004, a wealthy potato farmer entrepreneur and his wife donated their home, valued at $2.8 million, to the state for use as the mansion. Plans called for a renovation before being used by the governor.

ILLINOIS
Springfield

LAND OF LINCOLN AND THE CITY LINCOLN LOVED

A silver dome puts the finishing touches on this tall capitol whose city was home to one of our greatest Presidents.

STATE MOTTO

"State sovereignty, national union"

★ *Facts & Figures*

Architectural style	Neo-classical with French influence
Architect	John Cochrane and Alfred Piquenard
Exterior material	Bedford limestone and granite
Dome surface	Zinc (painted silver)
Building height (to tip of dome)	361'
Construction period	1868-88
First occupied	1876
Capital population (Census 2000)	111,454
Census estimate 2007	117,090
Direction capitol faces	East
Original cost	$4,315,591

60

The Past Remembered

FROM SOUTH TO NORTH

The State of Illinois was settled from south to north. The state capitals migrated in this direction as well. Kaskaskia served as the first capital in 1818-1819. Next, Vandalia, about 80 miles southeast of Springfield, served as the capital for 20 years which fulfilled a commitment the State made to that city. Then, it was Springfield's turn. Springfield was chosen for its central location. The present capitol is the second in this city and the sixth overall.

LAND OF LINCOLN

Abraham Lincoln, nick-named "Honest Abe," began his political career in Springfield. It was here the famous "House Divided" speech took place. Lincoln debated Stephen Douglas on seven different occasions throughout the State of Illinois. Though Lincoln lost the Senate race to Douglas in 1858, his stand on slavery gained him national prominence, helping him to become the Republican candidate for President. He called Springfield his home for twenty-four years until 1861 when he relocated to Washington, D.C. to become the nation's sixteenth President. The present capitol was built after his death.

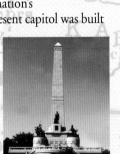

A postcard with a 1911 postmark sends Christmas greetings from "Ed" in Springfield to "Miss Eva" in Galveston, Texas.

A QUIET PLACE

The land on which the present capitol sits was donated to the state to serve as a final resting place for Abraham Lincoln. However, Mrs. Lincoln did not want the late President buried in the center of town. She

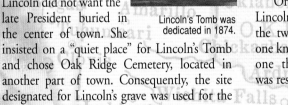

Lincoln's Tomb was dedicated in 1874.

insisted on a "quiet place" for Lincoln's Tomb and chose Oak Ridge Cemetery, located in another part of town. Consequently, the site designated for Lincoln's grave was used for the new capitol.

SAVED BY THE FIRE

Some felt a central location should not be the deciding factor for a capital since the state's center was so far from the heavily populated Chicago metropolis. Though construction was underway, political pressure took precedence and some thought the Capitol should be moved out of Springfield. The General Assembly was scheduled to meet in Chicago during the fall of 1871. However, these plans were thwarted due to the Great Chicago fire which devastated the city. This calamity allowed Springfield the time it needed to solidify the city as the capital's permanent location

IDLING AWAY

Construction lasted nearly 20 years with work being stalled several times. It began with the passing of the 1870 constitution which limited construction funding. In 1877, the funds appropriated for construction ran dry and suspicion of corruption led to several investigations. A depression caused further delays. Adding to the woes of completing the project, newspaper accounts report that ten men lost their lives in construction accidents. For a five-year period, the project was completely idle. All of these unforeseen obstacles contributed to renewed efforts to abandon the existing project and relocate to either Peoria or Chicago. Finally, in 1884, additional funding was approved and the building was completed in 1888.

FANTASY TOWERS

Original drawings indicate that statues of Lincoln and Douglas were to be mounted on the twin towers of the capitol. Although no one knows for certain why this did not happen, one theory is that a shortage of funding was responsible.

Statues of Lincoln and Douglas near the front entrance.

An Allen & Ginter card, distributed in 1889, shows the capitol. The back of this miniature card shows a list of the 41 state capitols at the time. It also states "One picture packed in each box of ten cigarettes."

An 1889 photo, though faded over the years, shows the capitol over a century ago. On the reverse is a newspaper clipping describing the building. It states in part: "The flag staff above the dome is 364 feet high. On it the American flag floats higher from the plane of the earth than at any other point in the world."

A special edition license plate shows the Illinois capitols.

Pearls of Wisdom

"A house divided against itself cannot stand ..."

Abraham Lincoln — June 16, 1858
From a speech at the
Old State Capitol

Historical Happenings

1800

1900

1818 | **1837** | **1871** | **1877** | **1888**

President Monroe grants statehood

Approval to relocate to Springfield

Relocation plans to Chicago thwarted by Great Chicago Fire

First legislative session in new capitol

Capitol completed

The eye of the inner dome.

⭐ The Inside Story

Pillars supporting the inner dome appear to be granite. In reality, they are scagliola, a plaster composite material made to look like granite or sometimes marble.

24 X 24 X 24

Illinois' interior dome is one of the most majestic. The relief work in the dome is produced from plaster cast moldings. There are 24 sections that make up the dome's interior. There are also 24 columns and 24 stained glass panels or partitions. Other than being symmetrical, the reason 24 was used is unknown.

MURAL, MURAL ON THE WALL

The state's "Favorite Son," Abraham Lincoln, is immortalized in several murals depicting his life and contributions to the State of Illinois and the nation. A 40 foot mural on the landing of the grand staircase depicts the Illinois Indians meeting with George Rogers Clark. This mural was painted directly on the wall. Several statues of Illinois statesmen are also on display. Among them is Civil War General John A. Logan, credited with establishing the first Memorial Day.

HONEST ABE OR ESCAPE ARTIST

During a time when Abraham Lincoln served as a state representative the State occupied a church as temporary quarters. In order to avoid a quorum, he was said to have crawled out a church window.

Relief work encircles the dome.

On the landing of the Grand Staircase is the George Rogers Clark mural.

A view of the rotunda from the second floor.

Notice the intricate detail in the ceiling of the governor's office.

1918
Statues of Lincoln
and Douglas placed
on grounds

1932
Dome
reconstructed

1988
Renovation
completed

2000

★ Claim to Fame

ABOVE AND BEYOND

Among domed capitols, Illinois' capitol height to the tip of the dome is second to none at 361'. It is 74' taller than the U.S. Capitol. Higher yet is the distance to the top of the flag pole which is 405'. However, the building structure, which only includes the top of the dome, is the "benchmark" for determining the official height of a capitol.

RED ALERT

A ladder leading to the flagpole is attached to the cupola. The ladder enables workers to service the flags. Because of its lofty height, a sensor is connected to a red light that comes on when visibility decreases to a certain level to warn approaching aircraft.

Statues of Lincoln and Douglas were planned to be mounted atop the twin towers in front of the dome. However, the project never materialized.

It is 405' to the top of the flag pole.

A menagerie of marble can be seen near the governor's office.

★ For What it's Worth

THROW THE BOOK AT 'EM

Would you believe a book riot? In 1875, at the Old State Capitol, members of the Illinois House threw books at each other. The unruly behavior was triggered by an unpopular speaker.

CAPITOL IN TOW

During the Old State Capitol's reconstruction, the building was dismantled and stored at the State Fair grounds. In researching the story, a rather preposterous account was discovered. It stated that the "Old State Capitol was jacked up and moved to the State Fair Grounds"— an impossible task considering its size. However, the Old State Capitol was "jacked up" about 1900 to add a new lower floor during the time that it served as the county office building.

INDIANA
Indianapolis

THE HOOSIER CAPITOL

Stained glass and skylights accent the Hoosier capitol. An octagonal dome and a quaint little chapel display colorful designs and shades of decorative glass.

STATE MOTTO

"Crossroads of America"

★ Facts & Figures

Architectural style	Renaissance Revival
Architect	Edwin May and Adolph Scherrer
Exterior material	Indiana (oolitic) limestone
Dome surface	Copper
Building height (to tip of dome)	235'
Construction period	1878-88
First occupied	1887
Capital population (Census 2000)	781,870
Census estimate 2007	795,458
Direction capitol faces	South
Original cost	$1,980,969

The Past Remembered

The Indiana Territory was created in 1800 with the legislature, known as the Assemblies, meeting in Vincennes for thirteen years. The first territorial capitol, built in 1805, is still in existence though it has been moved to another location. In 1813, the legislature moved into a stone building in Corydon. This building became the first state capitol and today is a state historic site.

INSTANT CAPITAL

At the time of statehood in 1816, it was apparent that Indiana's growing population was expanding more rapidly to the north. In response, the U.S. Congress granted four square miles of public land in the central part of the state to be designated as a new capital city. This allowed the state to relocate its capital from Corydon, near the southern border of the state. Because the new location was not yet populated, it did not have a name.

Although several names were submitted, Indianapolis became the favorite. The name "Indianapolis" was derived from "city of" and "land of Indians" — a perfect fit since several different Indian tribes had occupied the territory prior to statehood. The site for the new capitol, as described in the State Constitution, was known as the State House Square.

In 1825, the legislature moved to temporary facilities in Indianapolis until a new capitol was completed in 1835. However, this building did not serve the state's needs for long. After only a few years, the limestone construction deteriorated and the state demanded a bigger and more modern facility. It was demolished in 1877 — before construction on the present capitol had begun.

"A CLEAR ARRANGEMENT"

When Indiana held a competition to choose an architect for the new capitol, twenty-four architects submitted designs for consideration. The design submitted by architect Edwin May, who moved to Indianapolis to enter the contest, won the competition. May's plan was known as "Lucidus Ordo," which in Latin translates to a "clear arrangement." He was paid a modest fee of two percent of the cost of construction for his services. Construction began in 1878, Mr. May died two years later. Ironically, his draftsman, a Swiss designer named Adolph Scherrer who was largely responsible for the design completed the project.

TOO CLOSE FOR COMFORT

During the construction of the capitol, many curious onlookers wandered onto the grounds to get a closer look. Unfortunately, some of these well-meaning citizens got a little too close. Reportedly, these "nosey pokers" disrupted the work being done in causing accidents and damaging materials. In response to these intrusions, the construction site was fenced off from the public.

A short distance away, a sculpture entitled, "*The Return Home*" frames the capitol. This monument, commemorating Indiana soldiers, was erected in 1902.

These early 20th century postcards show a trolley barn, horse carts and vintage automobiles near the capitol. The postcard showing the awnings was mailed in 1907.

An American flag, suspended from the dome, provides a kaleidoscope affect in this 1978 photograph.

A glass paperweight of the former Indiana capitol in Corydon.

A matchbook cover, c. 1950s features the capitol.

A tiny Allen & Ginter card, distributed in 1889, shows the capitol. There were 41 state capitols featured in this series. One picture was packed in each box of ten cigarettes.

Pearls of Wisdom

"*Winds of Heaven Never Fanned The Circling Sunlight Never Spanned The Borders of A Better Land Than Our Own Indiana.*"

Sarah T. Bolton — September, 1880
Poetry recited during a capitol ceremony
Seen on a plaque in the rotunda

A stereo card, c.1895, shows the capitol in its early days. A trolley line was installed in Indianapolis in 1893 — shortly after the capitol was completed. Note the cables in the picture presumably used by trolley cars.

Historical Happenings

1800

1816   **1825**   **1835**   **1888**

1900

President Madison grants statehood

Legislature convenes in Indianapolis

First capitol in Indianapolis completed

Capitol completed

★ The Inside Story

ROWS AND ROWS

The architectural style of the interior is primarily Italian Renaissance. Each floor is lined with two rows of marble pillars providing a stately ambiance to the hallways. A spacious corridor, 68 feet in width, divides the entire length of the building. On each side is a row of tall marble columns. The entire corridor spans three floors, from the first to the fourth floor and is illuminated by natural skylights.

THE HORSE BEFORE THE CAR

In the earlier years of the capitol's history, capitol staff rode horses to work. To accommodate the horses from staff and visitors, the first floor of the capitol was used as a stable. When cars replaced horses as a mode of transportation, the first floor stable was replaced with offices.

LAYERED EFFECT

Over the years, extensive changes have been made to the gasolier lighting fixtures, paint colors and the woodwork. A 1988 renovation revealed an incredible thirteen layers of paint. Color schemes and designs have now been restored to their original appearance.

DOME AFTER DOME AFTER DOME

Although not visible from the ground floor, there are actually three domes that comprise the dome's interior. The layered effect from the three domes provides a hidden light source to enhance the beauty of the stained glass.

Shades of blue and circles of red provide an iridescent effect in the octagonal dome's interior.

This colorful stained glass, located in the chapel features inlaid designs of the state bird—a cardinal—and a dove to symbolize peace; with a border depicting the state tree—a tulip tree.

Rows of marble pillars line the corridor of the atrium.

1962
Chapel
added

1964
Dome painted
gold epoxy

1978
Dome returned
to original copper

1988
$11 million
renovation completed

2000

★ Claim to Fame

IN GOOD FAITH

In 1962, Indiana became the first state to dedicate a room in its capitol for a chapel. In addition to providing a room for prayer and meditation for persons of all faiths, weddings are also permitted. Although Indiana was the first capitol with a chapel, other states have since followed suit. At last count, six capitols set aside a chapel room or space for legislators and citizens to express their faith in God. Although, the original chapel was located on the third floor, it moved to the fourth floor in 1970.

Adjacent to the capitol, fountains provide a peaceful and relaxing setting to "Capitol Park."

★ For What it's Worth

FOOL'S GOLD

The dome was never truly gilded with gold, but for a number of years it did have a gold appearance. During a refurbishing in 1964, the dome was painted with a gold-colored epoxy material. Although real gold was not used, the process was more expensive than gilding with real gold. It was believed the fake gold material would last longer than real gold.

In an effort to restore the capitol to its original copper appearance, a new "cladding" of copper was added to the dome during a roof replacement in 1978.

This 1978 photograph shows the "gold" dome, shortly before it was returned to copper.

IOWA
Des Moines

THE MULTI-DOMED CAPITOL

On a hill overlooking the city, the golden dome is highlighted by a green dome at each corner.

"Our liberties we prize and our rights we will maintain"

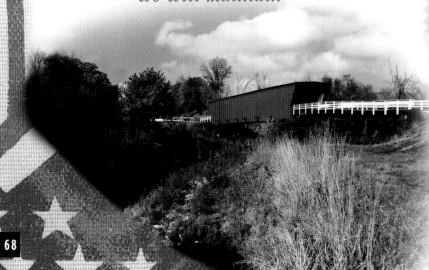

★ Facts & Figures

Architectural style	Neo-classical & Palladian
Architect	John C. Cochrane & A. H. Piquenard
Exterior material	Limestone, granite and sandstone
Dome surface	23 3/4 - karat gold leaf and four copper domes
Building height (to tip of dome)	275'
Construction period	1871-86
First occupied	1884
Capital population (Census 2000)	198,682
Census estimate 2007	196,998
Direction capitol faces	West
Original cost	$2,873,295

★ The Past Remembered

WESTWARD HO!

Prior to statehood, Iowa was part of Michigan and later the Wisconsin Territory. First located in Burlington as a separate territory, the capital was moved to Iowa City in 1842 where the first territorial capitol was built. This capitol served for seventeen years, but as Iowa's population grew, it was deemed inadequate for the state's needs.

As the country expanded westward, Iowa's population also grew to the west. Since Iowa City is located near the eastern border of the state, many legislators lobbied for a more central location as the capital. Although several sites were considered, a place known as Fort Des Moines was chosen in 1855. The site for the capitol became fixed when nine and a half acres of land were donated by local businessmen along with an offer to construct a building.

A compromise was made allowing the capital to relocate to Des Moines while Iowa City retained the state university. The old capitol in Iowa City was donated to the University of Iowa and now serves as a museum.

FARMERS TO THE RESCUE

The move to the new capital, a distance of 120 miles, was made in November 1857. The road between Iowa City and Des Moines was a stagecoach road that crossed streams without any bridges. At the time of the move, the ground was frozen and although most of the move went smoothly, a wagon carrying a large safe filled with gold and silver belonging to the state treasury bogged down in a snow drift because of the weight.

For several days it remained stranded until local farmers came to the rescue. They hitched ten yoke of oxen to a sled, pulling the safe free and delivering it to its new home.

THE OLD BRICK CAPITOL

The first capitol in Des Moines was a three-story brick building. Known as the Old Brick Capitol, it was located on the present site of the Soldiers' and Sailors' Monument. As the needs of the state outgrew this building, plans to build a more permanent capitol were made.

In 1871, John C. Cochrane and Alfred Piquenard were selected as architects to design the present capitol. Piquenard also designed the Illinois capitol.

A ROCKY FOUNDATION

Construction on the capitol began in 1871 using limestone for the foundation. However, the limestone cracked and crumbled during the first winter. Realizing a stronger foundation would be necessary to support the massive structure, the foundation was removed and rebuilt with a higher quality of stone.

A THOROUGH HOUSE CLEANING

In January 1904, a fire severely damaged the House chamber and the Supreme Court within a week before the legislature was scheduled to convene. Clean-up crews removed as much of the debris as they could and tarps were attached to the ceiling to cover holes left from the fire.

Despite the damage and unsightly conditions, the legislature convened as scheduled. According to newspaper accounts at the time, soot from the fire lingered throughout the session causing House members to "take daily baths."

SOARING GOLD PRICES

The cost of the original gilding of the dome was $3,500. It was re-gilded in 1905, 1927, 1965 and 1999. The latest cost to re-gild the dome had escalated to $400,000.

A divided-back, advertising postcard, mailed in 1908, shows a Mason car climbing the steps of the capitol.

Print of Dye

Dye

This image of the capitol was printed from a lithographic printing dye. The dye was hand-etched c. 1925.

This vintage photograph taken by Graeff-Oxford, NY is dated 1893. Note the grocer wagon with an East Locust Street address and the horse and buggy.

A celluloid button shows the capitol. It has a tiny American flag attached to it.

A capitol pennant from the 1950s

Pearls of Wisdom

"A state, like an individual, should present a decent exterior to the world — a grand building with noble lines and elegant architecture would be an inspiration and a stabilizing influence."

Representative John A. Kasson
1870

Historical Happenings

1800 — 1900

1838	1842	1846	1857	1886	1892
Iowa Territory created	Territorial capitol in Iowa City completed	President Polk grants statehood	Capital relocates from Iowa City to Des Moines	Capitol completed	Old "Brick Capitol" burns

![Suspended from the center dome]

Suspended from the center of the dome is the Grand Army of the Republic flag. Painted on canvass, it shows 13 stars. During a restoration, a sky with clouds was painted in the interior dome. Previously, a pale blue sky was painted in the dome.

Twelve statues encircle the inner dome

★ The Inside Story

ALL THE MARBLES

Iowa's interior features 29 varieties of hand-crafted marble. Shades of red and green and various other hues can be seen. There are 22 types of imported marble — mostly European but also from Mexico. Marble from four U.S. states are also represented to include Iowa, Vermont, Tennessee and New York. In contrast to the marble, all the wood except mahogany used in the interior is native to Iowa.

The rotunda area is lavishly adorned with 29 types of marble.

PHOTO FINISH

The largest reproduction of a photograph of its time, 26' long and 6' high, is on display on the first floor. Photographed in 1919 after the finish of World War I, it shows the 168th Iowa infantry, just returned from France, in front of the west side of the capitol.

IT'S THE LAW

The Law Library, located on the second floor, contains over 130,000 law-related books. The five story library has twin, iron circular staircases at opposite ends of the room for accessing the volumes of books.

The Law Library

This massive 26' long photo shows soldiers returning from WWI.

1897
Soldiers' and Sailors'
Monument completed

1904
Fire damages North wing
(House chamber)

1922
Flag emblem is
mounted in the dome

2000
2001
Fire damages
Old Capitol in
Iowa City

★ Claim to Fame

MIX AND MATCH

The distinguishing feature of the Iowa capitol is its five domes. In addition to the central dome that is covered with over 23 carat of firmly pressed, thin gold sheets, there are four smaller green domes at each corner. The green domes are covered with copper that has been tarnished by the weathering process. Each green dome is trimmed with gold leaf that appears as beads forming a rope. All five domes are topped by a lantern.

SPORTING TWO LINCOLNS

Although many capitols have a statue of Abraham Lincoln, Iowa is unique in that it has two Lincolns featured in statues at the capitol. One statue features Abraham, the other depicts his son, Robert Todd Lincoln.

OBJECTS MAY BE CLOSER THAN THEY APPEAR

In many instances, capitol ceiling domes are painted with images of stars or other scenes. Iowa's dome has a painted sky, but there is also a flag emblem that is mounted and stretched across the dome ceiling. From the rotunda floor, it looks as though the flag is painted on the dome ceiling. In reality, the flag emblem is painted on canvass and is suspended with piano wire well below the ceiling dome. Placed in 1922, it represents the Grand Army of the Republic, commemorating Civil War soldiers.

FAT AND WIDE

The Iowa capitol claims to have the widest of any of the capitol domes.

A reflected view of the capitol.

★ For What it's Worth

SLEEPING ON THE JOB

The former Supreme Court included a private study for the justices. There were five fold-up beds known as "Murphy Beds." On occasion, a court case would require a sleep-over at the capitol. When the beds were folded into the wall, a large mirror hid the bed. Although the Supreme Court is no longer located in the capitol and most of the Murphy beds have since been removed, one still remains.

AN UPSIDE DOWN VIEW

In 1948, an article appeared in *Life* magazine about a young Chicagoan who had visited "all 48" capitols in ten months. At each capitol, he did a headstand in front of the capitol and had a bystander take his picture. *Life* did a story and printed his pictures of the capitols along with his personal opinions of the "ten worst." He rated the Iowa capitol as the second worst commenting, "A terrible waste of materials." However, not many would share his opinion today. With its golden dome and four "green" domes, many would call Iowa one of the more beautiful capitols.

OFF ROAD

During the capitol's construction, the contractor Robert Finkbine devised a rather unique way to move the stone to the upper portions of the building. He constructed a winding dirt road to serve as a ramp which ended at the top floor. Mule wagons were then used to transport the heavy stones to the top.

KANSAS
Topeka

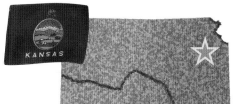

THE SUNFLOWER STATE ADDS A STATUE TO ITS DOME

Controversial murals and a birdcage elevator are featured at the Sunflower Capitol that took 37 years to complete.

"To the stars through difficulties"

★ Facts & Figures

Architectural style	French Renaissance (predominantly)
Architect	E. Townsend Mix and John G. Haskell
Exterior material	Kansas Limestone
Dome surface	Copper
Building height (to tip of dome)	306'
Construction period	1866-1903
First occupied	1869
Capital population (Census 2000)	122,377
Census estimate 2007	122,642
Direction capitol faces	North
Original cost	$3,200,589

The Past Remembered

The first territorial legislature met in Pawnee in 1855. The building where they met, now part of Fort Riley, is still in existence.

BUILDING YOUR HOUSE UPON THE SAND

In 1862, twenty acres of land in Topeka were donated to the state. It became known as Capitol Square. Although construction of the capitol began in 1866, the decision to use sandstone in the construction of the foundation proved costly. Within a year, the forces of nature had eroded the sandstone foundation into piles of sand. Consequently, the sandstone was removed and replaced with a new limestone foundation.

THE FINAL PIECE

Kansas built its capitol in sections spanning 37 years. The first phase, construction of the east wing, was completed in 1869. The west wing was added in 1881. Finally in 1903, the central section, which included the dome, was added which connected the east and west wings. The final piece, the statue atop the dome, was added in 2002.

BIG HOUSE ON THE PRAIRIE

When the first sections of the statehouse were completed, Topeka was surrounded by an untamed prairie. As a result, it was not uncommon for livestock and other animals to frequent the capitol grounds. To keep these animals off the grounds, some accounts indicate a stone fence was erected. As the town expanded, cries for a more modern fence resulted in replacing the wall with a "pig-tight" wooden fence.

CAVE OF THE WINDS

Prior to the west and east wings being connected, they stood alone as separate buildings with an open space between them. To shelter those traveling between the two wings, a covered-bridge structure was built to connect the two sections. Said to be like a wind tunnel, it became known as the "Cave of the Winds."

The Kansas capitol, lighted at night, has been the setting for several movies including *Truman*. These movies are often filmed at night when the capitol is not in use.

Alfred Landon, Governor of Kansas in 1936, lost his bid for President in a landslide loss to Franklin Roosevelt.

A stereoview card shows only the east wing and a fence around the capitol, c. 1870.

A Fred Harvey postcard sent by "Aunt Maggie", postmarked 1920, proclaims Topeka as one of the "handsomest capitals in the West."

Pearls of Wisdom

"I sincerely believe that in … the panel of John Brown, I have accomplished the greatest paintings I have yet done, and that they will stand as historical monuments."

John Steuart Curry — c. 1942

In 2001, Kansas adopted the image of the capitol on their license plate.

Historical Happenings

1800

1900

1861
President Buchanan
grants statehood

1869
Legislature
occupies east wing

1881
West wing added

1903
Capitol
completed

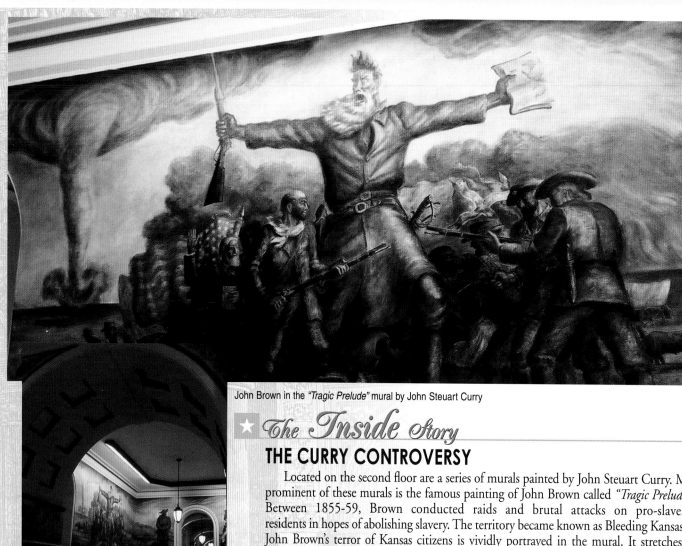

John Brown in the *"Tragic Prelude"* mural by John Steuart Curry

★ The Inside Story

THE CURRY CONTROVERSY

Located on the second floor are a series of murals painted by John Steuart Curry. Most prominent of these murals is the famous painting of John Brown called *"Tragic Prelude."* Between 1855-59, Brown conducted raids and brutal attacks on pro-slavery residents in hopes of abolishing slavery. The territory became known as Bleeding Kansas. John Brown's terror of Kansas citizens is vividly portrayed in the mural. It stretches 31' in length and is 11½' tall. This particular piece has generated controversy ever since it was painted at the capitol. In Curry's eyes, Kansas represented a struggle between the "free staters" and those who were pro-slavery. Some critics were quite vocal in expressing their dissatisfaction with his portrayal of Kansas in turmoil. They wanted a calmer, more tranquil image to characterize their state. Curry further complicated the matter by requesting that a section of marble be removed from the rotunda to extend his area of painting. The capitol committee denied his request. Consequently, he never completed all the murals he planned.

P.S.

Understandably, Curry did not appreciate the committee's denial to have the marble removed. As a postscript to the above story, he never signed his famous murals but he did paint a skunk family in the Kansas prairie on the Kansas Pastoral mural when he returned two years later after all the controversy. Over the years, a legend has been told that Curry added names to the "skunk family." Though authorities indicate this legend is untrue, Curry certainly left his mark on the Kansas capitol.

The dome interior

HEATING THINGS UP

The Kansas capitol had many built-in fireplaces since it was built before the advent of modern heating. On the second floor, there are eleven fireplaces!

1923	1942	1966	2000 2002
Birdcage elevator installed	Curry murals completed	Tornado damages dome	"Ad Astra" statue atop dome added

★ Claim to Fame

ALL CAGED UP

Located in the east wing, a hand-operated elevator often referred to as a cage elevator by some — because of its cage-like appearance — is still in operation. It was placed in service in 1923 and it is operated by an attendant. Kansas is the only capitol that has maintained this type of elevator. A House resolution was passed in 1976 for the preservation and maintenance of the elevator.

The cage elevator

Elevators like this — also referred to as a "birdcage" elevator by the profession — are rare, but do exist elsewhere.

TO THE STARS

In October 2002, a sculpture on top of the dome was added. Although the original design for the dome included a statue, over 99 years passed before the dome was complete. Sculpted by Richard Bergen and known as "Ad Astra," the bronze statue is 22' tall and weighs 4,420 pounds. The sculpture portrays a Kansa Indian shooting his arrow toward the North Star. The name of the sculpture was intended to reflect the state motto, "To the stars through difficulties."

Fountains and clouds add interest to this autumn setting.

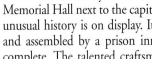
Table of the unknown prisoner

★ For What it's Worth

"POPS" ON ICE

In 1892-93, a third political party known as the Populist Party was successful in electing its members to the State and U.S. House of Representatives as well as other offices. However, the Republicans challenged the rightful control of those seats and a bitter fight for control of the Statehouse ensued. Some of the most appalling stunts included one party refusing to leave the chamber; having members arrested; locking out the other party members; breaking into the chamber with a sledge hammer; and barricading the door and turning off the heat in an attempt to "freeze" the others out. After what came to be known as the 1893 Legislative War broke out, the Populists agreed to have the matter settled by the courts. Eventually the Republicans were awarded control and the Populists were effectively put "on ice."

UNDESIGNATED GIFT

In the Secretary of State's office, which is located in Memorial Hall next to the capitol, a wooden table which has an unusual history is on display. It was hand-carved in the 1890s and assembled by a prison inmate taking over nine years to complete. The talented craftsman used several types of wood and formed it in the shape of a modified octagon. He carved intricate designs into the wood including an American flag, the Kansas seal and other images. When finished, the unidentified prisoner donated the table to the governor. To this day, the reason is unknown.

KENTUCKY
Frankfort

A NEW KENTUCKY HOME

In 1910, this capitol became the new home to the Kentucky legislators. The state spared no expense in lavishly landscaping the grounds.

STATE MOTTO

"United we stand, divided we fall"

★ Facts & Figures

Architectural style	Beaux arts
Architect	Frank Mills Andrews
Exterior material	Indiana limestone
Dome surface	English terra cotta
Building height (to tip of dome)	212'
Construction period	1905-10
First occupied	1909
Capital population (Census 2000)	27,741
Census estimate 2007	27,098
Direction capitol faces	North
Original cost (including furniture)	$1,820,000

★ The Past Remembered

IT'S FRANKFORT BY A NOSE

Lexington, Louisville and Frankfort all competed for the seat of government. Even though the first General Assembly met in Lexington, it selected Frankfort, the smallest of these towns, as the permanent capital. In addition to its river access, citizens of Frankfort offered the best site for the capitol and donated materials. Records indicate this included nails and panes of glass.

WAR BUCKS

Frankfort's first two capitol buildings were destroyed by fire. The third capitol, known as the Old State House, was built in 1830 and still stands today. The new capitol was completed in 1910 with the aid of $1 million from the Federal Government for Civil War and Spanish-American War reparations and services. The Kentucky legislature appropriated a similar amount of money to include furnishings and grounds. At $1.8 million, it was considered a bargain even in its day. Although the original amount appropriated for grounds was $50,000, the final cost amounted to $190,000. Today, it is evident that the additional cost was well worth the investment as Kentucky has one of the most beautifully landscaped capitol grounds.

HUNT PLACE

Original plans for the new capitol called for it to be built on the same site as the old. However, the architect's plans called for a larger site for the proposed footprint of the capitol. To accommodate the new capitol, a 33-acre farm known as "Hunt Place" was considered just right and was purchased.

SHARE THE WEALTH

Though the name commonwealth bears the same significance as "state," Kentucky is one of only four states to use this title. Virginia, from which Kentucky was formed, also preferred commonwealth, which means a "group of people banded together for a common good." Pennsylvania and Massachusetts also share the commonwealth designation.

This 1970s photo shows a view of the capitol. A 2003 photo shows a similar view from the same overlook. Notice the changes in landscape and the growth in vegetation.

This postcard shows a tobacco leaf encircling the capitol and declares "The Pride of Kentucky."

This 1912 postcard of the capitol shows banner flags suspended from the dome. The Kentucky River is in the foreground. The photo was taken from the site of Daniel Boone's grave, c. 1910, around the capitol's dedication. Apparently, car dealers were not the first to string banners to draw attention to what's new.

Pearls of Wisdom
"...wind around a spiral flight of seventy-eight steps, next ascend straight up a ladder of fifty rungs, and then crawl through a small opening in the floor of the lantern. The view is splendid, but the height too dizzy for the average person."

George A. Lewis — 1912
First Custodian of the Building
In describing the view from the dome

A brass pin with a blue ribbon, c. early 1900s, features the Kentucky capitol.

Historical Happenings

1800 — **1900**

1774
Daniel Boone leads settlers
into the Bluegrass area

1792
President Washington
grants statehood

1830
Old State Capitol
completed

The inner dome.

★ The Inside Story

WIDE OPEN SPACES

Known as the nave, the open space between the Senate and the House chambers provides a tunnel-like effect and an expansive and stunning view of the interior. Trimmed in Tennessee marble with Italian marble covering the floors in the corridors, it is 403' long. Georgia marble was used in the stairways and pilasters. Thirty-six monolithic columns, towering 26' in height and weighing ten tons each, support this nave area.

WILD BLUEGRASS COUNTRY

Each end of the nave has a different mural of Daniel Boone painted by Gilbert White. In one lunette, Boone is pictured with a group of explorers viewing the Bluegrass countryside. The other depicts the negotiation of the land with the Cherokees.

FRENCH CLASS

The design of the interior was greatly influenced by French architecture. The State Reception Room is modeled after a similar reception room of Queen Marie Antoinette in Versailles, France. The rotunda, as well as the dome, is copied from Napoleon's Tomb of the Hotel des Invalides located in Paris. Other features, such as stairways and banisters, are similar to the Paris Opera House. Murals in the reception room give the appearance of tapestries and depict the city of Versailles. Mirrors, chandeliers and fireplaces also contribute to the aristocratic class of French design. Mirrors are positioned to give the appearance of endless chandeliers.

Also in this room is an Austrian rug weighing over 1000 pounds. At the time it was made, it was reported to be the largest ever woven. During the weaving process, the loom broke three times due to the weight.

A bronze sculpture of Abraham Lincoln provides stately stature to the center of the nave.

The wide open spaces of the nave.

A many-faceted, stained glass skylight is mounted over the House of Representatives chamber.

1900 Governor Goebel assassinated in front of Old State Capitol

1910 Capitol completed

1952 Capitol Annex completed

1961 Floral clock installed

1998 Renovation completed

2000

⭐ *Claim to Fame*

KENTUCKY TIME

A giant floral clock accents the grounds. It sits over a pool of water with bubbling fountains, but does not tick nor does it make any noise. Instead, the hands of the clock sit idle and only move every sixty seconds when they make a sweeping motion covering one and a half feet. Installed in 1961 with design assistance from the Garden Club, it weighs 100 tons and is 34' in diameter. Over 10,000 foliage plants are meticulously placed to fill the basin of the clock. Quartz chips are inserted between the plants to spell "KENTUCKY."

HAND TOOLED

As with any capitol, visitors often marvel at the enormity and magnificence of the building. What is even more remarkable about Kentucky's capitol is that the only mechanical equipment used in its construction was a steam-powered concrete mixer.

NEIGHBORS AT ODDS

Although Kentucky remained loyal to the Union during the Civil War, the sentiments of its citizens were divided. Some men fought for the North while some joined the South. Kentucky holds the distinction that presidents of both sides, Abraham Lincoln and Jefferson Davis, were native sons. In fact, they were born just 60 miles apart.

Limestone columns frame the dome.

The north side, which is actually the front, is also gracefully landscaped.

⭐ *For What it's Worth*

FUNGUS AMONG US

During the dome's restoration, eight different types of fungus were found growing on the dome. Before the dome was re-assembled, a fungicide was used to destroy the damaging menace.

ALL DOLLED UP

Like several other state capitols, Kentucky displays miniature replica dolls of its First Ladies. The collection was started in 1971 with a new one added each time the administration changes. Periodically, the mold for the doll is changed in keeping with current styles.

LOUISIANA
Baton Rouge

HUEY LONG MAKES SHORT WORK OF A NEW CAPITOL

With Spanish moss hanging gracefully from sprawling oak trees and pink azaleas decorating the grounds, the towering capitol overlooks the muddy Mississippi.

STATE MOTTO

"Union, justice and confidence"

Facts & Figures

Architectural style	Art deco
Architect	Seiferth, Weiss and Dreyfous
Exterior material	Alabama limestone
Tower surface	White limestone
Building height (to tip of dome)	450'
Construction period	1931-32
First occupied	1932
Capital population (Census 2000)	227,818
Census estimate 2007	227,071
Direction capitol faces	South
Original cost	$5,000,000

★ The Past Remembered

ON HIGHER GROUND

In 1845, the legislature meeting in New Orleans, voted to establish a new capital site. The following year, they accepted an offer by Baton Rouge of a plot of high ground that overlooked the Mississippi River. The Old Capitol, as it is now known, was completed in 1849 and is still standing. In 1862, during the Civil War, it was taken over by Federal troops and sustained fire damage. As a result, the legislature moved back to New Orleans for twenty years. After extensive renovation, the legislature returned to the Old Capitol in Baton Rouge.

A postcard c. 1940 commemorates Huey Long's legacy.

THE KINGFISH RULES

As governor of Louisiana, Huey Long was so persuasive and controlling, some scholars have referred to him as a dictator. Known as the "Kingfish," his dream was to build a new capitol. Despite the fact that the economy was muddled in the Great Depression, Long spearheaded the necessary legislation to make his dream a reality in just fourteen months. In 1930, he was elected to the U.S. Senate but did not relinquish the governor's office until 1932. His decision not to resign was just long enough to influence the election of his handpicked successor.

SHARE THE WEALTH

In 1934, Huey Long and his associates wrote a booklet entitled *"Share Our Wealth."* In this writing, he expressed his belief that the nation's wealth should be more equally distributed and proposed a plan to make "Every man a king." Through radio broadcasts, he espoused his proposal, "We will allow no one man to own more than $50 million dollars," and

During the assassination of Louisiana legend, Huey Long, a stray bullet was lodged in this marble column and was left to memorialize the event.

organized *Share Our Wealth* clubs. He also proposed pensions for those over 60. In 1935, membership in the *Share Our Wealth* clubs was said to include nearly 4.7 million members.

A LONG SHOT

President Franklin D. Roosevelt became concerned about Long's growing national popularity and potential influence on the upcoming Presidential election. Long claimed that the Federal government attempted to withhold funding to Louisiana and had sent men to "dig up dirt" on his personal life. Long presented a transcript to the U.S. Senate of a "bugged assassination attempt" on his life.

In September 1935, Senator Long stood in the back of the Louisiana House chamber, lobbying state legislators to change their mind on a highly disputed bill. Amazingly, he successfully swayed the votes of several members and the bill passed. As he exited the House chamber, even though his bodyguards were present, the "Kingfish" was gunned down.

STANDING TALL

In selecting an architect for the new capitol, Huey Long bypassed the usual committee approach in personally selecting a firm. In so doing, he asked them to meet two criteria. These were that it be a skyscraper and secondly that it reflect Louisiana history. At 450 feet, it certainly is a skyscraper. The second condition was also met in that artisans sculpted Louisiana statesmen through various forms of art.

Huey Long's statue faces the capitol building he so cherished. Note the carving of the capitol.

HUEY PIERCE
1893 —
GOVERNOR — 19
UNITED STATES
1932 — 19

Extra! Extra! Headlines in The New York Times proclaim the assassination of Huey Long.

In 1970, the Senate chamber sustained one half million dollars in damage when disgruntled union members exploded sticks of dynamite. Note the close-up of a splinter of wood or possibly a pencil which was projected into a ceiling tile.

Pearls of Wisdom

"We have lived long but this is the noblest work of our whole lives..."

Robert R. Livingston —1803
Ambassador who negotiated the
Louisiana Purchase from France.
Inscription near capitol entrance

Historical Happenings

1800   1900

1803
Louisiana Purchase
signed

1812
President Madison
grants statehood

1849
Old State House
completed

1861
Louisiana secedes
from union

1928
Huey Long
elected Governor

Memorial Hall

The Governor's elevator doors

Former governors are immortalized on the
bronze elevator doors in Memorial Hall.

One of two white porcelain vases —
a token of friendship from France.

★ The Inside Story

TEN FLAGS OVER LOUISIANA

Memorial Hall features the ten flags that represent the governments which controlled Louisiana over the past 300 years. The architectural theme of the hall is Art Deco. It replaces a traditional capitol rotunda. Seven varieties of marble were used in the floor and walls. The floor is inlaid with travertine from Mount Vesuvius in Naples, Italy.

THE FRENCH CONNECTION

Two white porcelain vases, trimmed in gold and displayed on each side of the elevator doors, were given to the state by France as a sign of friendship. When donated in 1934, they were valued at $15,000 each. Today, they are considered priceless.

FOR THE GOVERNOR ONLY

An elevator in the capitol reads "For Governor Only." The restricted use of the elevator was intended for the "Kingfish" himself, Huey Long. During the Huey Long era, the governor's office was on the first floor. Today, it is located on the fourth floor, the highest floor this elevator reaches. Egrets, often mistaken for pelicans, are depicted on the elevator doors.

CAPITOL CORRECTIONS

Dining in the House of Representatives Dining Hall is a worthwhile experience. It is staffed by trustees of the Dixon Correctional Institute. Building maintenance and grounds keeping positions are also staffed by inmates. In so doing, the state provides meaningful work for minimum security prisoners and also saves tax dollars.

YOU ARE MY SUNSHINE

In 1940, Jimmy Davis along with Charles Mitchell wrote the song *"You Are My Sunshine."* The song, sung by Davis, earned a gold record award. Davis would go on to serve two terms as governor — 1944-48 and 1960-64. For several years, the governor held a spring concert to entertain the legislature. In 1961, after he had been criticized for purchasing a Cadillac, he rode his horse Sunshine to work — up the capitol steps! When asked about his peculiar behavior, he responded that he was just "showing Sunshine his office." As a postscript to the story, in 1977 his song was chosen as one of two state songs of Louisiana.

1932 Capitol completed

1935 Huey Long assassinated in the capitol

1940 Statue of Huey Long erected

1970 Senate bombing

1998 Renovation completed

2000

Early each spring, pink azaleas blanket the grounds of the Cajun capitol.

★ Claim to Fame

SKY HIGH

At 450 feet tall, and thirty-four stories high, Louisiana's is the tallest capitol. Note the resemblance to the Empire State building.

PRIESTLY PARISHES

Due to its Roman Catholic heritage, Louisiana is the only state that refers to its counties as "parishes." Also the French were the first to settle this region and thus French is a second language spoken by many.

Walkways in this formal garden lead to the centerpiece statue and grave of Huey Pierce Long.

The view from Observation Tower on the 27th floor. Beyond the gardens is downtown Baton Rouge while the Mississippi River is on the right.

★ For What it's Worth

ALL BETS ARE OFF

At the time of the capitol's completion, two local merchants debated how long the building would last. They each invested $2.50 in an interest bearing account at a compound interest rate of 4% with a local bank, wagering if the capitol would survive for 500 years. The heirs of the winning bet were to receive the proceeds in the year 2432 — a sum that would exceed two billion dollars! The bank was later released of its obligation.

A STICK MARKS THE SPOT

Before Louisiana was settled, French explorers traveled up the Mississippi River looking for higher ground when they noticed a red pole. Indians were said to have used the pole to delineate their hunting grounds by staining it with blood from animals that were killed during hunts. The spot became known as Baton Rouge, which in French means "red stick."

LONG LIVE THE KINGFISH

The colorful and dramatic life of Huey Long did not escape the notice of Hollywood. *The Kingfish*, a movie portraying Long's life and tragic death in the halls of the capitol, was filmed on location. *All the Kings Men* was also based on the life of Huey Long.

A fish-shaped, brass pin symbolizes the "Kingfish."

Forty-eight steps are inscribed with the states in the order of statehood. Alaska and Hawaii are etched on the 49th step as they achieved statehood after the capitol was completed.

MAINE
Augusta

A BULFINCH STATE HOUSE IS RECONSTRUCTED

A major facelift and expansion in 1909-10, including a new dome, allowed the capital to remain in Augusta.

STATE MOTTO

"I direct"

★ Facts & Figures

Architectural style	Classical Revival
Architect	Charles Bulfinch
1910 Addition/remodeling	G. Henri Desmond
Exterior material	Hallowell white granite
Dome surface	Copper
Building height (to tip of dome)	185'
Construction period	1829-32
First occupied	1832
Capital population (Census 2000)	18,560
Census estimate 2007	18,367
Direction capitol faces	East
Original cost	$138,991
1910 addition	$350,000

★ The Past Remembered

GROWING PAINS

Renowned architect Charles Bulfinch designed the capitol in 1829. Tucked away on a hillside overlooking the Kennebec River, this massive structure is an imposing sight. Bulfinch also designed the U.S. Capitol and the state house in Boston and the resemblance is unmistakable. However, as Maine's population grew, the original state house could not meet the growing facility needs of the legislators and citizens.

NOT CEMENTED IN PORTLAND

From the time Augusta was chosen as the capital, the people of Portland made repeated attempts to relocate the capital to its coastal city. Proponents favoring the move attempted to persuade the legislature to relocate every time the capitol's shortage of space became a topic of public discussion. In anticipation of being named the capital, the city of Portland began constructing a capitol building in 1836, and did so again in 1858. Each time, the legislature, by narrow margins, voted to remodel the building in Augusta instead.

THE WEST WING

In response to the need for additional space, an addition to the rear of the building was added in 1890-91. This addition, costing $150,000, blended well with the original Bulfinch design and became known as the West Wing. Although several Maine architectural firms competed for the bid, a Boston firm was awarded the contract. In response to the snub, the Portland Daily Press quipped, "No Maine architects need apply."

CAPITOL GAINS

In 1909-10, a $350,000 addition doubled the length of the capitol. However, as realized by architect G. Henri Desmond, adding this much size to the capitol caused the Bulfinch dome to seem disproportionately small in relation to the rest of the building. To solve the problem, the original dome was replaced with a larger one. As a result of these changes, the integrity of the original state house was maintained only in the portico and the wall directly behind it.

A "Now and Then" photo comparison. A postcard, c.1910, after the time of the latest addition, shows the capitol surrounded by lots of trees with the hillside at its backdoor. Other than the dome oxidizing to green, not much has changed.

This postcard was mailed to "Dear Friend Anna" in Ann Arbor, Michigan in 1908. It shows the capitol prior to the 1909-10 reconstruction.

A stereo card, c. 1880, shows the "Bulfinch capitol."

Pearls of Wisdom

"We hear that our Portland neighbors have adopted a beautiful plan ... that they might attract the State government out of that Granite cage at Augusta."

Bangor Times — July 3, 1858

Historical Happenings

1800

1900

1820	**1827**	**1832**	**1836**	**1860**	**1891**
President Monroe grants statehood	Augusta selected as capital	Capitol completed	Proposed capitol started in Portland	Move to Portland defeated in legislature	West wing added

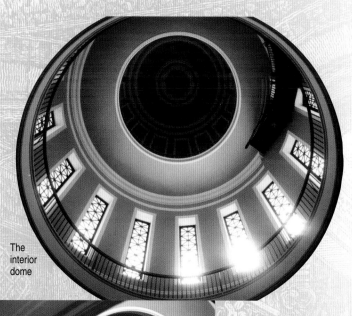
The interior dome

Two levels of balconies encircle the dome's interior.

A terra cotta bas relief depicts Civil War volunteers returning home.

★ The Inside Story

A TROPHY CATCH

Originally, the State Museum was housed in the capitol. At the time, trophy-size sport fish — for which Maine is famous — were displayed. Although the museum relocated in 1971, wildlife dioramas still exist.

A RIVER USED TO RUN THROUGH IT

Some years ago, a rather unique exhibit was on display at the capitol. The exhibit featured live trout and salmon that swam under a covered bridge. As capitol staffing and office space grew, there was no longer room for the water exhibit.

JUST PASSING THROUGH

A pass-through area is located on the third floor. This area, formerly referred to as Octagonal Hall, forms an octagonal shape and is now known as the rotunda. Though inner domes are generally visible from the first or second floors, this capitol is unique because the third floor rotunda is the first floor from which the inner dome is visible.

EYE SHADOW

Balconies above form a double ring around the eye of the dome. Windows in the upper part of the dome allow light to pass through and create shadows on the painted surfaces. The inner dome is covered with plaster and painted in earth tones.

A postcard, sent in 1910, features the Doric columns in the original Hall of Flags.

The Senate chamber, although not the original, was recently restored to its 1910 appearance.

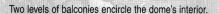

Maine

1910
North & south wings
added, dome replaced

1971
Capitol Museum
relocated

2000
2001
Renovation
completed

★ Claim to Fame

DRAWING THE LINE

In 1839, the boundary line between the British controlled Canadian province of New Brunswick and Maine was in dispute. Expecting an altercation, both countries mobilized some of its troops. The State, along with the U.S. government, assembled 50,000 troops for a possible conflict. However, in 1842 the dispute was settled without incident upon the signing of a treaty.

A LONG DRY SPELL

The Temperance movement has its origin in Maine in 1815. Although a society was organized the same year, a law known as the Maine Law, prohibiting the consumption and sale of alcohol was not passed until 1851. In the years that followed, twelve states or territories passed similar "Maine laws." The law remained in effect until National Prohibition was repealed in 1933.

A front row seat on the balcony provides a pleasing view of the surrounding area.

Ornamental ironwork frames the front walkway and Capitol Park.

White flowers of summer frame the green dome.

★ For What it's Worth

TOP DOG

In 1921, Governor Percival Baxter had an Irish Setter named Garry Owen. Garry was a special dog to the governor and also became a favorite with visitors to the capitol. Children on their way to school would stop and play with the dog. Garry's doghouse was painted green and white to match the governor's mansion. When the governor was in his office, the dog would wait patiently on a couch or on the floor for the work of the State to be finished. Garry even had a special pass to ride the railroad with his master. When the dog died in 1923, the American flag over the capitol was lowered to half-mast. Although a military official complained that it was inappropriate to lower the flag, the governor did not raise the flag until after the funeral.

NORWAY 14 MI
PARIS 15 MI
DENMARK 23 MI
NAPLES 23 MI
SWEDEN 25 MI
POLAND 27 MI
MEXICO 37 MI
PERU 46 MI
CHINA 94 MI

MARYLAND
Annapolis

GEORGE WASHINGTON WALKED THESE HALLS

To preserve the history of our forefathers, the integrity of the old capitol was maintained while adding new Senate and House chambers.

"Strong deeds, gentle words"

★ Facts & Figures

Architectural style	Georgian
Architect	Joseph Horatio Anderson
1902-05 addition	Baldwin and Pennington
Exterior material	Red brick
Dome surface	Wood-painted gray and white
Building height (to tip of dome)	179'
Construction period	1772-79
First occupied	1775
Capital population (Census 2000)	35,838
Census estimate 2007	36,603
Direction capitol faces	East
Original cost	£7,500 British sterling
1902-05 addition	$857,138

The Past Remembered

A SMOKIN' DEAL

The capital of the Province of Maryland was located in St. Mary's City. The first state house, a red brick building located on Saint Mary's Bluff, was built in 1676. Payment for construction was made with tobacco — the currency used by the province. The legislature was known as the "Upper and Lower Houses of Assembly." In 1829, the red brick state house was demolished. However, in 1934, a replica was built.

Tobacco leaves

ANNE ARUNDEL TOWN

In 1694, the General Assembly relocated to a place known as Anne Arundel Town. During the Assembly's first session, the name of the town was changed to Annapolis in honor of the soon to be princess. Additionally, the construction of a state house was approved. Shortly after it was built, the state house was struck by lightning. It survived but was destroyed by fire five years later in 1704. It was rebuilt in 1706 and was often referred to as the "court house." This state house was demolished when work on the current state house began in 1772.

HURRICANE FORCES

Although construction of Maryland's state house began in 1772, unforeseen circumstances prevented it from being completed until 1779. Initially, the construction suffered a setback due to hurricane damage. However, the American Revolution was the primary factor that delayed the capitol's completion. Once it was finished, however, the original copper cupola was a disappointment to some because it was considered disproportional to the rest of the building. Nature took care of the problem when another hurricane damaged the copper cupola, hastening its demise. A wooden dome replacement, which was completed in 1797, proved to be more durable and a "good fit" with the rest of the building.

ADDING ON

During the 1800s, the need for additional space was addressed by adding two annexes. Eventually, these additions became obsolete and were replaced with a west addition in 1902-05 which now houses the present House of Delegates and Senate chambers.

A mannequin of "George Washington" in the Old Senate Chamber.

A MOMENT IN TIME

An historic moment is captured in the Old Senate Chamber. A mannequin, that looks as if it is ready to take a step, depicts Washington resigning his commission. Complete with uniform and facial features, it was patterned after the famous Jean Antoine Houdon's sculpture which is located in the Virginia capitol.

MAKING HISTORY

Several notable events in colonial, state and American history have taken place in the state house. In 1783-84, prior to it becoming the capitol of Maryland, the Continental Congress met here for a period of nine months. Another historic event which took place here was the ratification of The Treaty of Paris, which ended the American Revolution in 1784. Also during this time, General George Washington resigned his commission as the Commander-in-Chief of the Continental Army. He retired to resume life as a farmer on his Mount Vernon estate, located on the Virginia side of the Potomac River. His retirement, however, was short-lived. In 1789, he returned to public service as the nation's first President. Washington was said to have visited Annapolis frequently.

ALL IS NOT IN VANE

Atop the dome is a 28' lightning rod, designed in accordance with Benjamin Franklin's specifications. Although its exact date of installation is unknown, the weather vane survived a severe hurricane in 1788 and remains in place today.

Washington Resigning His Commission, painted by Edwin White in 1859. Note the differences in the room as portrayed in the painting versus the recent photograph above.

Earliest view of the State House from the Columbian Magazine of 1789.

This postcard, mailed in 1908, shows the west side before it was replaced by the 1902-05 addition.

Pearls of Wisdom

"I close this last act of my official life, by commending the interests of our dearest country to the protection of Almighty God, and those who have the superintendence of them in His holy keeping."

George Washington — December 23, 1783
Old Senate Chamber

A pennant
c. 1950s

Historical Happenings
1800

1694
Annapolis designated as capital; relocates from St. Mary's City

1779
Capitol completed

1783
State House serves as nation's capitol

1788
Seventh state to ratify the Constitution

1797
Wooden dome replaces original cupola

The inner dome.

A seasonal view features a quilt show and the State House Christmas tree. Note the wide black line defining the old from the "new" section.

Tiffany skylights highlight both the House and Senate chambers.

★ The Inside Story

PIECES OF SILVER

Until a recent renovation, the Maryland Silver Room was a museum in itself. It featured pieces of silver from the U.S.S. Maryland silver set, donated to the Navy's ship in 1906. It also included historic documents included the only copy of the U.S. Constitution that still has the original seal intact. Plans call for the room to be converted into a recreated Old House of Delegates chamber.

MILLENNIUM LEAP

Black and white marble tiles cover the floor in the hallway leading to the legislative chambers. However, this checkerboard pattern is interrupted by a solid line of black marble that runs the width of the hallway. This line delineates the old section from the new. Effectively, it joins the 18th century with the 20th century.

REVOLUTIONARY PORTRAITS

The State House is home to several paintings by Charles Willson Peale. Famous for his American Revolutionary portraits, the Old Senate Chamber (renovation currently under way) features his historic painting, *Washington, Lafayette and Tilghman at Yorktown*. In 2006, another portrait of Washington by Peale sold at Christie's auction for $21.3 million!

RESTORING THE PAST

From 1772 to 1878, the Old Senate Chamber remained virtually unchanged. Due to its deteriorating condition, the chamber was rebuilt from the ground up in 1878, but was modernized as deemed appropriate. After several years, those dismayed by the modernization of the room received approval to restore the historic features. After considerable research, which included locating drawings, photographs and descriptions, the restoration of the Old Senate Chamber to its 1783 appearance was completed in 1905. The chamber is once again being restored. In the process, furnishings and paintings are in storage.

The Senate chamber features Italian marble walls and columns as well as portraits of Maryland's four signers of the Declaration of Independence.

1900 **2000**

1905
West annex replaces earlier addition; Old Senate Chamber restored

1996
Original acorn atop dome replaced

★ Claim to Fame

THIS OLD HOUSE

Although the legislature now meets in newer chambers within the state house, Maryland claims to have the oldest state house in continuous legislative use which dates to 1779.

A TOUGH NUT TO CRACK

The Maryland State House is also reported to have the oldest and largest wooden dome in the country. The beams, made of cypress wood, are held together by the original wooden pegs. In order to avoid the British tax, no nails were used. Atop the dome is a five-foot wooden acorn. The original acorn, said to symbolize wisdom, lasted over 200 years. During a restoration project in 1996, it was replaced with a new one as the wood had rotted beyond repair.

DOUBLE DUTY

The Maryland State House is the only current state capitol that also served as the national capitol. During 1783-84, the Maryland State House was host to the Continental Congress. Meeting in the Old Senate Chamber, such notable congressmen included future Presidents Thomas Jefferson and James Monroe. Although, Trenton also served as a U.S. capital location, they met in a different building from New Jersey's present capitol.

Maryland State House Christmas ornament

The west or "new" side of the state house.

The wooden dome was designed by architect Joseph Clark.

★ For What it's Worth

HAVIN' A BALL

On the night of December 22, 1783, a ceremonial ball was held to honor George Washington who was resigning his commission as Commander-in-Chief of the Army the following day. Washington is said to have danced with every woman present.

PAINTINGS DON'T LIE ... OR DO THEY?

In the stairwell to the second floor is the famous painting, *Washington Resigning His Commission*. The painting shows Mrs. Washington and other women on the floor of the Senate observing the momentous occasion. In reality, Martha Washington was out of town and there were no women on the floor at this historic event. During those days, women were forbidden on the Senate floor and were required to watch from the balcony.

360

The town of Annapolis, based on its original plat, is laid out in circles. The State House is in the inner circle, though not at the center. Streets radiate out from the circle and are named after the points of the compass. A larger circle, added later, extends further out with streets being named after additional points of the compass — Northeast, Southeast, etc.

LOOSELY SPEAKING

The origin of Maryland's state motto is Italian which means "Manly Deeds, Womanly Words." In recent years, the state changed the motto to "Strong Deeds, Gentle Words." However, when researched, it was discovered that the original translation was closest in meaning.

MASSACHUSETTS
Boston

THE BULFINCH STATE HOUSE OVERLOOKS BEACON HILL

Perched atop Beacon Hill and overlooking Boston Common, this historic capitol dates to John Hancock & Paul Revere.

STATE MOTTO

"By the sword we seek peace, but peace only under liberty"

★ Facts & Figures

Architectural Style	Neo-classical Federal
Architect	Charles Bulfinch
Exterior material	Red brick
Dome surface	23-karat gold leaf
Building height (to tip of dome)	155'
Construction period	1795-98
First occupied	1798
Capital Population (Census 2000)	555,400
Census estimate 2007	599,351
Direction capitol faces	South
Original cost	$133,333

The Past Remembered

"PASTURE-RIZED"

With more than two centuries of history, the Massachusetts capitol's past is littered with names familiar from history books. The grounds, on which the capitol sits, once belonged to John Hancock — the first signer of the Declaration of Independence and also the first governor. While Hancock owned the property, he used it as a cow pasture. In fact it was known as the "Governor's Pasture." The capitol's cornerstone was laid by Samuel Adams, governor in 1795, with the help of Paul Revere. On the grounds are statues of other Massachusetts notables, namely orator Daniel Webster, philosopher/educator Horace Mann, Mary Dyer and Anne Hutchinson, who died for their faith, and John F. Kennedy, our 35th President.

PATRIOT GAMES

Upon completion of the State House in 1798, the wooden dome was covered with whitewashed shingles. In 1802, Paul Revere and sons layered it with copper in hopes of eliminating the leaks. Next it was painted a stone gray. Then in 1861, it was painted gold. Finally, real gold leaf was applied in 1874. Gold has been the standard ever since with the exception of the World War II era when it was painted a "battleship gray" color. The name of the dome, known as the Bulfinch dome, is taken from the original building architect, Charles Bulfinch. Bulfinch was one of the architects for the U.S. Capitol building and also designed the original Maine State House.

COATS OF MANY COLORS

The dome is not the only material that has undergone a facelift. The brick has also seen many changes. Originally the brick was red. In 1825, it was given a coat of white paint. Next, it was painted a yellowish hue to match an addition. Then in 1918, it was back to white to match the addition of two marble wings. Finally all the coats of paint were removed in 1928 returning the brick back to its original red color.

Mums accent this Fall 1988 capitol grounds photo.

In 1910, "Daniel" mailed this card to "Bertha" stating "This is where I spend some of my pastime."

Mailed in 1907, this postcard was an advertisement for Old Home Week and Boston Baked Beans.

How has the capitol changed in the past 100 years? This postcard, sent in 1905, shows a curved driveway, a yellowish brick exterior and a gold dome. Note the presence of red and white awnings. Today, the driveway is gone, the brick is red, the dome has gold leaf and there are no awnings.

This stereocard bears a handwritten date of Apr 20, 1881 on the reverse side.

This postcard advertises Cross Shoes for women. It shows the stone gray color of the dome depicting the period prior to 1861.

Pearls of Wisdom

"[The] Boston State-House is the hub of the solar system. You couldn't pry that out of a Boston man, if you had the tire of all creation straightened out for a crowbar."

Oliver Wendell Holmes
1858

A postcard advertisement, c. 1900, shows the dome being polished with Sapolio "cakes." The reverse of the card reads in part "BETTER AND CHEAPER than soap, EMERY, ROTTEN STONE ... PRICE NEVER OVER 10c PER CAKE."

Historical Happenings
1800

1778 — Massachusetts becomes the sixth state to ratify the Constitution

1798 — Capitol completed

1802 — Dome covered in copper

1825 — Brick painted white

1855 — Brick painted yellow

1874 — Dome gilded with gold leaf

This stained glass skylight features the seals of the thirteen colonies. Located in Memorial Hall, the Massachusetts seal is in the center.

★ The Inside Story

THE GREAT HALL

Completed in 1990, The Great Hall is the newest addition to the capitol complex. With spacious skylights, it makes an open and inviting place for official functions and receptions. Flags from all of the Massachusetts communities are attached to the walls.

IT'S ABOUT TIME

Hanging from the ceiling in the Great Hall is an unusual piece of artwork that is also a clock. The artist was reportedly inspired by all the varied and unique clocks that are prominently seen in town halls, churches and meeting places in New England.

BREAKING THE MOLD

Ornate designs of wrought iron railings line the main staircase that overlooks the stained glass windows. To assure that the design remained unique, the molds were broken after they were cast. Displayed in the stained glass window at the top of the stairs are the Revolutionary seal along with early state and Royal family seals.

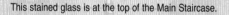

This stained glass is at the top of the Main Staircase.

The House of Representatives has 160 members.

Decorative iron railings provide a frame for the stained glass windows.

Flags of every community are displayed in the Great Hall. Note the unusual clock suspended from the skylight.

1895
Brigham addition completed

1917
East and West wings added

1918
Brick painted white a second time

1928
Brick restored to original red color

1990
Great Hall added

★ Claim to Fame

JUST SIGN YOUR JOHN HANCOCK

The deed or abstract to the capitol property truly has a John Hancock "signature." Before being deeded to the state, the land on which the Massachusetts state house sits was owned by John Hancock.

STATE VS. COMMONWEALTH

Massachusetts is one of four states — along with Pennsylvania, Virginia and Kentucky — known as a commonwealth. After citizens rejected the first draft of the state constitution, a second draft was written by John Adams who changed the name "State of Massachusetts-Bay" to "Commonwealth of Massachusetts." It is believed that Adams changed the name to make it clear that the second document was altogether different from the first. Massachusetts thus became the only state in the Union to change its name. Other than the name, there is no legal difference between the four Commonwealths and any other states.

A FALLEN PINECONE

Atop the dome's cupola is a pinecone. This was placed as a reminder of the lumber industry that played a major role of this area's early economic development. Though the pinecone remains, the wealth of Massachusetts no longer depends on pine trees.

STADIUM SEATING

During 1812, the membership of the House of Representatives grew to 749 members! With this many members, it was not only a challenge to conduct business, but grandstand seating was required. The membership was subsequently reduced and now stands at a more manageable 160.

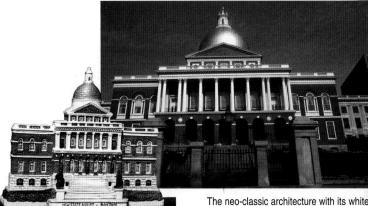

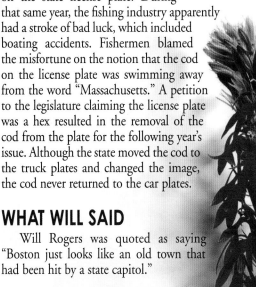

The neo-classic architecture with its white columns stands out against the red brick and gilded dome.

From the Guillon Atelier collection: *A Celebration of Architecture* handcrafted collection of Massachusetts' most cherished buildings. Courtesy of Facades, Boston

★ For What it's Worth

"CODNAPPED"

In 1784, a Boston merchant donated a wooden codfish to the House of Representatives as a reminder of the significance of the codfish industry to Massachusetts. It became a good luck charm. It first hung in the Old State House and was appropriately "transferred" upon completion of the present State House. Over the years, it became known as the "Sacred Cod" and was mounted above the gallery. In 1933, the Sacred Cod was "codnapped" by a fraternity from Harvard called the Lampoon. Eventually, it was returned to its rightful place in the House gallery.

FISHING LICENSE

In 1928, a codfish was depicted on the state license plate. During that same year, the fishing industry apparently had a stroke of bad luck, which included boating accidents. Fishermen blamed the misfortune on the notion that the cod on the license plate was swimming away from the word "Massachusetts." A petition to the legislature claiming the license plate was a hex resulted in the removal of the cod from the plate for the following year's issue. Although the state moved the cod to the truck plates and changed the image, the cod never returned to the car plates.

WHAT WILL SAID

Will Rogers was quoted as saying "Boston just looks like an old town that had been hit by a state capitol."

MICHIGAN
Lansing

CONSERVATIVE SPENDING RESULTS IN CREATIVE IDEAS

An elongated dome appears to pierce the clouds as it points to the skies.

STATE MOTTO

"If you seek a pleasant peninsula, look about you."

★ Facts & Figures

Architectural style	Renaissance Revival
Architect	Elijah E. Myers
Exterior material	Ohio sandstone and Illinois limestone
Dome surface	Cast iron, painted "buff" in color
Building height (to tip of dome)	267'
Construction period	1872-78
First occupied	1878
Capital population (Census 2000)	119,128
Census estimate 2007	114,947
Direction capitol faces	East
Original cost	$1,427,739

The Past Remembered

THE CANADIAN THREAT

In 1805, the city of Detroit was designated as Michigan's territorial capital. A former territorial courthouse served as the state capitol from 1837 to 1847. Based on its population and economic base, Detroit seemed a likely choice to continue as the capital. However, its proximity to Canada factored into the decision to relocate the capital further inland. At the time, there was concern over a possible attack — remembering that Detroit had been captured by British and Canadian forces in the War of 1812.

MICHIGAN, MICHIGAN

The nearness to Canada was not the only reason Detroit was not selected as the capital. Upon achieving statehood in 1837, many cities and towns began vying for the honor to become the capital. Communities considered included Ann Arbor, Grand Rapids, Jackson and Marshall. In 1847, after much debate, a more centralized location in Lansing Township, though almost completely undeveloped, was named the new capital. Land was cleared and a temporary capitol hastily built. A community soon sprang up around Michigan's "Capitol in the Forest." Briefly named Michigan, Michigan, it was changed to Lansing to avoid confusion. The "temporary" capitol served the state from 1848 until 1878.

NOT JUST A "COOKIE CUTTER" CAPITOL

As Michigan's population grew, a decision to build a more modern and larger capitol was made in 1871. In a national contest with twenty other architects, the Michigan legislature selected Elijah E. Myers, eventually considered to be one of the more renowned architects of the Gilded Age. He incorporated a different style of column for each of the first three stories — Tuscan, Ionic, Corinthian. The fourth floor was a composite of all three.

Michigan was the first of four capitols Myers designed. Modeling his design after the U.S. capitol, Myers started a trend with his classical revival style and central dome which became a hallmark symbol of democracy. Texas and then Colorado were so impressed with his design that they also selected him as their architect. Though Idaho selected a simpler design, they too employed Myers as architect for their former capitol. Many other states followed suit in adopting this architectural style for their capitol.

SAVE A LITTLE, SAVE A LOT

Completed in late 1878, Michigan's capitol was a lesson in conservative spending. Though the budget was slightly increased, the original budget was only $1.2 million. The architect and his contractors were challenged to improvise in the selection of materials. Despite these restrictions, they were able to accomplish a very decorative and pleasing appearance and completed the project within budget — a notable accomplishment during the Gilded Age.

ATOMIC REACTION

Over the years, growth in government rendered the capitol inadequate to accommodate the state's needs. After years of planning for a new one, the citizens of Michigan were asked to choose from seventeen architectural drawings displayed in the rotunda in 1969. A plot of land was also acquired. The ultra-modern designs were intended to represent a new age for Michigan's capitol — specifically the Atomic Age. Michigan's citizens were less than enthusiastic about the designs featuring a three-building complex with a plaza and a tower structure to replace a dome. In the end, the traditional capitol was saved when the project was tabled because of an economic recession. To address the need for more space, additional floors were created throughout the capitol by splitting rooms with high ceilings in half. In so doing, 50,000 square feet of additional floor space was created.

A postcard, postmarked 1911, commemorates the visit of President Theodore Roosevelt on May 31, 1907. Note Roosevelt's picture on the bunting over the entrance as a huge crowd gathered for the event.

A button acknowledging visitors to the capitol was formerly available to capitol visitors.

A 25-cent parking token depicts the capitol dome.

Michigan is known as the "Motor Capitol."

Pearls of Wisdom

The building "passes into the possession of the State not only free from debt, but absolutely free also from the odor of fraud."

Capitol dedication — January 1, 1879
House of Representatives Chamber

This postcard, mailed in 1911, shows a lone bicycle and Model T car. However, the postcard tells more about the past than just this. On the reverse side, the writer expresses her concern about a "little girl with scarlet fever." This disease, though not an epidemic, was still a concern to many people at the time. Today, traffic is one of the problems that are now out of control and a frequent topic of the day. Scarlet fever is now rarer than the automobile was in those days which is noticeably absent from the picture. The card, truly a contrast from today, points out how times have changed.

Historical Happenings

1800

1900

1805
Detroit designated capital of Michigan Territory

1823
First capitol completed in Detroit

1837
President Jackson grants statehood

1847
Lansing designated as capital

1848
Temporary capitol completed (until 1878)

1878
Capitol completed

★ The Inside Story

THE GLASS FLOOR

The first floor rotunda is comprised of 976 tiles of opaque glass set in cast iron. The floor was designed to present an optical illusion. The higher into the dome, the more sunken the floor appears. Children as well as adults are especially intrigued in viewing the opaque glass from differing vantage points.

SEEING STARS

A field of stars is seen when peering into the oculus (eye) of the dome. The stars are actually painted on the underside of the oculus. Intended to be inspirational, they symbolize progress for the future.

DOME WITHIN A DOME

The dome seen from the inside is a different dome from what is seen on the outside. In reality, there is a dome within a dome.

GOING AGAINST THE GRAIN

To cut costs, pine was used for interior doors, window trim and wainscot. Cast iron was used for columns. Then, in the 1880s, the pine was carefully hand painted to mimic walnut. Seven layers of paint were required to exactly match the color and grain of real walnut. Iron columns were painted to look like marble and nine acres of plain plaster walls and ceilings were painted with elaborate patterns and colors. No two rooms were painted alike! Even though it took five years to complete the work, money was saved because labor was cheaper than materials in the 1880s. Today, the opposite is true. Nevertheless, the capitol's unparalleled decorative paint was completely restored as part of the capitol's overall restoration, completed in 1992. The challenge and success of the project was recognized when the National Trust for Historic Preservation awarded the Michigan State Capitol the nation's top preservation award in 1992.

The inner dome

The House of Representatives Chamber

The Senate chamber

A school class tours the capitol. Children, intrigued with the glass floor, "spread their wings."

Timeline

1896 — Henry Ford drives a gas-powered quadicycle

1907 — Teddy Roosevelt visits capitol

1957 — Mackinac Bridge opens — connecting Michigan's two peninsulas

1969 — Designs for new capitol unveiled

1972 — Subdividing of floors completed

1992 — Restoration completed

2000

★ Claim to Fame

CRIME FREE

The history of state capitol construction, particularly during the Gilded Age, was often marked by corruption and abuse as this book has abundantly documented. Michiganders, however, can take great pride in the scandal-free construction of their capitol, considered a wonder at the time.

A REAL STRETCH

Michigan's dome is a rare sight in that its dome is narrower than other domes. The elongated dome, with its tall lantern at the top, gives the appearance of being stretched. During the early years of the capitol, some viewers commented that "from a distance at night [it] appears as a huge bird cage hanging in the air."

THE LIST GOES ON

It should also be noted that there are other "claims" that Michigan may make. As noted earlier, Michigan was the first state to hire Myers to design its capitol, launching his career as the architect who established the dome as a hallmark of democracy. The capitol's elaborate decorative paint, considered among the finest in the nation and completely restored, is one of the reasons the building was declared a National Historic Landmark in 1992. As it turned out, this step was influential in Michigan receiving honors for restoring this elaborate color scheme during its restoration completed in 1992.

A view from the front porch of the Governor's mansion on Mackinac Island.

★ For What it's Worth

OVERFLOW CROWD

During the cornerstone celebration in 1873, an estimated 35,000 people converged on Lansing to observe the gala event. At the time, Lansing's population was only 7,000 and the small town did not have enough hotels to accommodate so many out-of-towners. In response to the sudden influx of people, the citizens of Lansing were gracious enough to open their homes to house and feed the overflow crowd.

REMNANT FROM THE PAST

During the capitol restoration completed in 1992, a local citizen brought in a scrap of carpet which turned out to be a remnant of a carpet installed in the Senate Chamber in 1886 (it replaced the original, installed in 1878). The remnant had been stored in an unused chicken coop for many years. Plans call for the "Chicken Coop Carpet" to be copied and installed in the Senate Chamber when the current carpet is replaced.

MINNESOTA

St. Paul

THE NORTH STAR CAPITOL
A massive marble dome tops the Twin Cities Capitol.

"Star of the North"

★ Facts & Figures

Architectural style	Italian Renaissance
Architect	Cass Gilbert
Exterior material	White Georgia marble and St. Cloud granite
Dome surface	White Georgia marble
Building height (to tip of dome)	223'
Construction period	1896-1905
First occupied	1904
Capital population (Census 2000)	257,284
Census estimate 2007	277,251
Direction capitol faces	South
Original cost	$4,500,000

The Past Remembered

A RIVER RUNS THROUGH THEM

The twin cities, St. Paul and Minneapolis, are divided by the Mississippi River. Minneapolis, now the larger of the two, did not surpass St. Paul in population until the 1880s which was after the capital was chosen. One principal cause was Minneapolis' booming flour industry. Today, there remains a close rivalry between the two and St. Paul alone, is the the capital.

TALE OF TWIN CITIES

Minnesota's marble capitol is nestled in the business district of the smaller of the Twin Cities and adjacent to the Mississippi River. St. Paul has been home to the legislature since 1849. Meeting in various locations throughout the city, a permanent capitol was built in 1853 and enlarged twice thereafter. This capitol was destroyed by fire in 1881. A second capitol, built on the same site, served until 1905 when the present structure was completed.

TAKE YOUR PICK

In 1857, the legislature passed two state constitutions. Two rival conventions — one Republican and one Democrat — came up with similar versions. One major difference was that the Democratic version was passed without black suffrage. In a compromise move, Republicans removed black suffrage from their version. The two constitutions are on display at the Minnesota History Center.

MULTI-TASKING

The current capitol, designed by Cass Gilbert, competes proudly with the modern skyscrapers of the city. His design was chosen from among forty-one entrants. In addition to serving as the architect, Gilbert was in charge of the construction, the décor, including the Rathskellar, and he also submitted plans for the landscaping. Other accomplishments to Gilbert's credit were the Arkansas and West Virginia capitols.

WINE NO MORE

History records that the single largest ethnic group of immigrants to Minnesota was German. Not suprisingly, a café opened in the basement of the capitol in 1905 and was built with German accents and known as the Rathskeller. The German influence was also evident in the ceilings and arches with decorative drawings and paintings of eagles, squirrels, ribbons, oak and grape leaves. To complete the theme, the owners added 29 German scripted mottoes. A popular place at the time, it has been rumored, though not proven, that it served beer and wine to legislators as well as others. With the advent of World War I, and as the result of Americans disdain for Germans coupled with the temperance movement as the result of Prohibition, the mottoes were covered over. They remained this way until the layers of paint were carefully scraped away during an investigative project in 1985 which revealed the mottoes. Then in 1999, the German mottoes and artwork were restored. The Café is now open to the public and whether or not wine was ever served, it is no longer.

I'LL DRINK TO THAT

Of the 29 mottoes displayed in the café, many relate to drinking. As translated, these include "More people get drowned in the cup than in the creek." "Cheerfulness bring in with you, worry leave out-doors." "One for all — all for one." "Whether you eat or drink, say grace." and "Drink but don't indulge in drinking; speak but don't pick quarrels."

GERMAN CAFE IN BASEMENT. I. R. PATNO

A souvenir postcard booklet, mailed in 1906, included this historic photo of the Rathskeller.

The restored German Rathskeller.

Prior to restoration, this German motto was exposed. It is translated "One more for the bad weather."

MINNESOTA STATE CAPITOL

Vintage automobiles suggest the legislature, in this photo postcard above and photo below, is in session.

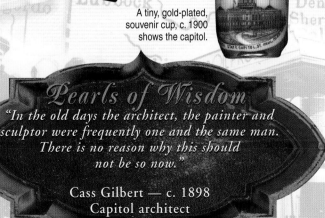

A tiny, gold-plated, souvenir cup, c. 1900 shows the capitol.

A photo postcard showing the Mississippi River with the capitol in the background was used as an invitation to a dinner party in 1910. Sent on June 13 for a party on the 15th with a one cent stamp bears record to the fact that in the early 1900s postal cards were often delivered the same day as sent.

Historical Happenings

1800

1900

1853

First capitol completed

1858
President Buchanan grants statehood

1881
First capitol destroyed by fire

1883

Second capitol completed

In 1990, the capitol staff illuminated the crystal chandelier for the visit.

The Capitol rotunda

The elaborately decorated Governor's Reception Room has a ceiling trimmed with gold leaf.

An arched skylight is over the second floor grand staircase.

The Senate chamber

★ The Inside Story

Cass Gilbert designed the chambers of the House, Senate and Supreme Court to have similar features yet have their own personality. Though each has arches, skylights and murals, the designs are unique. During recent restorations, great care was taken to identify and restore original color schemes and furnishings.

SYMBOLIC STENCILING

The interior is lavishly decorated with many forms of art. Walls and ceilings, reflecting a French influence, display Minnesota symbols — North Stars, gophers, corn, wheat and Lady Slipper flowers. Well known artists were also contracted to produce murals. The Rathskellar reflects German symbolism in its arches and lettering. Over twenty types of stone, including marble from France, Italy and Greece, were used in the interior.

A SPORTING EVENT

A crystal chandelier with 92 lights is suspended from the rotunda ceiling with a 28-foot chain. The chandelier is normally illuminated only on special occasions such as the governor's inauguration and Statehood Day.

An eight-pointed star is the symbol of the North Star State. The glass star is outlined in brass and is inlaid in the center of the rotunda floor.

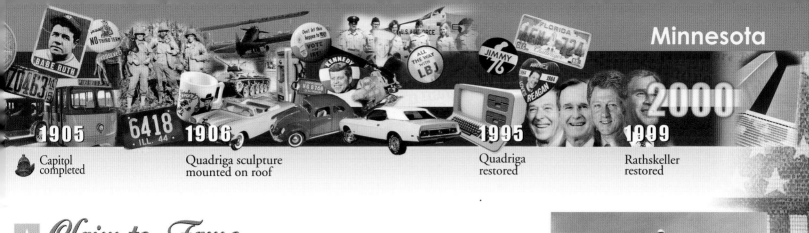

1905 Capitol completed

1906 Quadriga sculpture mounted on roof

1995 Quadriga restored

1999 Rathskeller restored

2000

★ Claim to Fame

SENATE SENIORITY

Minnesota makes the claim that it has the largest numerical senate, comprised of 67 members, the most of any state.

A FRENCH ACCENT

A gold-leafed, hollow copper chariot, led by four horses and guided by two female figures is mounted at the base of the dome. A male figure rides the chariot. Each statue was made from hammered copper sheets. The sculpture, known as "The Progress of the State," often referred to as the Quadriga, was used in lieu of a traditional pediment. Sculpted by Daniel Chester French and Edward Potter, it was the subject of controversy as some thought it inappropriate for Minnesota.

French, who received $35,000 for his work, is most famous for his sculpture of Abraham Lincoln of the Lincoln Memorial. The symbolic figures, holding a banner "MINNESOTA" and a horn of plenty are said to represent agriculture and industry with the forces of nature working together to bring prosperity to the state.

A charioteer led by two female figures with horses, known as the Quadriga, is mounted in front of the dome.

Minnesota, gem of the north, Both fields and forests tell thy worth. Our love and praises thou dost win, Emblem dear is the moccasin.

MOCCASIN MINNESOTA STATE FLOWER

STATE CAPITOL ST. PAUL MINN.

Note the state flower was referred to as a moccasin species.

★ For What it's Worth

SENATE SLUMBER PARTY

In 1937, a group of nearly 200 protestors, known as the People's Lobby, forcibly took control of the Senate chamber. The group, which included about 50 women, made themselves at home by lounging on the furniture, eating, giving speeches, singing songs and finally settling down to sleep for the night before vacating the next morning.

MISTAKEN IDENTITY

Minnesota's state flower, the Lady Slipper, is also known as a moccasin flower. This flower is depicted in wall and ceiling stenciling. In 1893, the legislature unknowingly designated a species not native to Minnesota as the state flower. Not until 1902 was the mistake corrected.

MISSISSIPPI
Jackson

UNSOLVED MYSTERIES ABOUND AT THE "CAPITOL OF LIGHTS"

An overwhelming display of lights illuminates the interior but sheds no light on mysteries within.

"By valor and arms"

⭐ Facts & Figures

Architectural style	Beaux Arts
Architect	Theodore C. Link
Exterior material	Georgia granite and Bedford limestone
Dome surface	Terra cotta
Building height (to tip of dome)	180'
Construction period	1901-03
First occupied	1903
Capital population (Census 2000)	184,256
Census estimate 2007	175,710
Direction capitol faces	South
Original cost	$1,093,641

The Past Remembered

LeFLEUR'S BLUFF

The town of Natchez served as the first capital until a more central location known as LeFleur's Bluff was chosen in 1821. In honor of General Andrew Jackson, the name LeFleur's Bluff, was changed to Jackson. A brick capitol was built that same year. In 1839, it was replaced with what is now known as the Old Capitol. This second capitol survived attacks on the city by General Sherman's army in the 1860s as well as demolition attempts in the 1950s due to neglect.

"CAPITOLIZING" A PRISON

As the Old Capitol became unable to meet the growing needs of the state, a new site was chosen. The site chosen for the New Capitol was the old state penitentiary. In dismantling the prison, bricks were salvaged and later used in the construction of the capitol. To further minimize the cost of construction, the state utilized inmates from the new state penitentiary. With the help provided by these extra workers, the walls and foundation were completed in less than a year.

MILLION DOLLAR CAPITOL

Even though many states funded their capitol through tax increases or bond issues, Mississippi found their money elsewhere. The Illinois Central Railroad owed the State back taxes which, along with the settling of lawsuits, netted the State slightly over a million dollars for capitol construction. It became known as the "million dollar capitol."

A CIVIL CELEBRATION

The dedication in 1903 of the capitol was a special celebration. A New Orleans newspaper published a special 40-page section on the neighboring state's new capitol. The Illinois Central dispatched sixteen passenger trains to transport those traveling to Jackson to see the ceremony. Night trains converged from all directions bringing visitors, including Civil War veterans, to the gala event. Confederate veterans, dressed in their gray uniforms, pitched tents on the grounds and represented a significant number of those in attendance. However, many just came to see the well publicized capitol of lights.

CHARRED CHIMNEYS

During the Civil War, General Sherman's Army marched through Jackson on three occasions. Each time they torched the city. After the third assault, all that remained was a city of charred chimneys and a few homes, including the governor's mansion. Although books and records were taken from the Old Capitol, it suffered no structural damage. The devastation of Jackson was so complete that it was appropriately christened the name Chimneyville.

LOOK OUT BELOW

The eagle mounted atop the dome stands eight feet high and has an impressive wing span of fifteen feet. Made of solid copper and gilded with 14 karat gold leaf, it cost only $1,500 at the time. In addition to the eagle "looking out from above," there are also lion's heads placed at each corner of the base of the dome.

The eagle atop the dome.

"LEST WE FORGET"

In 1912, a monument to Confederate women was placed in front of the capitol. Each side of the monument is engraved with an inscription, one of which was authored by Jefferson Davis, as a tribute to womens role in the Civil War. Wives, daughters, mothers and sisters are honored. The north side inscription, honoring sisters, concludes with the motto, "Lest we forget."

A colorized postcard, requiring a one cent stamp shows the capitol built in 1839 with a gold dome, though it was never gold.

This early photo, mounted on cardboard and yellowed over the years, shows the capitol void of landscaping. On the reverse side, a printed message reads "New Capitol" and "Rolls of film No. 1 or 2 Brownie Camera developed for 15c."

A postcard with a 1906 postmark shows the capitol soon after completion but prior to any trees being planted.

A stereocard, c. 1902, shows the capitol under construction with an incomplete dome. The card indicates it is a "Selected Subjects" of the "Tourists Series" published by Montgomery Ward & Co, Chicago. It also states the "new capitol" is "on Illinois Central Railroad."

Pearls of Wisdom

"First a little circuit of incandescents flashed out, then another and another as the switches were turned, until it seemed that an enchanted palace was being reared by invisible fingers."

Author unknown — 1903
Initial lighting ceremony

A school class listens intently to a capitol tour guide.

Historical Happenings

1800 — 1900

1803 Acquired by U.S. in Louisiana Purchase

1817 President Monroe grants statehood

1821 Jackson approved as permanent capital

1839 Old Capitol completed

1861 Mississippi secedes from Union

1863 Jackson destroyed by Union army

The Inner Dome

The Senate

The House of Representatives

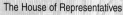

The rotunda

"M" for Mississippi

These unsigned stained glass portraits are thought to be Tiffany's.

★ The Inside Story

LET THERE BE LIGHTS

Throughout the capitol, Mississippi's capitol is "burning" with lights. There are 4,750 light bulbs lighting the interior with 750 clear lights in the rotunda area alone. In addition, natural lighting from skylights as well as a glass floor provides an overwhelming show of light.

A REAL EYE-CATCHER

Ascending the stairs to the third floor, three panels of arched, stained-glass artwork are a real eye-catcher. The panels, appearing to tell a story, are not signed by the artist. Although it is conjectured they were created by Tiffany's, the identification of the artist remains a mystery.

NOT ALL BLACK AND BLUE

Upon entering the main vestibule, the visitor sees black and blue — marble that is. Interior walls are trimmed with a combination of Black Belgian marble and blue Vermont marble. The rotunda features Italian white marble with a border of jet black marble from New York. In all, there are eleven types of authentic marble, costing over $100,000, throughout the capitol. Scagliola, an art form of marble, was also used in the columns and other places. Although many colors are displayed, the deep black color is enhanced by the intense sources of light.

1903 Capitol completed

1934 Capitol redecorated

1961 Old Capitol restored

1982 $19 million restoration completed

2001 Mississippi votes to keep Confederate flag

2005 Hurricane Katrina damages Old Capitol

2008 Old Capitol restored again

★ Claim to Fame

PROMENADE AROUND THE COLONNADE

At each end of the capitol is a semi-circular façade — a unique architectural feature among state capitols. Like "bookends," each end of the capitol appears to hold up the interior of the building. Each wing is comprised of a series of Corinthian columns, known as a colonnade, and is capped with a saucer-style dome. One wing houses the Senate and the other the House of Representatives. As an aside, William Strickland, the architect for the Tennessee capitol, had previously used a similar design in 1834 for the Stock Exchange Building in Philadelphia.

JUST IN CASE

Completed in 1903, the capitol was possibly the first all-electric building in Mississippi. However, either the designer or state officials did not have complete confidence in Thomas Edison's new invention of electricity as some fixtures include a gas jet outlet — just in case the electric fixtures were deemed inferior.

THE SOUTH RISES AGAIN

In April 2001, Mississippi voters were given a choice of a new state flag design or to keep the flag it had been using since 1894. The new design was absent the Confederate emblem. When the votes were tallied, the old flag won by a two to one margin. With South Carolina and Georgia acquiescing to interest groups to change or remove their flag, Mississippi is the only state to retain the Confederate image. The Confederate emblem shows 13 white stars on a blue X with a red background.

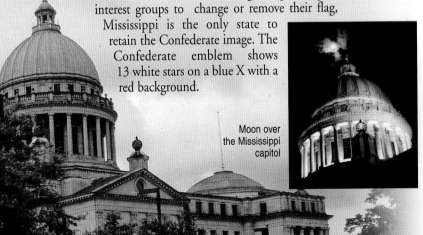

Moon over the Mississippi capitol

Note the colonnade and semi-circular façade at the side of the capitol.

★ For What it's Worth

MYSTERY SOLVED

During a restoration of the interior and removal of one of the walls, a safe was discovered. Although previously the safe used by the State Treasurer's office, it had long ago been forgotten as it was hidden behind a false wall. Once re-discovered and realizing the safe was locked and after an intense search for the combination, efforts to open it were abandoned. Those aware of the mystery of the locked safe wondered if it would ever be solved and whether there was anything of value locked away. In hopes of uncovering hidden treasure, some "want to be safecrackers" tried their hand at opening the safe over their lunch hour. Then, one day someone succeeded with the right combination and amazingly the safe swung open! To everyone's disappointment, the safe was empty.

CHECKING OUT SO SOON?

During the Civil War, as troops from both sides moved into and out of Jackson, a hotel known as the Bowman House was one of the few buildings still standing. On May 13, 1863, General Johnston of the Confederate army had established headquarters at the Bowman House. The next day, Johnston "sounded the retreat" and evacuated the city. On that same day, General Sherman moved in, hoisted the Stars and Stripes atop the capitol and set up his headquarters at the same hotel.

MISSOURI
Jefferson City

A SHOW ME CAPITOL
Overlooking the Missouri River, the "Show Me State" showcases its capitol with fabulous displays of art and stained glass.

STATE MOTTO

"The welfare of the people shall be the supreme law."

Facts & Figures

Architectural style	Roman Renaissance
Architect	Egerton Swartwout and Evarts Tracy
Exterior material	Carthage and Phenix marble
Dome surface	Carthage and Phenix marble
Building height (to tip of dome)	262'
Construction period	1913-1918
First occupied	1918
Capital population (Census 2000)	39,636
Census estimate 2007	40,564
Direction capitol faces	South
Original cost	$4,044,153

★ The Past Remembered

GO WITH THE FLOW

In 1812, the Missouri Territory was formed out of the Louisiana Purchase. For a period of nine years, the legislature met in various locations in the city of St. Louis, including the Missouri Hotel. Later, it convened in nearby St. Charles. With the advent of the steamboat and exploration of the Missouri River, the legislature specified that the permanent seat of government would be located on the Missouri River and within 40 miles of the Osage River. In 1821, a section of public land overlooking the Missouri River, which was virtually unpopulated, was chosen to be the capital. It was named the "City of Jefferson."

TESTED BY FIRE

As with other capital cities, Jefferson City survived attempts to relocate the capital. The first capitol — now the site of the Governor's Mansion — was built in 1826 but was destroyed by fire in 1837.

MURPHY'S LAW

In 1911, the second capitol was struck by lightning, caught fire and burned. Reportedly, this fire would not have been as devastating if the firefighters, some of whom were volunteers, had been better equipped. Other factors contributing to its demise include a water main break, insufficient water pressure and the time it took to reach the capitol, which was located on a hill.

FIRE SALE

The capitol fire inspired others to promote the idea to relocate the capital. Newspapers, including the *St. Louis Post Dispatch*, seized the opportunity to sell the idea of a move. The city of Sikeston offered a plot of land and $3 million to entice a capital relocation. However, since the state constitution designated the City of Jefferson as the capital, relocating the capital would require voter approval. Unfortunately for proponents of the move, the next general election was two years away, so obtaining voter approval would have to wait. In the end, the capital was not "for sale." In this same year, Jefferson City was officially established as the capital, ending the rivalry to relocate.

DESIGN COMPETITION

An architectural contest was held in which 69 architects submitted drawings for the new capitol. The Commission Board unanimously selected the New York firm of Tracy and Swartwout.

A 13-foot statue of Thomas Jefferson, after whom the capital was named, greets visitors on the front steps.

An artist's rendering shows the first capitol c. 1840.

Capitol after the fire

Capitol before the fire

A matchbook distributed by the Capitol Brewery of Jefferson City.

An early postcard shows the architect's plan to conceal the railroad tracks from the Missouri River view.

A marble paperweight depicts the north side of the capitol.

Pearls of Wisdom

"I come from a state that raises corn and cotton and cockleburs and Democrats, and frothy eloquence neither convinces nor satisfies me. I am from Missouri. You have got to show me."

Willard Duncan Vandiver — 1899
Speech at a naval banquet in Philadelphia

Historical Happenings

1800 — 1900

1804
Missouri becomes known as Gateway to the West

1821
President James Monroe grants statehood

1826
Jefferson City selected as capital; first capitol built

1837
First capitol destroyed by fire

The much acclaimed *"A Social History of the State of Missouri"* by Thomas Hart Benton, 1936.
(© T. H. Benton and R. P. Benton Testamentary Trusts/Licensed by VAGA, New York, NY)

With 5,700 square feet of stained glass artwork, the capitol resembles a cathedral.

The Eads Bridge presents an optical illusion as though it is moving and changing direction as you pass by the artwork.

The inner dome

Murals surround the inner circle that leads to the interior dome.

Murals around the rotunda

★ The Inside Story

SURPLUS CAPITAL

While many states ran short of funds to complete their capitol, a special property tax levy gave Missouri a $1 million surplus. Even though the capitol was complete, the attorney general ruled that the money be spent on the capitol. Legislators decided to use the remaining monies to furnish the building with murals, stained glass and other decorative works using the best craftsmen of the time. These projects were accomplished over a 12-year period.

DECK THE HALLS

The hallways of the first floor were used to house the Missouri State Museum. The capitol's original design included natural lighting to illuminate these museum displays. One hallway, aptly named the History Hall, features artifacts and stories of Missouri history. The other, Resources Hall, features the natural resources found in the state.

JUST ORDINARY PEOPLE

In 1935, Thomas Hart Benton was commissioned to paint a mural on the four walls of the House Lounge. The mural, *"A Social History of the State of Missouri,"* was completed in 18 months but was soon greeted with criticism from legislators. The people portrayed were ordinary people, not Missouri's favorite sons. Among the people portrayed were laborers, settlers, slaves and farmers as well as Jesse James and Huck Finn. One legislator was said to remark, "We're more than a coon dog state." Benton chose to depict the character of Missourians in the role they played in the development of the state. More realistic than what politicians desired, the mural became a source of ridicule and controversy.

THE ART OF TIME

Paintings known as lunettes are displayed throughout the second floor. Forty-one half-moon shaped paintings depict the history and resources of the state. Although Benton's murals receive a great deal of attention, there are many other murals that deserve recognition. These include a series of earlier murals painted by a group of artists from Taos, New Mexico with the theme "Missouri, the Mother of the West."

1911 — Lightning strike ignites fire that destroys second capitol on site

1918 — Capitol completed

1936 — Benton mural completed

1965 — Gateway Arch in St. Louis completed

2000
2001 — Renovation completed

★ *Claim to Fame*

THE WIDE MISSOURI

The Grand Stairway measures 65' from wall to wall. The State claims that it is the widest interior staircase of any building in the world. Another significant feature is the entrance door. Finished in bronze, the massive door measures 13' x 18' feet.

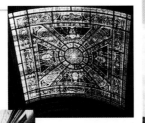

The Grand Stairway and stained glass artwork above the staircase.

JUST A WHISPER

Although other capitols have spaces in which a whisper can be heard from a great distance, the Missouri capitol is unique in that the architect designated a gallery and hired an acoustics expert to achieve such ends. Above the fifth floor near the top of the dome is a place known as the Whispering Gallery. A soft whisper uttered close to the inside wall can be heard on the opposite side of the dome, a distance of 65'. The voice actually travels around the perimeter to the opposite side.

PANELS OF PINK

The exterior of the marble dome features 16 carved panels around its diameter—the only capitol with such a feature. Adding a pinkish accent to the dome, each panel is 5' x 9'.

Surplus funding made the *Fountain of the Centaurs* possible.

★ *For What it's Worth*

FISHING FOR AN ANSWER

The origin of the word *Missouri* is from a Sioux Indian tribe known as the Missouris. But the meaning of the term is not so clear. Possible interpretations include "wooden canoe people," "those who have big canoes" or "town of the large canoes."

EGG ON THEIR FACE

Benton used a powdered, paint material made with raw egg yolks to paint his ordinary people. Known as egg tempera, he painted directly onto the walls instead of on canvass. Oftentimes, while working on the mural, a visitor would wander in to watch. On occasion, when Benton thought the visitor fit the image he was trying to portray, he would add their face to the mural.

Another view of *"A Social History of the State of Missouri"* by Thomas Hart Benton, 1936. (© T. H. Benton and R. P. Benton Testamentary Trusts/Licensed by VAGA, New York, NY)

MONTANA
Helena

HELENA, A TOWN THAT MADE A NAME FOR ITSELF

The Wild Wild West lived up to its name in Montana. Today, the mystery of the naming of Helena is still uncertain.

STATE MOTTO

"Gold and Silver"

★ Facts & Figures

Architectural style	American Renaissance
Architect	Charles E. Bell & John H. Kent
1912 addition	Frank Mills Andrews, Charles S. Haire, John C. Link
Exterior material	Columbus sandstone
1912 addition	Montana granite
Dome surface	Copper
Building height (to tip of dome)	165'
Construction period	1899-1902, 1909-12
First occupied	1902
Capital population (Census 2000)	25,780
Census estimate 2007	28,726
Direction capitol faces	North
Original cost (including furnishings)	$540,000
1912 addition	$650,000

The Past Remembered

FOLLOW THE GOLD

In 1862, prospectors struck gold in an area that became known as Bannack. Many prospectors and entrepreneurs moved to this town and as a result, it was designated the first capital of the Montana Territory. Soon after, however, gold was discovered near Virginia City and as gold seekers moved on to the new strike, the capital followed. In 1869, an election was held to decide which of these towns would be the capital. Before the election results were tallied, a fire destroyed the office where the ballots had been sent. But this was not to be the final vote on the capital's location.

LAST CHANCE

In 1864, a group of prospectors returning from a northern expedition had all but given up on finding gold in Montana when they decided to try an area that had been overlooked. Known as Prickly Pear Creek, it was located midway between what is now Yellowstone and Glacier Parks. Gold, indeed, was discovered and a gold camp arose. Miners referred to it as Last Chance Gulch but changed the name to Helena just a few months later. Over the next several years, their last chance efforts led to a harvest of over $3.5 billion in gold and silver.

MAKE EVERY VOTE COUNT

As Helena was centrally located on the stage route and because of its new-found wealth, it became a hub of trade in the region. This greatly enhanced the likelihood of Helena becoming the the territorial capital. Thus in 1874, another election was held for that very purpose. The ballot read "For Helena" or "Against Helena." The outcome was hotly contested. There were accusations of votes from one county not being counted and other charges of vote switching. After all was settled, Helena was declared the winner and became the capital in 1875, a title it has held ever since.

MINING THEIR OWN BUSINESS

When Montana achieved statehood in 1889, copper mining had become a major industry within the state. Once this happened, mine owners, who were known as Copper Kings, were able to exert significant influence over the political affairs of the region. A fierce rivalry between copper magnates soon developed with one wanting Anaconda and the other Helena to be declared the capital. Both poured huge sums of money into an upcoming election and used the power of newspapers to sway votes. They also courted voters with champagne and expensive cigars. Accusations of "buying votes" and bribery were rampant. After concentrated efforts by these copper magnates to sway the vote, an election in 1894 confirmed Helena once again for the coveted title of state capital.

GET OUT OF DODGE

A year after this final election, the legislature authorized $1 million to build a capitol. Before construction began, it was learned that the capitol commissioners intended to defraud the state. The commissioners were ultimately promptly dismissed and like a scene from an old western movie, they hastily saddled their horses and rode out of town. A new commission was appointed and responded to the scam by cutting the budget by $350,000 and redesigning the capitol.

DON'T RAIN ON MY PARADE

Construction of the capitol finally began in 1899 and was completed in less than four years. A dedication celebration was held on July 4, 1902 with thousands attending. Despite an unrelenting rainstorm, the festivities went ahead as planned except for a parade which had to be postponed.

Each summer, meticulously planted flowers proclaim Montana as king. This 1984 photo shows a long-standing tradition, started during the 1902 dedication, to spell out MONTANA.

Leather postcards were individually hand-made from 1904-08 and were banned by the U.S. Postal Service in 1909. This one features the Montana capitol.

This postcard has a May 28, 1909 postmark. The writer states, "It is quite cold up here and we are expecting another snowstorm. It is quite different from La Junta (Colorado) weather." The writer adds, "Can't you go to the fair in Seattle and stop at Helena?"

A private mailing postcard, with a 1905 postmark bears the stamped address of Mrs. Jennie Frankfort on Fifth Avenue in Helena. The address was traced to a business known as the New York Dry Goods Company.

A plate, depicting the Montana capitol, was made in Germany by Wheelock.

A hinged, copper notepad, measuring 2"x3", is embossed with the capitol.

The state flower, the bitterroot, is engraved on the side of the legislative desks.

Pearls of Wisdom

"There is but one thing about the whole building that puts a bad taste in the mouth —"
"Oro y Plata" — gold and silver.
(inscribed on the cornerstone)
That is not a good motto for any state.
It is a good motto for a miser."

Editor, Helena Independent
July 4, 1902

Historical Happenings

1800   1900

1864	1875	1876	1889	1894	1902
Montana Territory established	Territorial capital relocates from Virginia City to Helena	Battle of the Little Bighorn	President Harrison grants statehood	Voters select Helena as state capital	Capitol completed

The Charles Russell painting. Listening to a capitol guide telling the story of this priceless painting is worth the visit. Note Russell's signature and the ram's horns.

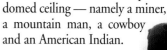

The painting *Driving the Golden Spike* depicts the completion of the Northern Pacific Railroad at Gold Creek in 1883.

Ascending to the second floor, the Big Sky Country illuminates these majestic stained glass windows on the Grand Stairway. The staircase is illuminated by a barrel-vaulted skylight.

Note the Christmas colors in the rotunda.

The interior dome.

★ The Inside Story

SWAP MEET

The Montana capitol is home to a masterpiece painting of nationally acclaimed artist, Charles M. Russell. The painting, 25' long and 12' high, depicts Lewis and Clark seeking to secure horses from the Montana Indians to carry them over the Bitterroot Mountains.

Enroute, Lewis and Clark encountered the friendly Salish Indians in southwestern Montana. After a warm greeting with the help of several translations, the smoking of peace pipes and the trading for horses, Lewis and Clark were on their way. This remarkable scene, painted in 1912 by Charles Russell, is on display in the House of Representatives and is titled *Lewis and Clark Meeting Indians at Ross' Hole*.

SECRET PASSAGE

The Governor's Reception Room was designed in an English Tudor style, furnished with oak and marble, and has ornamental fireplaces. Beside one of the fireplaces is a secret or hidden door that leads to the governor's private office.

COWBOYS AND INDIANS

During the restoration process, it was learned that red and green were the original, prominent paint colors in the rotunda. Officials were pleasantly surprised with the combination despite being a little concerned that they were "Christmas colors." A frontiersman is represented in each corner of the domed ceiling — namely a miner, a mountain man, a cowboy and an American Indian.

1905
General Meagher
statue dedicated

1911
Charles Russell
mural completed

1912
East and West
wings completed

1916
Jeanette Rankin
elected as first
Congresswoman in U.S.

2000

2001
Renovation
completed

2006
Mystery of
stature solved

★ Claim to Fame

HOW DO YOU SAY IT?

Many stories and articles have been written about how Helena got its name and how it should be pronounced. One version claims that in 1864, a few months after the gold camp was founded, the name Helena was chosen at a town meeting. The pronunciation was to follow Webster's Dictionary, which meant the accent was on the second syllable as in "Hel-ee-na." However, some years later, locals changed to accenting the first syllable, pronouncing the name "Hell-e-na." This tradition stuck through the years. To add to this distinction, although 21 states report a town named Helena, Montana has this unique pronunciation.

STRIKING IT RICH

The gold strike brought many people into Helena and many did in fact strike it rich. In a two-year period, it is estimated that $3.5 billion in gold was extracted. At the time of

statehood, the town of Helena had the most millionaires per capita in the U.S.! The town was so wealthy, affluent individuals competed to see who could build the most extravagant mansion. To this day, this part of the town is known as the "Mansion District."

INDEPENDENCE DAY

The people of Montana are proud of their capitol and independence and have tied key events to our nation's Independence Day. On July 4th, they dedicated the cornerstone in 1899, the capitol in 1902 and the General Thomas Francis Meagher statue in 1905.

The cornerstone

Above it all—the capitol is a landmark seen for miles around in the small town of Helena.

★ For What it's Worth

FINDERS KEEPERS

While the capitol was being constructed, a 17-foot tall statue arrived at the railroad station that no one came to claim. Although the label identified the shipper as a foundry in the east, there was no record of who ordered it or where it was to be placed! Part of the problem was that the former capitol commissioners had absconded with most of the records. Adding to the mystery, the foundry records from where the statue was ordered were destroyed in a fire! Absent any evidence or spokesperson as to where the statue was intended, a decision was made to place the statue atop the dome.

STAKING HER CLAIM

But this was not the end of the story. In 2006, a Pennsylvania woman contacted the Montana Historical Society inquiring if her grandfather's statue was still atop the dome. Historians were able to confirm that indeed the woman's claim was true. It was also learned that the Belgian-born sculptor, Edward J. Van Landeghem, had named the statue "Montana."

BEAT THE CLOCK

Prior to 1975, legislative sessions were limited to 60 day periods. Often legislative business remained even though the session was officially over. In order to continue the session, the Sergeant-at-Arms would cover the clock with a cloth and leave it there until all matters had been considered. In some cases, the overtime lasted several days. When some members threatened court action, the practice ceased.

The statue "Montana" is perched atop the capitol dome.

NEBRASKA
Lincoln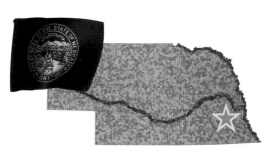

TOWER ON THE PLAINS

A "Sentinel" of the Plains, the Nebraska capitol towers over the landscape. The Nebraska legislature also stands out as the only state with a unicameral legislature.

"Equality before the law"

★ Facts & Figures

Architectural style	Art Deco
Architect	Bertram Grosvenor Goodhue
Exterior material	Indiana limestone
Dome surface	Gold glazed tiles
Building height (to tip of dome)	400'
Construction period	1922-32
First occupied	1924
Capital population (Census 2000)	225,581
Census estimate 2007	248,744
Direction capitol faces	North
Original cost (including furniture)	$9,800,440

The Past Remembered

RECYCLING THE SITE

Omaha was the site of Nebraska's two territorial capitols. In 1867, soon after statehood and despite much disagreement, the legislature decided to relocate the capital south of the Platte River. The site chosen was a small community known as Lancaster which was then renamed as Lincoln. All three state capitols were built on this site. The previous two capitols were poorly built. The second one, completed in 1888, was considered to be in disrepair in just a few years.

A CROSS WITHIN A SQUARE

In 1920, a national competition was held to choose an architect that would design a capitol to better accommodate the needs of the state. The winning plan was submitted by Bertram G. Goodhue, a New York City architect. The jury based its decision on utility, economy and choosing a "monument worthy of Nebraska." Goodhue's plan for the capitol, a break with tradition, was known as a "cross within a square." A 400' tower, the central office structure, is in the center of the square. Four interior courtyards surround the tower and divide the square. In so doing, it forms a cross.

THE SPIRIT OF THE PIONEER

Goodhue also wanted the capitol to reflect a central theme for its artwork and every feature associated with it. Both the pioneer and law are represented in this central theme. To accomplish this, he employed the services of mosaic designer Hildreth Meiere, sculptor Lee Lawrie, and Dr. Hartley Alexander. This unity of theme is embodied in sculptures, inscriptions and other forms of art.

CURB APPEAL

The landscape design was created to carefully frame prominent views of the capitol for those walking or driving around the site. Much like the appearance of the building itself, the landscape on the perimeter lawn is more subtle in color and plant material while the interior of the building is much more colorful. Similarly, the interior courtyards were designed to be the flower gardens of the site.

PAY AS YOU GO

Nebraska's constitution prohibits the State from going into debt or to have deficit spending. This legal restriction required that the capitol, with a cost of nearly $10 million, be constructed as funds became available. To avoid a budget deficit, the capitol was constructed in four phases. As a result of this pay-as-you-go approach, Nebraska's capitol took ten years to build, but was paid in full when completed in 1932.

THE FINISHING TOUCHES

In 1924, the architect Bertram Goodhue died. The successor architect, William Younkin, took over the project. The tower was completed in the third phase.

Some features of the original design were left out of the construction. These included fountains in the interior courtyards and twenty murals. However, these twenty murals were added later beginning in 1956 with the last one accepted in 1996.

SOWING THE SEEDS

The tower has 18 stories and is topped with a gold dome. Atop the dome is a 19' statue

Abraham Lincoln receives a tribute to the capital named after him.

known as The Sower. Designed by sculptor Lee Lawrie, the bronze figure is said to be "sowing the seeds of life to the winds."

LINCOLN'S LINCOLN

At the west entrance of the capitol is a bronze statue of Abraham Lincoln. The Gettysburg Address is carved into the wall behind the statue. Sculpted by Daniel Chester French in 1912, it has been on the grounds since that time and thus predates the current capitol.

License plates from 1940 and 1941 display the capitol. Nebraskans were proud of their capitol.

A bottle cap and soda from a cherry beverage, popular in the 1940s and 50s, features the capitol.

This book by Leonard R. Nelson, with a uniquely embossed cover, was copyrighted in 1931 just prior to the completion of the capitol.

An aerial view c. 1940s, taken by an unidentified photographer, shows the unique design of the capitol and how it "towers" over the surrounding area.

Pearls of Wisdom

"With malice toward none, with charity for all, with firmness in the right as God gives us to see the right, let us strive on to finish the work we are in …"

Abraham Lincoln — March 4, 1865
Inscribed in Memorial Hall

This postcard shows the previous capitol that was torn down to make room for the present capitol.

A photo postcard showing all parking spaces in use suggests the legislature was in session. Note the late 1930s autos.

Historical Happenings

1800   **1900**

1867	1912	1920	1924	1925
President Andrew Johnson grants statehood	Lincoln statue added to the grounds	Bertram Goodhue chosen as architect	Architect dies	Old capitol razed

★ The Inside Story

The Memorial Chamber, on the 14th Floor, depicts "heroes" of wars prior to 1922.

Indian symbolism decorates the doors to the East Chamber.

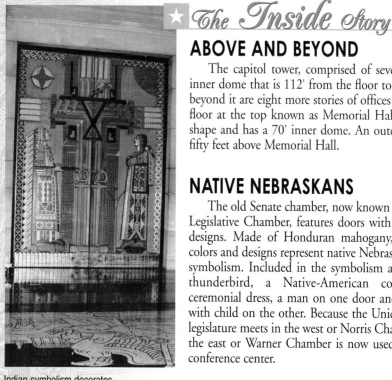

The Great Hall   The vestibule ceiling

One of the four courtyards divided by the cross.

Black-and-white marble mosaics define the rotunda.

ABOVE AND BEYOND

The capitol tower, comprised of several sections, has an inner dome that is 112' from the floor to its peak. Above and beyond it are eight more stories of offices with an observation floor at the top known as Memorial Hall. It is octagonal in shape and has a 70' inner dome. An outer dome is another fifty feet above Memorial Hall.

NATIVE NEBRASKANS

The old Senate chamber, now known as the Warner Legislative Chamber, features doors with hand-carved designs. Made of Honduran mahogany, the bright colors and designs represent native Nebraskan Indian symbolism. Included in the symbolism are corn, a thunderbird, a Native-American couple in ceremonial dress, a man on one door and a wife with child on the other. Because the Unicameral legislature meets in the west or Norris Chamber, the east or Warner Chamber is now used as a conference center.

CONTINUING THE CENTRAL THEME

The rotunda, with a mosaic tile floor made of black-and-white marble features hand-cut designs. The jet-black is from Belgium and the white is from Italy. The center design is known as "Earth as the Life Giver."

INSIDE OUT

The unique design of the capitol is not just a 400' tower and although is difficult to describe in words, was a well-thought-out plan. The base or lower office square is 437' on each side. Inside this square, a cross is formed which in turn defines four courtyards. Within each section of the cross are flower gardens, grass and a tile walkway. Although these spaces are open to the air and are outside of the main building, they are actually within the structure.

1930 — The *Sower* mounted on dome

1932 — Capitol completed

1934 — Unicameral adopted

1956 — Murals added

1996 — Thematic murals completed

2000

★ *Claim to Fame*

BRINGING DOWN THE HOUSE

Governments normally operate under a two-house system — a senate and a house of representatives. However, Nebraska is the exception to this rule. In breaking with tradition, Nebraska voted to conduct its business with only a one-house legislature. Known as a Unicameral, members are elected on a non-partisan basis and are known as senators. Adopted in 1934, Nebraska's intent was to become more efficient and thus create a cost savings. This was partially prompted by the depression and the "dust bowl." The change allowed the state to reduce its number of required legislators. The Unicameral first convened in 1937 and reportedly has resulted in significant cost savings to the state. Currently, 49 senators make up the one-house legislature. From time to time, other states including Alaska, Montana and Oklahoma have considered changing to a one-house legislature.

A view from the observation floor.

Above the north entrance is this inscription and a pioneer sculpture.

The dome with the *Sower* atop

A NEW ERA

Nebraska, the Cornhusker state, became the first state to construct a capitol radically different from the traditional domed capitol. This innovative design was the first high-rise capitol. Louisiana and North Dakota soon followed suit. Oregon's capitol, though not a high-rise, also departed from a traditional dome. Nebraska was also the first state to incorporate native or indigenous culture into its architectural emphasis. Inscriptions and symbolism seen throughout the building depict historic events and people representing the dual theme of the evolution of western democracy as a form of government paralleled with the natural and human history of Nebraska as a region.

★ *For What it's Worth*

"O" WHAT A STREET

Lincoln is reported to have the longest, straight main street anywhere. Known as O Street, the pavement stretches a total of 60 miles, extending through other towns. Allen Ginsberg, a poet, also considered it noteworthy as it is the subject of his poem, Zero Street.

A REAL RIP-OFF

The Tower on the Plains, as it is known, is also a target for violent winds. In April 2001, a violent windstorm ripped a two-ton section of copper sheeting off the roof of the capitol.

THE JURY IS IN

In 1920, the jury charged with choosing the best design for the capitol expressed the following remarks — that the capitol be:
1) "free from binding traditions;"
2) that "it makes no pretense of belonging to any period of the past" and
3) that it be "a State Capitol of the Here and Now."

NEVADA
Carson City

A SILVER LEGACY

From the silver mining days to the silver coins of the casinos, Nevada continues to generate wealth and attract tourism from around the world.

"All for the country"

★ Facts & Figures

Architectural style	Italianate/Neo-classical
Architect	Joseph Gosling
Exterior material	Sandstone
Dome surface	Fiberglass-painted silver
Building height (to tip of dome)	120'
Construction period	1870-71
First occupied	1871
Capital population (Census 2000)	52,457
Census estimate 2007	54,939
Direction capitol faces	West
Original cost	$169,831
(1906 Library Annex)	$66,482

The Past Remembered

A GAMBLE PAYS OFF

In 1858, Carson City was founded by Abraham Curry who had the foresight to set aside ten acres for a capitol. The site became known as the Plaza. Although Carson City was not centrally located within the territory, it was the choice of the legislature. Silver City, Virginia City and Dayton also competed to be declared the capital. Ironically, one of the first acts of the territorial legislators in 1861 was to enact a law that made gambling a felony! Years later, gambling casinos and the silver coin brought untold wealth and tourism which were instrumental in shaping Nevada's future.

NO SILVER, NO STATEHOOD!

Known as the "Silver State," Nevada's silver and gold mining established a legacy and a source of wealth in the state from the time it was being settled. In 1870, the Federal government established a United States mint to produce gold and silver coins in Carson City because of its proximity to the source. However in the 1890s, the demand for silver had drastically declined as did the state's population. Before federal legislation was instrumental in restoring the price and thus demand for silver, there were cries to strip Nevada of its statehood.

FOR PETE'S SAKE

Upon the capitol's completion in 1871, the contractor, Peter Cavanaugh, had spent more money on the project than he was paid by the state. This was said to be due to his attention to details and pride in his work. Through the graciousness of the legislature and in recognition of Mr. Cavanaugh's diligence to give the State "their money's worth," members voted to reimburse Mr. Cavanaugh for his excess costs.

OVERBOOKED

After many years of accumulating books and reference materials, the state library which was housed in the capitol, had outgrown its space. There were so many books that librarians began storing the excess books in the dome. The added weight in the dome caused concern that too much stress was being put on this high point of the building. In 1906, a library addition was added at the rear of the capitol. The library annex was octagonal in shape and included its own dome. Eventually, the library became "overbooked" once again and was relocated to another building. Although the library annex still exists, it has been converted to office space for the capitol staff.

SOMETHING OLD, SOMETHING NEW

Although Alaska is reported to have the smallest capitol, Nevada has the second smallest. As has been the case with many capitols, population growth precipitated the need for more office and meeting space for legislators and staff. Discussions and plans were made for a new capitol coupled with the potential of demolishing the old. Although the dome was restored in 1969, an extensive $6 million renovation including removing and rebuilding of interior walls, was completed in 1981. To accommodate the growth, a new legislative building was built in 1970 — just a short walk from the capitol.

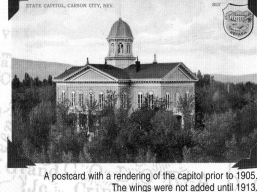

Vines growing up the sandstone walls add a special touch to the Library Annex. The octagon-shaped building with its silver domes is now used for office space

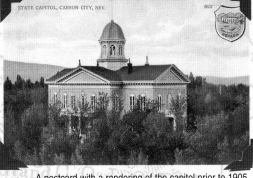

A postcard with a rendering of the capitol prior to 1905. The wings were not added until 1913.

Diagonal parking was in vogue as shown in this photo postcard showing automobiles c. 1930.

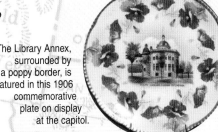

The Library Annex, surrounded by a poppy border, is featured in this 1906 commemorative plate on display at the capitol.

Pearls of Wisdom

"... a large, unfenced, level vacancy, with a liberty pole in it, and very useful as a place for public auctions, horse trades, mass meetings and likewise for teamsters to camp in."

Samuel Clemens (aka Mark Twain) — 1861 Who relocated to Carson City and helped set up the Territory — in describing the capitol site

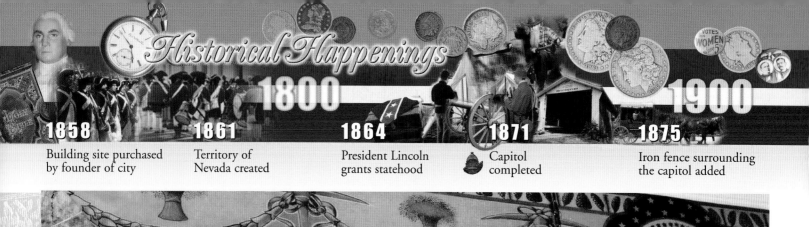

Historical Happenings

1800

1900

1858
Building site purchased by founder of city

1861
Territory of Nevada created

1864
President Lincoln grants statehood

1871
Capitol completed

1875
Iron fence surrounding the capitol added

The three-foot wide ornamental frieze.

The Assembly chambers in the Legislative Building.

Alaskan marble lines the floors and walls. Staircase railings and balusters are made of black walnut.

A Victorian façade.

The "Nevada Lincoln," a painting of Abraham Lincoln painted in 1911 is displayed in the Assembly Hall of the Legislative Building. Around 1950, a bullet hole was discovered in the picture. It has since been patched.

★ The Inside Story

FROM "PINES TO VINES"

Ornamental friezes — elongated murals 400' long — wrap the corridors in the capitol. Added in 1917, a three-foot wide top frieze represents northern Nevada while a nine-inch wide lower one represents the southern part of the state. The drawings on these friezes symbolize the state's resources and industries and are referred to as "pines to vines." The top border displays pine cones while the lower border, just above the marble wainscot, shows grapes. Mining and agriculture, chief industries of Nevada are also depicted. A list of twenty-one minerals, native to Nevada, is on a scroll.

VINTAGE VICTORIAN

Victorian charm greets visitors to the capitol. Double-arched panes of French crystal glass encased in wood trim and painted white are mounted over a pediment. Double doors below the pediment with beveled glass add to this inviting entryway. Although most glass panes have been replaced over the years, these panes do date back to the Victorian era.

BATS IN THE BELFRY

Originally, the inner dome was open to the rotunda below. However, it was closed during a renovation project in 1977. Elliptical in shape, it allowed light and air to penetrate through to the floor below. The opening allowed bats to enter and congregate in the dome area. On occasion, they would swoop down to the floor and startle visitors and staff passing by.

122

1903
President Theodore
Roosevelt visits the capitol

1906
Library building
added

1913
Two wings
added

1970
Legislative building
completed

1981
Building interior
completely rebuilt

2000

★ Claim to Fame

A WESTERN UNION

Although, the reasons for Nevada statehood are largely political, they are often misstated. In 1864, as the Civil War was drawing to a close, supporters of President Lincoln wanted to ensure not only his re-election but also the continuation of his policies toward the Confederate states. Nevada was thought to be a key state in accomplishing these goals. Another important issue involved the proposed Thirteenth Amendment which would abolish slavery. If Nevada was elevated to statehood, expectations were that Nevada's vote would support this amendment. Time was imminent that statehood be granted. Approval of the state constitution by Congress was a precursor to Nevada becoming a state. Nevada's legislature was willing to do whatever it took to achieve statehood and thereby cast the necessary votes. To accomplish this end, the entire Nevada Constitution was telegraphed to Washington at a cost of $3,416 enabling Congress to approve the proposed document.

BUCK FIFTY A PRAYER

In 1861, legislative sessions were opened with prayer. At the time, a clergyman was paid $1.50 per day to open the session and pray for the legislative proceedings. In order to cut costs, a member of the legislature who also happened to be a minister, agreed to pray for free!

★ For What it's Worth

THE SILVER RUSH

Although the dome was originally oxblood in color, the dome atop the capitol was later painted a silver color. The "Silver Rush" — an influx of people seeking to discover silver or gold in the territory — helped to influence Nevada's quest for statehood. Despite having less than one-sixth the population required to be considered for statehood, Nevada's request was approved. Thus, it is no surprise that Nevada's capitol and library annex are graced with a bonanza of silver domes.

The Legislative building (in the foreground) now houses the Senate and Assembly.

Since 1875, this iron fence has surrounded the grounds of the capitol.

HEMMED IN

In 1875 shortly after the capitol was completed, there were many teamsters traveling into town hauling various supplies and goods. Once they arrived in town, their work animals — namely oxen, mules and horses — were often unhitched from their wagons and left to roam. The women of Carson City complained of animal droppings on the capitol grounds. The complaints stemmed from the fact that the floor length hems of their skirts were being soiled by these unwelcome deposits and the odor from the animals was also offensive. In response to their complaints, the legislature approved funding to construct an iron fence to surround the capitol grounds and to ward off the unwelcome visitors. This original fence still stands as a nostalgic remnant of Carson City's frontier days.

THAT PIONEER SPIRIT

After the legislature approved the funding to construct a fence, several bids were considered. Although the erection of the fence was awarded to other contractors, the low bid to supply the iron fencing and gates was that of Hannah Clapp, a school teacher and her friend, Eliza Babcock. This award was a remarkable achievement in pioneer days both for the entrepreneurs as well as for the capitol commissioners in awarding a contractor bid to women. Reportedly, they netted over $1,000 for the job, a considerable sum for its day. Over the years, the story has been told and retold — with varying degrees of truth. One such version insinuates that the commissioners were not aware that Ms. Clapp's initials, H.K. stood for Hannah K. However, Ms. Clapp was well known in this small community and archival records refute this claim.

THE SILVER PARTY TICKET

Nevada's silver mining industry also had an effect on its politics. For the period from 1895-1903, Nevada citizens shunned the traditional Republican and Democratic candidates for governor and instead elected members from the Silver Party.

NEW HAMPSHIRE
Concord

THE RULE OF THE COMMON PEOPLE
Although small in size, New Hampshire boasts the largest membership in its House of Representatives of any state.

"Live free or die"

★ Facts & Figures

Architectural style	Eclectic
Architect	Stuart James Park
Exterior material	Concord granite
Dome surface	23³/4 carat gold leaf over copper
Building height (to tip of dome)	150'
Construction period	1816-19
First occupied	1819
Capital population (Census 2000)	40,687
Census estimate 2007	42,392
Direction capitol faces	East
Original cost	$82,000

The Past Remembered

HOMELESS

From 1782 to 1808, New Hampshire did not have a permanent capitol. During this period, the legislature met in eight different towns — Concord, Amherst, Charlestown, Dover, Exeter, Hanover, Hopkinton and Portsmouth. Until the legislature finally decided to locate in Concord, New Hampshire was the only state without a capitol.

HOMEGROWN

In 1814, three communities competed for the capital. The legislators stipulated that the building be granite. With a granite quarry located nearby, the town of Concord had the inside track. As a further inducement, Concord offered to donate the granite. The state prison was also located in Concord and thus labor for cutting and shaping the granite was also free. The ability to use prison labor and homegrown materials enabled the state to hold the cost of construction to approximately $82,000.

NOTHING BUT A FROG POND

When the legislature announced its decision to locate the capital in Concord, a disagreement arose over which part of town would become the site for the capitol. One site under consideration, known as the "Green lot," was met with opposition and said to be "nothing but a frog pond." However, proponents of the "frog pond" location, with a little help from the governor and the local newspaper, were successful in persuading the legislature to construct the capitol on this site.

KANGAROO COURT

In 1864, the legislature was considering expanding the capitol. In response, Manchester made a generous cash offer to lure the capital away from Concord. The legislature was agreeable to relocate the capital but offered the town of Concord a chance to keep it. They issued an ultimatum to the town of Concord which specified that a new street south of the capitol was to be built to replace its unsightly

surrounding area. The ultimatum was accepted and work on the new street proceeded until one property owner refused to allow his house to be relocated. As the deadline for completion was the next Monday, the mayor and its citizens came to the rescue. Although the property owner pleaded to wait until Monday when the courts would be open, the mayor and others removed the final obstacle on the Sabbath so that a court injunction would not stop their work. Despite the owner's protest, the new street was open to traffic and became what is now known as Capitol Street. This allowed Concord to retain the capital.

THE BIGGEST, BRIGHTEST AND BUSIEST

In 1909, after several decades of growth, the legislature voted again to double the size of the State House. This gave Manchester one more opportunity to try and steal away the capital from Concord. A Manchester merchant boasted that his town had grown into the "biggest, brightest and busiest" of any town in the state and therefore had earned the right to be the capital. They backed their argument with an offer of a building site and $1 million. A Manchester newspaper charged that the town was being treated unfairly and that their offer was not being taken seriously. Heated debates ensued over which city was most deserving. Manchester held rallies, sponsored entertainment and showed proposed sites but all efforts were in vain. In the end, the legislature affirmed Concord by a vote of 277 to 69.

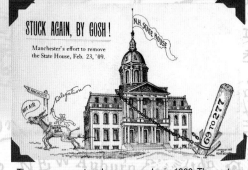

These penny postcards were popular in 1909. The cartoon shows the State House "staked to Concord" while a state representative unsuccessfully tries to pull it to Manchester. Although the bill was defeated, these postcards became souvenirs of the failed attempt to relocate the capital.

Erected in 1891, the Memorial Arch commemorates war veterans. The overlay photo, taken during the construction of the Arch, shows a cobblestone street and a horse and buggy.

A model of the State House commemorates the sesquicentennial with this 1969 Ezra Brooks liquor decanter. The bottle, standing 11½" tall, was made by the Heritage China Company.

"SAFE AND RELIABLE" BAKING POWDER

Is especially recommended as the most healthful baking powder in the market, being entirely free from any adulteration whatever. One trial will convince any intelligent consumer that "Safe and Reliable" has no equal, and your grocer will refund your money if not perfectly satisfied with it. Ask your grocer for "Safe and Reliable" Baking Powder and insist on having it. A set of Capitol Cards (50 in set) sent to any address on receipt of 4 cents in stamps.

GRANGER & CO., Buffalo, N. Y., U. S. A.

The back of this miniature trading card for baking soda states, "One trial will convince any intelligent consumer that 'Safe and Reliable' has no equal."

This matchbook cover, c 1935, was issued to counteract the lack of advertising after the Great Depression. Issued by the Diamond Match Co., they were sold at five 'n' dime stores for a penny.

This postcard bears a 1906 postmark. Note the dome was not gilded at the time.

Historical Happenings
1800

1788	1815	1819	1865	1891
Ninth state to ratify the Constitution	Concord selected as state capital	Capitol completed	Dome is gilded with gold leaf	Memorial Arch erected

★ The Inside Story

STADIUM SEATING

A 400-seat auditorium is home to the House of Representatives. Also known as the General Court of New Hampshire, it is virtually a volunteer legislature. Serving as a state representative is considered an honor. Representatives are said to truly represent a cross section of New Hampshire and are from all walks of life. Seats are arranged side-by-side as in a stadium or auditorium. There is no room for desks.

MY CUP OF TEA

From 1969-73, during the administration of Governor Walter R. Peterson, First Lady Dorothy Peterson invited various women's groups for tea and social occasions at the State House. Reportedly, she asked that they bring their own cup and saucer to be served. Many of the invitees left their cups and saucers for the first lady to keep. The gifts became a permanent collection at the capitol. At last count, there are 100 sets in a glass cabinet.

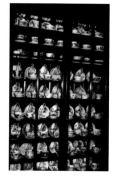

BATTLE FLAGS

Upon entering the main entrance, glass cases display more than 100 flags. The Hall of Flags, as it is known, displays flags carried by New Hampshire soldiers from the Civil War and succeeding wars.

MAKING A SCENE

The main floor features an exhibit of miniature Revolutionary War scenes. These dioramas depict the New Hampshire regiments in service to the country.

The 400-seat House of Representatives.

This colorful stained glass is located on the main floor.

The Senate chamber murals

A diorama depicts a Revolutionary War scene.

1910
Second addition completed

1938
Hurricane blows eagle off dome

1957
Eagle replaced

1976
Refurbishing completed

★ Claim to Fame

A FULL HOUSE

New Hampshire's House of Representatives, 400 members strong, boasts the largest governing body of any state. In fact, it is the fourth largest legislative body in the world! Only the U.S. House of Representatives, the British House of Commons (one house of Parliament) and the Indian House of People have larger memberships. In 1943, due to population growth, the membership had swelled to 443. That same year, a constitutional amendment was passed capping the number at 400. Roll call is said to take 23 minutes.

IF IT AIN'T BROKE, WHY FIX IT?

The New Hampshire legislature is unique in that it has met, and continues to meet, in its original chambers since completion of the State House in 1819. Although the original chambers of other capitols are older, each of their legislatures now meets in a different room in more modern chambers.

THE GOVERNOR'S COUNCIL

A five-member board, called the Executive Council or Governor's Council, dates back to 1784. It acts as the approving authority for certain actions and contracts in concert with the governor. Elected by the people, its purpose is to serve as another check and balance of state government. For the record, Massachusetts also has a similar board.

★ For What it's Worth

IN WAR AND PEACE

Standing 6 feet 6 inches tall, with nearly a 5-foot wingspan, a golden eagle perches on a gold ball atop the dome. The original eagle, known as a war eagle, was carved in 1818. Made of wood and painted gold, the original was held together by wooden pegs and had long wing tips. Upon assessing its condition after 140 years of use, it was replaced with a copper eagle replica. However, it is now known as a "peace" eagle and is gilded with gold leaf.

PAY FREEZE

As noted, New Hampshire has more representatives than any other state. Two other facts are also worthy of note. It has the highest per capita ratio of representatives to its citizens. Secondly, the representatives are paid only $200 for a two-year term. Except for the mileage allowance, the pay has remained the same since 1889. In essence, New Hampshire employs a volunteer legislature.

THE PEOPLE RULE

Most representatives are ordinary citizens who have no experience in drafting legislation. Since only a few are attorneys, the ideas for laws of these ordinary citizens are refined by legal assistants. This has been the case since the early days. In 1849, a survey revealed the occupations represented at the time. A partial list of these included a bookbinder, a brickmaster, a sea captain, a stable keeper, a ticket master, a teacher, a stage proprietor, six deputy sheriffs, nine clergyman, five physicians, two taverners, 13 lawyers, 25 merchants and 161 farmers.

CLOSE ENCOUNTERS

Although New Hampshire is criticized for not having enough professional law makers, advocates argue that there are advantages. This democratic form of representation often results in citizens being able to know their representative personally, thus they are able to converse with them.

The golden leaves of Fall frames the golden dome in this 1988 photo.

NEW JERSEY

Trenton

ACROSS THE DELAWARE

With the Delaware River at its back door, the New Jersey State House has survived numerous additions and reconstructions in over two centuries of existence.

STATE MOTTO

"Liberty and Prosperity"

★ Facts & Figures

Architectural style	Eclectic
Architect (original)	Jonathan Doane
1845 addition	John Notman
Exterior material	Indiana limestone
Dome surface	23½ karat gold leaf over copper sheeting
Building height (to tip of dome)	145'
Construction period	1790-92 (original building only)
First occupied	1792
Capital population (Census 2000)	85,403
Census estimate 2007	82,804
Direction capitol faces	North
Original cost	£4,242

The Past Remembered

EVOLUTION OF A CAPITOL

Constructed in several phases, the New Jersey State House has evolved over the years and bears little resemblance to the original building. Although the original architectural style was said to be Georgian, additions include American Renaissance, Victorian, French Academic Classicism and Second Empire. During these growth spurts, offices such as the Senate and General Assembly chambers were relocated to more suitable rooms. With so many different additions and styles, the building has its own unique character.

Historical records indicate that the original 1792 building cost, complete with bell tower, was 3,992 British pounds, 3 shillings and one half pence. In addition, the land cost 250 pounds and 5 shillings.

FIRE AND ICE

In March 1885, a major fire of undetermined origin caused extensive damage to the building. During the fire, both the Delaware River and nearby fire hydrant were frozen, preventing the fire from being quickly extinguished. Fortunately, the governor's office and both Senate and General Assembly chambers remained unscathed by the blaze. This event caused some lawmakers to seek a relocation of the capital to Newark or Elizabeth. However, their efforts failed to materialize as repairs and improvements to the existing building were undertaken.

HISTORY PRESERVED

During the 1960s, due to the deteriorating condition of the State House and shortage of functioning offices, a master plan was discussed to demolish most of the building. Fortunately, those in favor of historic preservation prevailed. The dome and rotunda phase of building renovation was completed in 1999. During the restoration process, the dome was stripped to its iron frame and refurbished.

"DIMES FOR THE DOME"

In 1997, a fund raising project to restore the dome was undertaken. Aptly named "Dimes for the Dome," students from elementary schools throughout the state participated in raising over $48,000 — the exact amount needed to regild the dome.

This view shows an unpaved street in this early 1900s postcard.

An old postcard c. 1910 shows an illuminated capitol.

Streets near the State House are narrow and adjacent buildings are in close proximity. Thus, taking pictures of the entire capitol without a wide-angle lens, as in this 1981 photo, can be a challenge.

In a photo dated 1929, the South and East Facades are reflected in a water power canal, commonly known as the Sanhican Creek. Trenton's proximity to water helped to enable early industries to thrive here. During the Depression, the water canal was paved over to provide for a modern road system.

A "Local View" postcard that was never mailed shows awnings, a woman walking with a handbag and automobiles from an earlier day.

The mid-day sun illuminates the state seal in this stained glass artwork.

Historical Happenings

1800

1787
Third state to ratify the Constitution

1792
Capitol completed

1846
Rotunda, first dome and wing added

1872
Building extended

1885
Major fire occurs

1889
Wing added and dome gilded with gold

Natural light illuminates a salmon color painted in the upper rotunda.

The chamber of the General Assembly.

Plows on the seal pay tribute to the state's farming industry.

In years past, a Christmas tree decorated the rotunda during this festive time of year. The space is now occupied by a statue of Lincoln.

The *Glory of New Jersey*, a three-foot porcelain sculpture, is a unique attraction.

Added in 1903, this circular stained glass skylight is above the Senate chamber.

★ The Inside Story

INSIDE PASSAGE

Buildings in the capitol complex are linked via an underground passageway, which was built in 1995. It is used extensively by staff to walk between the State House, State House Annex and other areas.

FIGHT TO THE FINISH

The General Assembly floor was once the scene of a literal fight for majority control. In 1878, when some Democratic and Reform party members defected to the Republican caucus, a new Speaker was duly elected. However, the remaining members refused to relinquish control of the General Assembly to the new Speaker. Instead, a brawl broke out among the members. Later on, when tempers had cooled, the new Speaker assumed his proper role.

SHADES OF MELLOW YELLOW

Shades of pale yellow are the predominant colors throughout the capitol as is evident in both the Senate and General Assembly chambers. It is also found in the stained glass artwork in the rotunda. Although some of the marble is genuine, scagliola or faux marble was used in the Senate chamber and adjacent corridors. The General Assembly room features figures depicting Liberty and Abundance — though different from the state motto. These are located on top of the arch above the podium. A huge brass chandelier, attributed to Thomas Edison, hangs from the ceiling.

THE BIRDS AND THE BEES AND THE RED OAK TREE

A small tree loaded with little yellow birds is enclosed in a case just off the rotunda. Known as The *Glory of New Jersey*, a three-foot-tall porcelain sculpture created in 1995 depicts four of the state's symbols: the red oak, gold finch, honeybee and purple violet.

LADYBUG, LADYBUG

On a leaf at the base of the tree sculpture is one little ladybug. It was placed there in recognition of New Jersey's first woman governor, Christine Todd Whitman. The sculpture, commissioned by the Friends of the State House, was crafted by the Boehm Porcelain Factory.

1900	1906	1912	1991	1999
Center wing extended	East wing replaced	Front of capitol extended	South Addition completed	Dome restoration completed

Claim to Fame

SURVIVAL OF THE FITTEST

Completed in 1792, the original building bears little resemblance to today's capitol. New Jersey's capitol has survived more changes to its existing building than any other capitol. Despite the many reconstructed portions of the capitol, the original structure has survived but is obscured by newer construction. Due to fires, annexes, expansions and tunnel connections, the capitol today is an expansive mix of various spaces.

Because original walls lie within the current capitol structure, the first construction date places it as the second oldest, next to Maryland, in continuous use of state capitols. There are those who would argue that Virginia's capitol is older. Although technically true, the qualifier for this distinction is that the State of Virginia seceded from the Union for a period of time and therefore lost its continuity of statehood. Nevertheless, both capitols hold the distinction of existing for more than 200 years.

TEMPORARY DUTY

A second notable claim of New Jersey is that the city of Trenton served as the U.S. Capital in 1783 and 1784 when the Second Continental Congress met here under the Articles of Confederation. The Federal government selected Trenton as the nation's permanent capital, but changed it in favor of Washington D.C. following objections from George Washington.

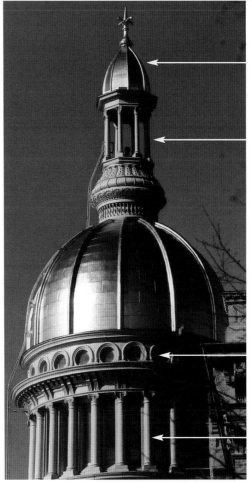

Cupola
Lantern
Roundels
Colonade

An atypical dome with some unusual design features.

The Delaware River, which separates New Jersey and Pennsylvania, was the site of General George Washington's famous crossing. The ensuing surprise attack on enemy soldiers in Trenton was the turning point of the Revolutionary War. New Jersey's capitol is the only one to afford a view of an adjacent state.

For What it's Worth

DUAL CAPITALS

Until 1702, there was an East and a West Jersey. Each had its own capital, neither of which was Trenton. Thus, there were dual capitals. Known as provinces, each province had its own proprietor.

ON THE ROAD AGAIN

In 1776, the Revolutionary War impacted governments in many ways including the ability for lawmakers to meet. New Jersey was no exception. The Legislature, continually on the move, did not have a permanent meeting place and was forced to convene in various locations throughout the state. It wasn't until after the United States Constitution was ratified in 1790 that Trenton was selected as its capital.

NEW MEXICO
Santa Fe

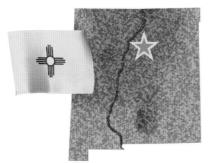

OLD SANTA FE CULTURE
An emphasis on historical Santa Fe strongly influenced the design of the capitol. Pueblo Indian symbolism is seen throughout the building.

"It grows as it goes"

★ *Facts & Figures*

Architectural style	Pueblo Indian adobe
Architect	W. C. Kruger
Exterior material	Stucco
Dome	None
Building height	60'
Construction period	1965-66
First occupied	1966
Capital population (Census 2000)	62,203
Census estimate 2007	73,199
Direction capitol faces	East
Original cost	$4,676,860

The Past Remembered

A RELUCTANT CONGRESS

Even though New Mexico was colonized before the Pilgrims landed at Plymouth Rock, it was one of the last states to be granted statehood. The U.S. Congress rejected New Mexico statehood on several occasions. Possible reasons include the relatively remote location, a population with diverse cultures and residents who primarily spoke languages other than English.

THE SPANISH KINGDOM

Originally known as the Spanish "Kingdom of New Mexico," this land first progressed to a Mexican province known as Nuevo Mejico. During the Mexican-American War in 1846, Santa Fe was captured and became a U.S. territory that included Arizona. In 1912, New Mexico became the 47th state. Over the years, it has not only retained its multi-cultural heritage, but has enhanced it.

ALL THE WAY WITH SANTA FE

For a period of twelve years beginning in 1897, legislators were deeply divided over efforts to relocate the capital from Santa Fe to Albuquerque. Legislation allowing for relocation, known as "Capital Removing Bills," was introduced in every session. However, the controversy ended when the U.S. Congress designated Santa Fe as the permanent capital.

IN A ROUND ABOUT WAY

The unique circular design or "donut shape" of the present capitol was also the subject of much controversy. The Chamber of Commerce, Board of Realtors and other groups opposed the design claiming it was too modern and "did not conform to the Santa Fe historical building code." However, the height of the building does conform to the historic building code of Santa Fe as it measures only three stories.

THE ROUNDHOUSE

Most state capitols simply refer to their capitol building as the capitol. Some call it their state house. In Santa Fe, locals refer to it as the "Roundhouse" because of its circular design. The design was chosen to symbolize the native Indian kiva, a tribal meeting place that was round in shape.

ONCE UPON A DOME

Prior to the "Roundhouse," New Mexico did have a domed capitol which stood as the territorial capitol. Its traditional appearance was said to help influence the cause for statehood achieved in 1912. It continued to serve as the state capitol until 1950, at which time the dome was removed to blend with the territorial style of architecture. Still in existence, it is part of and is known as the Bataan Memorial Building.

What's a family vacation without a trip to the state capitol? This 1978 photo shows the height of the rotunda as well as the atrium affect. It also shows one of the times the family accompanied the author on one of the many capitol photographing stops.

Note the traditional dome of the earlier New Mexico capitol. Eventually "decapitated," it became part of the Battan Memorial Building. The postcard bears a 1907 postmark.

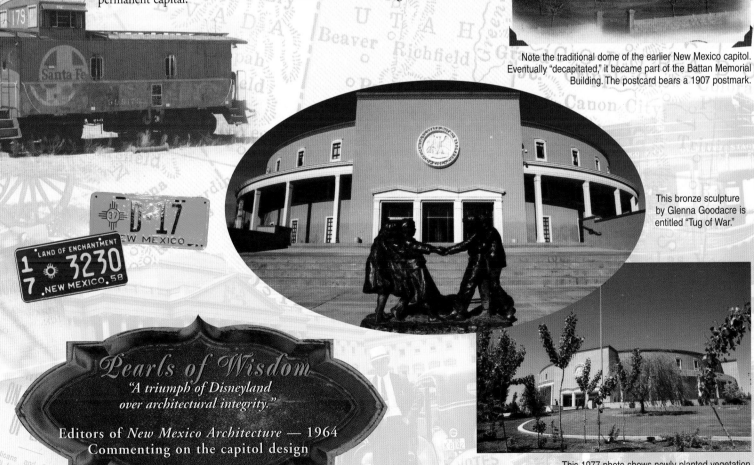

This bronze sculpture by Glenna Goodacre is entitled "Tug of War."

This 1977 photo shows newly planted vegetation.

Pearls of Wisdom
"A triumph of Disneyland over architectural integrity."

Editors of *New Mexico Architecture* — 1964
Commenting on the capitol design

Historical Happenings

1800

1900

1610
Santa Fe becomes capital of "Kingdom of New Mexico"

1833
Santa Anna becomes President of Mexico

1850
New Mexico designated as a territory, but denied statehood

1898
Spanish American War

The skylight of stained glass is said to represent an Indian basket-weave pattern. The colors are typical of much local artwork.

★ The Inside Story

ZIA SUN SYMBOL

Like no other capital, New Mexico modeled its flat roof building in the shape of a Zia, an Indian sun symbol. The round building is also said to reflect the circle of life.

As you enter the rotunda area, the Great Seal of the State, inlaid with native turquoise, is in the center of the floor. The bars, extending outward from the seal in all four directions form another design of the Zia Indian sun symbol. Looking upward, the interior dome is lined with sand and turquoise colored glass. Colorful flags of the New Mexico counties and trailing plants hang from the balconies.

In addition to the Zia symbolism of the building, the state seal portrays the Mexican eagle holding three arrows.

CULTURAL MAGNET

Today, events such as the Opera, the Fiesta, the Spanish Market, the Indian Market and the Music Festival featuring Indian arts and crafts are held in Santa Fe. Although small in population, Santa Fe attracts hundreds of thousands of visitors each year who come to enjoy and appreciate the wealth of culture present in this festive atmosphere. In continuing this theme, New Mexico's unique blend of cultures is reflected in the design and theme of its state capitol.

The state seal appears on the rotunda floor while county flags are draped from the upper floor.

Continuing the circle effect, the House of Representatives is in a semi-circle.

1900 — Bataan Memorial Building (former capitol) completed

1912 — President Taft grants statehood

1916 — Pancho Villa raid on New Mexico

1966 — Capitol completed

1992 — $25 million renovation completed

2000

★ *Claim to Fame*

OLDER THAN DIRT

New Mexico has the oldest capitol building in the United States. Though never a state capitol, the Palace of Governors was built in 1610 and served the Kingdom of New Mexico at that time. It is also one of the oldest public buildings in the United States.

ON A HIGH

With an elevation of 7,199' above sea level, Santa Fe claims to have the highest altitude of any state capital.

LIMITED EDITION

Although many capitols are modeled after the U.S. Capitol, the unique circular design of the New Mexico capitol is a one of a kind.

The Palace of Governors

Artwork abounds around the capitol.

★ *For What it's Worth*

FAMOUS COOKIES

In 1989, New Mexico became the first state to adopt an official state cookie. Known as the biscochito, this cookie is most often eaten during celebrations. Its anise flavor is said to have originated as an ancient custom of the Spaniards.

ON THE WINGS OF EAGLES

The state seal features two eagles. If you look closely, you will see the American bald eagle shielding a smaller Mexican eagle, symbolizing New Mexico's change in sovereignty.

Much of the art displayed in the capitol is on loan. This sculpture, by Estella Loretto, is entitled "Earth Mother."

NEW YORK
Albany

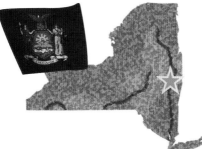

THE EMPIRE STATE CAPITOL—ECLECTIC MASTERPIECE

This unique design was the most elaborate of its time. Even with a price tag of $25 million, the capitol was scaled back from the original plan.

"Ever upward"

★ Facts & Figures

Architectural style	Eclectic
Architect(s)	Thomas Fuller, Leopold Eidlitz & Henry Hobson Richardson, Frederick Law Olmsted and Issac Perry
Exterior material	Maine gray granite
Dome surface	No dome
Building height	221'
Construction period	1867-99
First occupied	1879
Capital population (Census 2000)	95,658
Census estimate 2007	94,172
Direction capitol faces	East
Original cost	$25 million

The Past Remembered

NEW YORK.
Map on Pages 28-29.

An engraving c. 1867 shows the proposed capitol design with a tower at its center.

DOUBLE THE TIME, DOUBLE THE COST

It took a thousand workers more than three decades to complete the five-story building. In all, five architects contributed to the capitol's design. Toward the end of the project, work progressed day and night to finish the job. Newspapers at the time ridiculed the project as never-ending and costing a fortune. The final cost, $25 million, was double the amount of the cost of the nation's capitol in Washington, D.C.

A postcard c 1910 shows a busy street scene with trolleys and horse-drawn carriages.

GREAT EXPECTATIONS

A blend of four architectural designs, New York's capitol is certainly grandiose. In many respects, it takes on a medieval or Gothic appearance. Originally designed by Thomas Fuller, a native of England, the plan called for a huge tower in the center of the structure. Though his design was approved, the capitol commission eliminated the tower after Fuller departed as architect. The decision was based on the evaluation by outside engineers who decided the foundation would not support the tower's weight. Among the enhancements by other architects after Fuller's departure were the addition of the Million Dollar Staircase and a different design for the legislative chambers.

"THE CAPITOL IS BURNING"

Fire! Fire! A postcard photo shows the capitol in flames.

On March 29, 1911, a fire started on the third floor of the capitol. The fire was detected during the early morning hours before most people were awake. In spite of this, word spread quickly, awakening the sleeping city. Reportedly, phone calls were made exclaiming, "The Capitol is burning." Although, many people thought it was an early April Fool's joke, some were able to look out their window to see the capitol in flames. Two days after the fire, the body of a 78-year-old night watchman was discovered in a fourth-floor corridor. He was the only casualty of the fire.

Though the fire's cause was never determined, investigations suggested faulty wiring. There was one rumor that it started with a discarded cigar butt from a legislator.

This early Twentieth century postcard shows a congested area surrounding the capitol.

THE "BIG APPLE" LOSES TO ALBANY

One might expect New York City to be the capital of New York, and although it was considered, the smaller city of Albany was selected. In an effort to sway legislators in its favor, Albany made a generous offer to provide land in a prime public location as well as provide payment for a portion of the building.

IN SINKING SAND

As was the case with many other capitols, the construction phase did not go smoothly. One significant challenge was the discovery of both clay and a layer of quicksand during the excavation. To remedy the situation, an over-dig was required in which the sand was replaced with clay and concrete.

COOKING THE BOOKS

Just when it was presumed the building would be a total loss, the fire slowed when water from the fire hoses cascaded through the papier-mâché ceiling in the Assembly Chamber. Ironically, this material had not been authorized by the legislature. Attempting to cut costs from a solid oak ceiling, the contractor mixed papier-mâché with the oak. Though the fire caused major damage to the western side of the building, the capitol survived. The State Library with many valuable books and manuscripts from colonial days suffered major damage. However, some significant documents were rescued by the heroic efforts of librarians and others.

The west side of this stately capitol also has curb appeal as seen in this 1986 photo.

An early 1900s silver spoon depicts the capitol.

A capitol memento with an oval mirror is on the opposite side, c 1905.

A pennant, c 1950s proclaims Albany the capital.

Pearls of Wisdom

"There are two things which the State Capitol at Albany may confidently be relied on to furnish: an enduring opportunity to spend large sums of money, and an occasion for speculation as to when, if ever, the huge pile will be finished."

New York Tribune — 1896

Historical Happenings

1800

1788
Eleventh state to ratify
the Constitution

1797
Albany designated
as capital

1871
Cornerstone
laid

1885
Statue of Liberty
arrives in New York

1897
Million Dollar
Staircase completed

The Million Dollar Staircase

Stairs converge from opposite directions
onto a center step and then descend to
the next level.

The Governor's Reception Room

The seating in the Senate chamber is
arranged in a semi-circle.

Two huge fireplaces grace one end
of the Assembly Chamber.

Faces were not the only carvings.

Intricate carvings are embedded
in each of the stone pillars of
the Million Dollar Staircase.

★ *The Inside Story*

THE MILLION DOLLAR STAIRCASE

A massive four-story staircase climbing 119 feet, originally known as the Great Western Staircase, contains 368 steps — that is if you count all flights in each direction. However, starting at the bottom and proceeding straight to the top, it is only 139 steps. Hundreds of detailed carvings of faces, animals and other objects are featured on the sandstone walls supporting the staircase. Over 200 stone cutters and carvers, many of whom were European immigrants, worked on the project for 14 years. This beautifully detailed staircase is illuminated by sunlight from a glass skylight above. The cost of the staircase exceeded one million dollars, thus it aptly became known as the Million Dollar Staircase. In 2005, a $2.5 million restoration of the staircase was begun.

LET'S FACE IT

Henry Hobson Richardson was the original architect for this grand staircase. Isaac Perry added a plan to carve 77 famous faces and other designs in the red sandstone that makes up most of the staircase. The stone carvers themselves added a number of smaller faces, called the "Capitol unknowns" that are thought to be the friends and relatives of the carvers.

THE GREAT COVER-UP

Originally installed in 1897, the skylight above the staircase has two layers. The lower or laylight as it is known, is 55 feet above the fourth floor. The fire of 1911 destroyed the skylight but it was rebuilt shortly thereafter.

In 1942, during World War II, it was feared that the Germans were going to bomb some U.S. cities during the night. In order to block out the light, the skylights were covered with a wallpaper-like fabric to minimize the possibility that light would shine through and become a landmark as there was an arsenal only a few miles north of the capitol.

LET THERE BE LIGHT

The skylight remained covered until the 1960s. At that time, workers removed the glass, much of which was broken, and replaced it with a slate roof. Finally in 2002, after about 60 years of darkness, the state decided it was time to restore the skylight. With the re-opening of the skylight, the stone carvings on the staircase are now illuminated and can be seen as they were intended. The cost of the roof and skylight restoration project equaled the initial cost of the entire staircase — $1 million.

1900

1899
Capitol
completed

1911
Fire destroys library
and much of western
side of capitol

1942
Skylight over Million
Dollar Staircase covered
due to WWII bombing fears

1973
Empire State
Plaza completed

2000

2002
Skylight uncovered
after 60 years of
darkness

★ Claim to Fame

SLIPPERY SLOPES

New York's black-slate-and-red-tiled roof is unique among state capitols. Other features which set this capitol apart are the corner pavilions covered with red terracotta tiles, the steep-sloped ridges and turret peaks, and the differently styled dormers for each side which were designed by different architects.

A STYLISH LEGISLATURE

During the early stages of planning the capitol, the New York legislature made history in legislating the style of architecture for the capitol. There is no other known instance in which a legislature enacted a law stipulating architectural style. The 1877 law stipulated Italian Renaissance as the capitol's architectural style. However, the design was modified several times, which resulted in a mix of styles.

A close-up view of one of the steeples.

The skylight after being restored.

★ For What it's Worth

TEMP TO PERM

Although Albany was designated the capital in 1797, it was not approved as the permanent seat of state government at that time. Officially, Albany did not become the permanent capital of New York until a 1971 law designated Albany as the capital.

THE CASE OF THE MISSING CORNERSTONE

A cornerstone ceremony was held during the initial stages of construction. This gala event took place in 1871 and was attended by thousands. In the haste and confusion of the day, the cornerstone was not marked so that it could later be identified. It has never been located.

STEPPIN' OUT

Strange as it may seem, the steps leading to the front entrace are seldom used. Tackling 77 steps seems to be a deterrent to employees and visitors alike — except those desiring a bit of a workout. Alternatively, people enter through the lower level and take the elevator to the upper floors.

NORTH CAROLINA
Raleigh

THE CROWNED CAPITOL

Raleigh, named after the English explorer Sir Walter Raleigh, has a dome appropriately topped with a crown. The building was modeled after a Greek temple.

STATE MOTTO

"To be rather than to seem"

Facts & Figures

Architectural style .... Greek Revival

Architect .... Ithiel Town, Alexander Davis and David Paton

Exterior material .... Gneiss

Dome surface .... Copper

Building height (to tip of dome) .... 98'

Construction period 1833-40

First occupied 1840

Capital population (Census 2000) 276,093
    Census estimate 2007 375,806

Direction capitol faces .... East

Original cost $532,682

The Past Remembered

UNION SQUARE

In 1792, the legislature which had been meeting in various locations since the Revolutionary War, purchased 1,000 acres of land in order to create a new city which would serve as the capital. The plan was to model the city after Philadelphia, the nation's capital at the time. Five public squares were sectioned off and the central square was designated Union Square. The first state house to stand on the Square was completed in 1796.

A COSTLY BREAK

In 1831, a careless mistake resulted in the destruction of the first state house on Union Square. In an effort to make the roof fireproof, workmen applying zinc sheets over the shingles decided to take a break. In their absence, a pot filled with hot lead turned over catching the roof on fire and completely destroying the building. The tragedy prompted proposals to relocate the capital to Fayetteville. One motion to relocate to the Cape Fear area failed by a single vote.

STANDING ALONE

A lone statue of George Washington stands in the rotunda — even though the original plans called for stairways. In 1836, the architect, David Paton wrote a letter to William Strickland (later the architect for the Tennessee capitol) asking for advice regarding the proposed stairway. Mr. Strickland's response was that a stairway in the rotunda would "impair the effect of the room." He went on to say, "The Statue of Washington should stand alone, as a work of art...." The current statue is a 1970 reproduction of the one sculpted by Antonio Canova in 1820. The original was destroyed at the time the first state house burned.

LOOKS GREEK TO ME

The design for the new capitol, though very similar to the first except larger, was modeled after Grecian temples including the Parthenon in ancient Greece. Styles featured include Doric, Ionic and Corinthian. Ithiel Town and Alexander Jackson Davis are credited with the architectural design of this cross-shaped building. In 1835, they were replaced by David Paton who made some enhancements to the original design of the interior. Completed in 1840, the cantilevered overhang in the rotunda area is unique among state capitols.

SPARE THE CAPITOL

In 1865, when the city of Raleigh was under siege by General Sherman and the Union Army, the North Carolina governor knew that the capitol was at risk of being destroyed. In a valiant move, and most likely his last order as governor, he sent a peace delegation to ask Sherman to spare the capitol. General Sherman obliged.

Dedicated in 1948, this statue features three North Carolina-born presidents, Andrew Jackson, James Polk and Andrew Johnson.

The Veterans' Monument stands tall on the north side of the capitol.

A postcard, mailed April 1910, features the city's namesake, Sir Walter Raleigh, and does a little bragging on the North Carolina capital.

The State Library room interior was re-created to appear as it did in 1856.

Mailed in 1907, this photo postcard shows a vintage automobile and some electrical and telephone poles west of the capitol.

"How would you like to be here?" is written on the back side of this postcard mailed to Lynchburg, Virginia in 1908. The dome was never orange as depicted on the card. According to historians, it was pale green at the time.

Pearls of Wisdom

Raleigh is "unconvenient with commerce" and would never "rise above the degree of a village."

A North Carolina legislator — 1831
Remark made concerning relocating the capital

Historical Happenings

1800 — 1900

1789 Twelfth state to ratify the Constitution

1792 Raleigh chosen as capital site

1831 First State House on site burns

1840 Capitol completed

1861... Secession Convention votes to secede from Union

The inner dome is 97½ feet above the floor.

The Senate chamber in the State Legislative Building is equipped with the latest technology.

★ The Inside Story

A HOUSE WARMING

Considering that the state house was completed in 1840, heating a building of that size was quite a challenge. To effectively accomplish the task, designers included 28 fireplaces.

GREEK BY DESIGN

Grecian design greatly influenced both the interior and exterior of the capitol. The House of Representatives was modeled after a Greek amphitheater. Its semi-circular shape has galleries for public viewing and a vaulted ceiling. An historic portrait of George Washington painted by Thomas Sully hangs in this chamber. It is one of the few items saved from the 1831 fire of the first state house. The Senate is said to resemble a temple in Athens known as the Erechtheum. The legislature now holds its sessions in the State Legislative Building.

THE THIRD HOUSE

As was the case with other capitols during Reconstruction (the years following the Civil War in which states were restored to the Union), liquor was served in the capitol. A bar on the second floor was located in a committee room. Legislators often conducted much of their business and negotiating in this room. Its influence was considered substantial enough to refer to it as the "Third House."

The original Senate chamber

The original House chamber is semi-circular in shape. It was known as the House of Commons until 1868. All legislative furniture was made locally between 1838-40.

Antonio Canova's Statue of George Washington in the rotunda.

A unique feature of the second floor is the cantilevered gallery.

A model of the capitol is on display in a hallway.

1865
Union Army occupies capitol. General Johnson's Army surrenders to General William T. Sherman.

1963
Legislative Building completed

2000
Ten-year comprehensive restoration completed

⭐ Claim to Fame

A CROWNING AFFAIR

The green dome, with an oxidized copper covering, has an ornamental feature known as an anthemion crown and is a distinguishing characteristic of the North Carolina capitol. Patterned after a Greek temple, it is also referred to as a honeysuckle crown.

A HOUSE DIVIDED

North Carolina was the first state to construct a separate building to house its legislature. The State Legislative Building was completed in 1963 and houses the North Carolina General Assembly. The Governor's office remains at the capitol.

The crown atop the dome is known as an anthemion crown.

⭐ For What it's Worth

JOY RIDERS

The exterior walls of the capitol are made of gneiss, a form of granite. This stone was cut from a nearby quarry. In order to deliver the material, an "Experimental Railroad" was constructed in which wooden carts were pulled by oxen, horses and mules. Local citizens were fascinated by its novelty. The track, a little over a mile in length, was so popular that a special car was added for the express purpose of providing rides for these "joy riders." The ride advertised that the horse "was guaranteed not to run away."

LOOK BEFORE YOU LEAP

In 1865, with Union troops occupying Raleigh during the Civil War, a U.S. Army Signal corpsman, Lt. George C. Round, was assigned to set up a lookout station atop the dome of the capitol. Unable to see what was on the inside of the crown and thinking it would be a flat roof, he hastily leaped into the center of the crown. To his astonishment, he landed on a glass skylight. Although he broke through the glass, he managed to hang onto a wire netting. With glass falling through to the rotund floor 97 feet below, he was able to hoist himself back up to safety.

On April 26, 1865, using colored signal rockets, Lt. Round sent the "last signal message" of the war that evening "Peace on earth, goodwill to men."

The State Legislative Building, completed in 1963, houses the Senate and House chambers.

NORTH DAKOTA

Bismarck

CONTEMPORARY CAPITOL

North Dakota's modern design incorporated highly functional, yet attractive features into its capitol.

"Liberty and union, now and forever, one and inseparable"

★ Facts & Figures

Architectural style	Art deco
Architect	Holabird and Root
Exterior material	Indiana limestone
Dome surface	No dome
Building height	242'
Construction period	1932-34
First occupied	1935
Capital population (Census 2000)	55,532
Census estimate 2007	59,503
Direction capitol faces	South
Original cost	$1,977,000

The Past Remembered

BISMARCK ON A ROLL

In 1883, Bismarck was selected as the capital of the Dakota Territory. Six years later, it was divided into two states — North and South Dakota. The first capitol was built a year later with Bismarck continuing to be the North Dakota capital. According to historians, key factors considered in selecting Bismarck as the seat of government include its central location, its proximity to the Missouri River and the Northern Pacific Railroad which ran through Bismarck. As is often the case, politics also factored into the decision.

TAKING IT TO A HIGHER LEVEL

After a fire destroyed the first capitol in December of 1930, the legislature acted quickly to rebuild even though it was during the Great Depression. After much deliberation and although various designs were considered, the legislature decided that they would build a tower structure instead of a traditional domed capitol. Their reasoning was that a domed capitol would be "uneconomical" as it is typically costly to maintain and results in unusable space. Another factor was that their goal was to divide the building by function.

When the capitol was completed, they had successfully addressed each concern. Useable space inside the capitol is rated at 80 percent. By comparison, Minnesota's domed capitol, though a beautiful building, has just 29 percent useable space! As for dividing it by function, the west wing houses the legislature with an entry space. The adjacent tower houses the administration. Later, the judicial wing was added to the east wing, completing a capitol with each branch of government.

OUT OF THE MAINSTREAM

North Dakota's capitol was not the typical capitol of its day. Not only is it geographically removed from main stream America, it also was a departure from a traditionally domed capitol. Though constructed in the early 1930s, it represented a contemporary approach to building trends which gives the impression it may have been built decades later.

NOT JUST HO HUM

The capitol complex, though very functional, has several attractive and somewhat unique features that distinguish it from other capitols. Unlike most traditional capitols, there is an observation floor on the 19th story which provides a panoramic view of the countryside. On a clear day, visibility can reach 35 miles. Often, the Missouri River can be seen winding its way downstream. There are also historic photos and exhibits on display on the observation floor.

Placed in 1910, the "Sakakawea" statue is the oldest feature on the grounds.

An early 1900s postcard shows an artist's rendering of a proposed capitol that was not to be.

A postcard c. 1910 shows the previous capitol. In 1930, a fire destroyed this building.

Fiscus trees soften the stellar walls of the atrium in this 1989 photo. Artificial trees later replaced the live trees.

JR263 PEACE GARDEN STATE NORTH DAKOTA
ND 10-324 1913

Pearls of Wisdom
"I never would have been President, if it had not been for my experiences in North Dakota."

Theodore Roosevelt — c. 1910
Speech at Fargo

A photo postcard, mailed in 1937 shows a vintage automobile on its way to the capitol.

Historical Happenings

1800

1900

1883
Bismarck named capital of Dakota Territory

1884
First capitol completed

1889
President Harrison grants statehood

★ The Inside Story

MEMORIAL HALL

Once known as Memorial Hall, the Great Hall is one of the highlights of the capitol's interior. The floors are made of Tennessee marble, the walls are Montana travertine and the railings are solid bronze. Massive pillars wrapped in bronze extend from floor to ceiling. The bronze in the building is so extensive that its replacement cost is estimated to exceed the original cost of the building.

MONKEY BUSINESS

The walls of the entrance hall to the Secretary of State's office are paneled with California walnut. Each panel was spliced to create a left and right side. This area is referred to as the "Monkey Room" because visitors often claim to see monkeys in the wood grain. Depending on one's imagination, other animals seen include rabbits, lions and buffalo. There are also "special appearances" by E.T. and Garfield the Cat. Possibly, a more appropriate name would be the Animal Room. This intriguing and rather curious corridor adds a unique touch to this modern capitol, and is a special attraction for children.

ATRIUM SPACE

The atrium that connects the judicial wing with the main office building is one of only a few true atriums constructed in a capitol. It's a four-story open space with artificial fiscus trees and other foliage, which add a bit of the outdoors to an otherwise closed-in feeling of the interior. The floors in the atrium are made of terrazzo marble. A spacious view of the upper floors can be seen from the atrium. Balconies from the upper floors complement the two-way view.

FACE OFF

Unlike many capitols, there is very little symbolism in the North Dakota capitol with the exception of the elevator doors. Four sets of images that depict North Dakota life and history are sculpted into the bronze of the doors. The top set of these images portrays an Indian with a tomahawk on the left door while the right door has a soldier with a musket. When the doors are closed, the two face each other and are said to "illustrate the struggle between the white man and the Indian."

Bronze pillars line The Great Hall.

Depending on your imagination, all sorts of animals can be seen in the grain of the wood.

Curved lighting accentuates the semi-circular rows of legislative desks in this chamber.

A wheat chaff is at the base of these light fixtures.

The "white man and the Indian" is bronzed into the elevator doors.

1930 First capitol destroyed by fire

1932 Voters reaffirm Bismarck as capital

1934 Capitol completed

1973 Capitol remodeled

1981 Judicial wing completed

1985 Arboretum Trail added

2000

★ Claim to Fame

WHAT A BARGAIN!

North Dakota's capitol is considered the most economical capitol ever built. The construction cost was only 46 cents per cubic foot, which was considered quite a bargain when compared with the other high-rise capitols built in the same era. Louisiana's capitol was constructed at a cost of $1.00 per cubic foot while Nebraska's final cost was $1.10. As noted earlier, useable space is rated at 80 percent, while Louisiana's capitol is rated at 70 percent and Nebraska's at 50 percent.

GOING TO THE MALL

The North Dakota capitol is set on a vast amount of acreage. The large grassy area in front of the capitol is called a "mall." Various activities and civic events are held here, mostly during the summer months due to the cold Bismarck winters. Events range from art and craft shows and flea markets to formal occasions such as weddings. Various sculptures and artwork are also located throughout the capitol grounds. A nature trail known as the Arboretum Trail leads to flower gardens, ornamental trees, memorials and sculptures as it winds it way through the mall and surrounds the building.

The view from the observation floor

Lighted at night, the towering capitol of the north provides a dramatic impression that can be seen for miles.

★ For What it's Worth

MAKING CENTS OF HIGHER WAGES

Shortly after construction began on the capitol, the laborers went on strike for higher wages. Hired at 30 cents per hour, they demanded 50 cents. When tempers flared, a small riot ensued. At the governor's request, the National Guard was called in to calm the opposing sides. Eventually, work on the capitol resumed.

A TREE FROM A BUSH

During North Dakota's Centennial celebration in 1989, President George Bush was present to help plant an American elm tree from the White House grounds. This started a campaign to plant 100 million trees in the state by the year 2000. Although the goal of reaching this number was not achieved, records maintained by the State Forester show that over 74 million trees were officially planted as of Arbor Day 2001 — an amazing achievement.

ANOTHER STORY TO TELL

Officially, the building has nineteen stories. However, since the ground floor is not numbered, there are actually twenty floors. The top two floors are the observation floor and above it, the penthouse.

Fall colors soften the stark lines of the capitol.

OHIO
Columbus

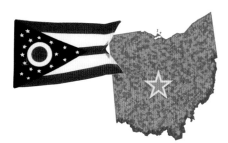

MARCHING TO A DIFFERENT DRUM

A pennant-shaped flag and Grecian style architecture featuring a drum instead of a dome sets this capitol apart.

"With God all things are possible"

★ Facts & Figures

Architectural style ....Greek Revival

Architect(s) ....Henry Walters, Nathan B. Kelly,
Isaiah Rogers & William R. West

Exterior material ......Brick and Columbus limestone

Dome surface ....Columbus limestone

Height of building (to tip of dome) ....158'

Construction period 1839-61

First occupied 1857

Capital population (Census 2000) 711,470

Census estimate 2007 747,755

Direction capitol faces ....West

Original cost $1,359,121

The Past Remembered

OHIO DISCOVERS COLUMBUS

At the time of statehood in 1803, the town of Chillicothe which is located south of Columbus, served as a temporary capital. In 1809, due to political pressure, the capital moved to Zanesville. A couple years later, it went back to Chillicothe.

Then, in 1812, the legislature decided that the permanent capital should be centrally located. In searching for the perfect location, an undeveloped site in the central part of the state was chosen instead of an existing city. The site was named Columbus after the explorer Christopher Columbus. A brick building, constructed in 1816 on the present grounds, served as the capitol until 1857.

In 1833, the National Road was built through Columbus. This helped to spur the growth of this start-up community and promote a more modern capitol.

A coaster, c. 1940s, depicts the previous capitol in Chillicothe.

DESIGN OF DEMOCRACY

The top three entries in a competitive design contest were combined into the beginning plan for the new capitol. The designs were based on a Grecian temple, which is a hallmark symbol of democracy.

Construction lasted twenty-two years before the capitol was considered complete. During the course of construction, at least seven architects, including painter Thomas Cole, added their input and made changes to the original design. Ultimately, the original design was changed, and no one person can be credited as the capitol's architect.

CONSTRUCTION MORATORIUM

Soon after construction began in 1839, problems developed. The State intended to primarily use prison labor but a cholera epidemic forced the State to seek additional laborers. However, this newly hired help went on strike, refusing to work with prisoners who had survived the cholera, fearing spread of the disease.

A year later, progress was again delayed when the legislature unexpectedly repealed the decision to build a new capitol. For six years, work on the capitol was halted while the legislature considered a possible relocation. Though work resumed in 1846, it was not until the previous capitol burned in 1852 that real progress began to be made.

LOOKS GREEK TO ME

Unlike most capitols which have a traditional dome, Ohio has a drum-shaped cupola. During construction, there was much debate over which design would be more fitting for the Greek revival architectural style. Although the cupola is flat, the interior dome provides a distinctive touch.

A SOLID FOUNDATION

According to a booklet by the Secretary of State's office published in 1955, construction began in 1839 and "Foundation walls 12' thick (15' at the corners) were put down." It goes on to say that "Present-day workmen who have had occasion to cut through the walls agree that the men of 1839 were truthful when they reported that they were erecting 'no temporary building'."

LINCOLN'S LEGACY

In 1861, Abraham Lincoln traveled to Columbus and visited the newly completed capitol. During his visit, he not only addressed the Ohio legislature but also learned of his Presidential election victory.

A few years later, the body of Abraham Lincoln, en route to Springfield, Illinois laid in state at the capitol as thousands paid their respects in proceeding through the rotunda. In his honor, the governor's office has been restored to its appearance during his visit.

A stereoscopic card reads: "made expressly for the Kresge and Wilson Syndicate," and shows a winter scene at a busy corner of the capitol, c. 1890s. Note the utility pole at the center.

Mailed to "Miss Nelllie" in Washington D.C., this postcard bears a 1904 postmark.

A postcard with a 1906 postmark shows the House and Senate chambers.

A photo postcard, dated 1913, shows vintage automobiles, a cable car and passers by dressed in attire reminiscent of the day.

Pearls of Wisdom
"The most honest of state capitols, sincere and forthright."

Frank Lloyd Wright
Architect

A glass jar, c. 1902 and filled with orange pekoe tea, featured the Ohio capitol.

A pinback with a 1901 date by the M.C. Lilley & Co. shows the capitol.

149

Historical Happenings

1800

1900

1803
Chillicothe designated capital

1809
Capital relocates to Zanesville

1812
Capital moves back to Chillicothe

1816
Columbus designated as capital

1839
Construction begins

1852
First state house on site burns

The inner dome

★ The Inside Story

RETURN ON INVESTMENT

During construction, critics complained that the legislative chambers were extravagant and that too much money was being spent on materials and the elaborateness of the design. Today, the chambers are considered to be the two most beautiful and magnificent rooms in the capitol. It proved to be money well spent.

OHIO — THE MOTHER OF PRESIDENTS

A glass skylight painting of the Great Seal of Ohio is set in the center of the inner dome. Around the building there are eight hearing rooms named after the eight U.S. presidents who were from Ohio. One of Ohio's nicknames is "the Mother of Presidents."

CIRCLES OF PROGRESS

The tiled rotunda floor is made of 4,892 blocks of black and white marble squares. In the center of the rotunda are 13 blocks of different shades of marble representing the original 13 states. Surrounding this group are three circles containing 32 "sunburst" points representing the states at the time the floor was completed. The circles represent territories which later became states.

Circles of progress in the rotunda floor.

Black and white tile accent the circular-shaped rotunda.

ALL OVER THE MAP

In 1993, an atrium was added. On the floor of the Map Room and below the atrium is a marble outline of the state and each of its counties. Names of each county appear on the county outline. Seven types of marble were used to make the map. This room, which connects the Statehouse with the Senate Building, was originally the capitol garage.

The map room

The House of Representatives

1861 — Capitol completed

1901 — Senate Building (originally Judiciary Annex) completed

1902 — Pennant-shaped state flag adopted

1993 — Atrium connecting to the Senate added

1996 — Renovation completed

2000

★ *Claim to Fame*

A "CREW CUT" DOME

Instead of a traditional dome, the Ohio capitol has a drum-shaped cupola with a flat top roof and looks as though the dome had a crew cut. Although plans called for a different style of dome, due to construction problems and financial constraints, the design was changed to a drum. As the capitol was built before the Civil War, domes had not yet become the standard or hallmark of capitols as was the case later in the century.

PENNANT FEVER

Ohio is the only state that has a pennant-shaped flag, a departure from the traditional rectangular flag. Actually, it is a double-pennant shape. It is also known as a "swallow tailed" or burgee flag. The flag itself is highly symbolic. The shape represents valleys and hills that comprise the geography of Ohio. The stripes represent roads and rivers. The white circle symbolizes the "O" for Ohio and the red disc in the center of the circle is the "eye of the buck," similar to the nut of the Buckeye tree and the buck deer — thus the "buckeye state." The thirteen stars surrounding the "O" represent the original thirteen states. Four additional stars represent the next four states with Ohio being the seventeenth.

★ *For What it's Worth*

CONGRESSIONAL OVERSIGHT

Due to an oversight, it wasn't until 1953 when the U.S. Congress officially set Ohio's date of statehood as March 1, 1803. No specific reason was given for the 150 year delay.

A stained glass mosaic, formerly hung in the rotunda dome from the 1920s until 1965, depicts the state seal. Rediscovered during the 1990's restoration, it is now displayed on the ground floor of the capitol.

A view from above the capitol.

CAPITOL COVER-UP

As noted earlier, construction of the capitol was halted for several years. During the delay, the foundation was covered over with dirt until a decision was made to resume construction.

PEN' PAL

As was the case with many state capitols, labor from the state penitentiary was used for construction. During the renovation in the 1990s, writings and graffiti were uncovered. Historians were able to trace a sketch with the author's name that was found etched on a wall to a prisoner who served his time during 1846-1849.

RUN, DON'T WALK

Before the atrium was added to connect the State House and the Senate Building, there was an open space between the buildings. Pigeons would congregate in this gap and on the rooftops above. The space became known as Pigeon Run as pigeons showed no mercy to passers by. Needless to say, it was safer to run than walk in the gap.

A RED CARNATION

In 1904, the red carnation was designated as the state flower. However, there is a story behind why the state adopted this rather simple flower. William McKinley, one of the eight Ohio presidents, was known for always wearing a red carnation on his lapel. It is in his honor that the carnation was chosen.

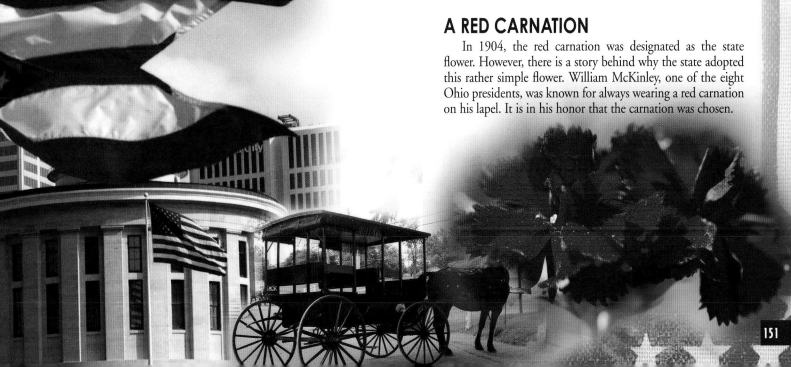

OKLAHOMA
Oklahoma City

"SOONER" OR LATER A DOME

For years, oil was drilled from beneath the capitol grounds. Although Oklahomans would have preferred to see the dome much sooner, it became a reality during 2002.

STATE MOTTO

"Labor conquers all things"

★ Facts & Figures

Architectural style	Greco-Roman
Architect	S. Wemyss-Smith & S.A. Layton
	Dome - Frankfurt Short Bruza Associates
Exterior material	Indiana limestone
Dome surface	Architectural pre-cast concrete & cast stone
Building height (to tip of dome)	243'
Construction period	1914-17
	Dome 2001-02
First occupied	1917
Capital population (Census 2000)	506,132
Census estimate 2007	547,274
Direction capitol faces	South
Original cost	$1,515,000
	Dome $21,000,000

The Past Remembered

STOLEN PROPERTY?

At the time of statehood in 1907, the town of Guthrie served as the temporary capital. In 1910, the choice of a permanent capital was put to the voters. In a landslide victory, Oklahoma City was chosen over rivals Guthrie and Shawnee. Upon hearing the results, Governor Haskell ordered the Secretary of State's office to drive to the capitol in Guthrie on Saturday night (the day of the election) when the election results were known, retrieve the State Seal and bring it to Oklahoma City. By the time it took for all this to happen and with a further delay due to a flat tire, it was Sunday morning. The Seal was wrapped in brown paper and delivered to the Governor in Oklahoma City. Once citizens of Guthrie learned of the "secret and sudden" removal, they claimed the Seal was "stolen" and appealed to the Supreme Court. Although the State Supreme Court did void the election due to a technicality, it was to no avail as a special session of the legislature adopted Oklahoma City as its permanent capital.

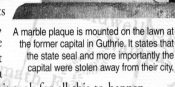
A marble plaque is mounted on the lawn at the former capital in Guthrie. It states that the state seal and more importantly the capital were stolen away from their city.

A 1913 postcard portrays proponents of the capital relocation from Guthrie to Oklahoma City.

DOMELESS

Construction of the capitol began in 1914 — which included plans for a dome. But as it progressed, costs began to exceed budget projections. In light of the blown budget and in the face of World War I, legislators decided to defer inclusion of the dome. Though the capitol was completed with a capped top, thus being "domeless," structural engineering to support a dome was incorporated into the building. After seeing the flattened top, some referred to the capitol as "Old Baldy." After the war, costs had escalated such that adding a dome would have doubled the original cost of the building.

HIGH HOPES

For several years after the capitol was completed in 1917, citizens fully expected that the dome was forthcoming. Until 1930, the State Directory, as well as other media including postcards, showed the artist's rendering of the capitol with a dome. Other plans that never materialized included a Memorial Arch at the entrance to the grounds to commemorate World War I.

LUCKY STRIKE

In 1942, oil was discovered beneath the capitol. The discovery produced a windfall of additional revenue to the state. Instead of using these unexpected funds to add the intended dome, legislators chose to spend the excess for other projects and uses.

SOONER OR LATER

In 1963, legislation to approve a dome was again rekindled. This time, a revolving restaurant was included in the proposal. As in the past, the Oklahoma legislature rejected the measure. Over the years, the debate over adding the dome continued to surface in legislative discussions. Finally in May of 2000, the State announced plans to add the long-awaited dome in time for its Centennial Celebration in 2007. With the approval, $1.25 million of State funding was authorized toward the $21 million project. Most of the remainder of funds needed was from private donors through efforts of the Centennial Commission. Construction lasted a year and a half and culminated in a grand celebration and dedication in November 2002 — well ahead of the Centennial Celebration. The dome is 80 feet in diameter and rises 155 feet above the roofline. A seventeen-foot statue named *The Guardian* tops the new dome. The statue represents a Native American warrior and was sculpted by Oklahoma Senator Kelly Haney, a Native American.

Whoops! A postcard, mailed in 1911, shows the much anticipated rendering of the dome that was put off for about 90 years.

A postcard showing 1920-30s vintage automobiles.

Oil wells dotted the landscape during the 1940s and 50s in this photo postcard.

A summer day in 1995 as the capitol appeared before the dome was added.

A memento from the dome dedication in 2002.

Pearls of Wisdom
"The foundations of justice are that no man shall suffer wrong"
Cicero (Roman orator) — c. 63 B.C.
Inscribed on a marble wall in the Supreme Courtroom

Historical Happenings

1800

1900

1889

1907

1910

The "Oklahoma Land Run" — settlers stake their claims to free land

President Theodore Roosevelt grants statehood

Voters approve Oklahoma City as permanent capital

★ The Inside Story

OKIE DOKIE

The capitol interior is lavishly decorated with unique artwork and architecture. The rotunda features portraits of renowned Oklahomans including Will Rogers and Jim Thorpe. In the center of the rotunda is a representation of the Great Seal made from five different varieties of tile. A large star represents Oklahoma as the 46th state. Forty-five smaller stars, placed in between the points of the large star, represent the other states which preceded Oklahoma to statehood. The five points of the large star represent the Indian tribes of Oklahoma.

THE BLUE ROOM

Covered with blue carpet and modeled after a similar room in the Virginia capitol, the Blue Room is reserved for the Governor's receptions, bill signings and other special occasions. Mirrors, at each end of the room, are trimmed in 24 karat gold paint. Just outside the Blue Room is an area used to showcase items of interest including tokens of friendship bestowed on the governor by visiting foreign dignitaries.

SPIRITED BALLERINAS

Toe-stepping ballerinas are the focal point of the mural entitled *"Flight of Spirit."* Painted in 1991 by Chickasaw Indian artist Mike Larsen, the mural pays tribute to five American Indian ballerinas from Oklahoma who achieved international fame in the 1920s and 30s.

The multi-colored interior dome after the exterior dome was added

Murals depicting World War I reside over the grand staircase.

An ice sculpture at the celebration of the new dome.

Thousands attended the dome dedication in November 2002.

From the floor below, a ring of lights encircles a mural of ballerinas in white.

1917 — Capitol completed

1942 — First oil well drilled beneath the capitol

1963 — Bill to approve dome defeated

1986 — Hidden staircase uncovered

2000 — Legislature authorizes $1.25 million for dome

2002 — Dome added

★ Claim to Fame

PETROLEUM PETUNIAS

Oklahoma is the only capitol with a known oil well beneath its building. In 1941, Phillips Petroleum drilled three degrees off center from the center of the building striking oil at a depth of 6,618 feet. The bottom of the well is approximately one and a quarter miles directly beneath the capitol. Officially named Capitol Site #1, the well was nicknamed Petunia #1 for the flowerbed located at the point where the drilling took place. In all, 1.5 million barrels of oil and 1.6 billion feet of gas were extracted resulting in over $1.1 million in revenue to the state.

Initially, there were 24 working oil wells on the grounds. In 1986, after pumping for 44 years, "Petunia #1" was considered dry and was capped. As a landmark remembrance to the "oil era," Phillips Petroleum was allowed to modify the normal procedure for capping a well so that it appears as an active well. Although Petunia #1 is dry, there is still an active gas well located on the grounds.

When oil was struck beneath the capitol, an oil derrick with a Phillips 66 logo became a familiar site.

★ For What it's Worth

OFFICE SPACE

A beautiful marble staircase, concealed for thirty-five years, was uncovered during the 1986 restoration. As the need for more office space within the capitol grew, the stairway had been walled up at the top, sealed on both sides and converted to office space during the early 1950s. Today, both visitors and staff use the staircase.

JUMPIN' THE GUN

In 1889, the federal government offered settlers an opportunity to obtain public domain land in the Oklahoma Territory. Land was offered on a "first come, first served" basis, requiring settlers to stake a claim to this free land. Known as the "Oklahoma Land Run", the rules stated that all entrants were to start at the same time when a shot was fired at noon. Although covered wagons, those on horseback and those running awaited the noonday start, it was later learned that some settlers started sooner than others as they jumped the gun on the official noonday start and hid out on their claim during the night. They became known as "Sooners." Although the unfair start was scorned by many at the time, in 1908 the University of Oklahoma adopted the nickname "Sooners" for their sports teams.

The addition of the dome was celebrated with the largest fireworks display in Oklahoma history.

OREGON
Salem

PIONEERING A NEW DESIGN
The Pioneer spirit is embrazoned in this non-traditional capitol design

"She flies with her own wings"

★ Facts & Figures

Architectural style	Modern Greek
Architect	Francis Keally
Exterior material	Vermont white marble
Dome surface	Vermont white marble
Building height (to tip of dome)	168'
Construction period	1936-38
First occupied	1938
Capital population (Census 2000)	136,924
Census estimate 2007	151,913
Direction capitol faces	North
Original cost	$2.5 million
Wings (1977)	$12.5 million

The Past Remembered

GOING HOMELESS

In 1849, prior to statehood, the Oregon legislature met in Oregon City. However, they had no building to call home. Instead, they met where they could find room including a Methodist church and a hotel.

TESTED BY FIRE

The first capitol in Salem was completed in 1855. Just 12 days after completion, this territorial capitol burned to the ground. Charges surfaced that the fire was set by jealous citizens from neighboring communities but nothing was ever proven. For the next 21 years, the legislature conducted state business in rented facilities in Salem. Despite statehood being achieved in 1859, the first capitol was not rebuilt until 1876.

OREGON'S TRAIL TO THE CAPITAL

When the Salem capitol burned in 1855, the legislature allowed voters to decide where the capitol would be located. An election resulted in Eugene defeating Corvallis by a close margin. Because of the close vote, two more elections were held. By then, the electorate had become disenchanted with continuing elections and stayed away from the polls. Eugene defeated Salem 2,539 to 444 in the third and final election. However, Washington authorities had other plans for this territorial possession as they overrode the election and reconfirmed Salem as the capital.

THE LONG ROAD TO STATEHOOD

On February 14, 1859, Congress granted statehood to Oregon. However, the news of the decision was sent via Panama and did not reach the new state for over a month. Except for Salem, the good news generated little excitement.

RISING OUT OF ASHES

The second capitol, which was completed on the same site in 1876, had a traditional dome and was cherished by many. It served as the capitol until April 1935 when it too was destroyed by fire. Although reported by a janitor on duty, the fire spread quickly from the basement and the building became a pile of ashes in only two hours leaving nothing but the shell.

Shortly after the fire, a design competition was held for the third and current capitol. Choosing between 126 designs, the Capitol Commission unanimously selected the design of Francis Keally of the architectural firm of Trowbridge and Livingstone of New York. Instead of a dome, the design included a tower with a vertical column or fins symbolic of the tall fir trees in Oregon. The architect's inspiration for the tower was said to be taken from a picture in a book of a Persian tower.

THE PIONEER SHAKES IN HIS BOOTS

In 1993, a 45-second earthquake with a magnitude of 5.6 rocked the capitol. *The Oregon Pioneer,* atop the capitol, was shaken loose from its base and moved a fraction of an inch. Engineers theorized that if the quake had lasted a few more seconds, it might have toppled the *Pioneer* and its base, which weighs almost 10 tons. If the statue had fallen through the roof, it could have been disastrous. The following year, the rotunda and tower underwent a $4.3 million strengthening to minimize the effects of any future earthquake.

BACK TO THE FUTURE

A nostalgic and unusual feature on the grounds is a gazebo. A familiar sight during the era of the previous capitol, it was removed after the 1935 fire. A new one was added to the grounds in 1982 as a reminder of the past. Sections of the Corinthian columns left standing after the 1935 fire are also featured on the grounds.

Column remnants from the Old Capitol are on display.

Known as the *Circuit Rider*, this statue commemorates the clergy who delivered the Gospel to the Oregon Territory. Missionaries, known as Circuit Riders were instrumental in helping Oregon to achieve statehood and locating the capital in Salem ...the inscription reads in part "the ministers of the Gospel wh, as circuit riders became the friends, counselors and evangels to the pioneers."

This pioneer sculpture is at the front of the capitol.

Published by the Pacific Novelty Company, this early postcard shows the former capitol and gazebo.

A photo postcard shows vintage 1937-38 automobiles parked outside the "new" capitol.

1843
Oregon Trail Wagon Train arrives with 900 settlers

1852
Congress confirms Salem capital of Oregon Territory

1855
Territorial capitol completed, then burns

1859
President Buchanan grants statehood

1876
Second capitol on site completed

The inner dome features 33 stars.

★ The Inside Story

SEEING STARS AND EAGLES

Thirty-three stars lie at the center of the dome's interior. Rising 106 feet above the rotunda floor, the stars symbolize Oregon's place in statehood. The outer circle of the dome is decorated with eagles and torches.

CANVASSING THE ROTUNDA

The rotunda features murals which depict Oregon history. Four additional murals leading to the House and Senate show the state's prominent industries. The artists, Barry Faulkner and Frank Schwarz, painted the murals onto canvass. They were then glued onto the walls, which are lined with rose travertine from Montana.

A ROCKIN CAPITOL

In 1982, a showcase displaying rocks and minerals of Oregon was added to the capitol exhibits. Rocks and mineral clubs from around  the state maintain the display. Every few months, the exhibit is changed to show different minerals.

The Senate in session. The mural depicts the news of Oregon statehood.

Staircases leading to the House and Senate are square in design.

A 1959 commemorative coin marks the 100th anniversary of Oregon statehood.

A bronze replica of the Oregon State Seal is embedded at the center of the rotunda.

1935
Fire destroys
previous capitol

1938
Capitol completed;
Gold Pioneer mounted

1977
Capitol expanded and
Wings added

2000
1993
Dome reinforced due to
earthquake damage

★ Claim to Fame

FEDERAL BAILOUT

The fire that destroyed Oregon's previous capitol occurred during the Great Depression. The Federal government came to Oregon's rescue under Franklin Roosevelt's New Deal. The PWA (Public Works Administration) subsidized the construction of the present capitol and the Federal assistance paid for 45 percent of its cost.

THE "GOLD MAN"

Atop the tower is a statue known as The *Oregon Pioneer*. Cast in bronze and gilded with gold leaf, it is 23 feet high and weighs eight and a half tons. The statue is of a man carrying an ax and a piece of canvass, possibly a wagon cover, and is sometimes referred to as the "Gold Man." The statue can be viewed up close by ascending 121 spiral stairs to the top of the tower starting from the fourth floor. In addition to viewing the city of Salem, on a clear day Mt. Hood and other mountains of the Cascade and Coastal Ranges can also be seen.

A close-up of The "Oregon Pioneer."

Black-eyed Susans decorate the capitol in this 1983 photo.

★ For What it's Worth

JUST CRY WOLF

In 1843, prior to statehood, an historic meeting took place in which British delegates were called to a meeting "to declare war on predatory animals." However, the meeting was actually to hold a vote as to whom they wished to be governed by — the United States or Britain. The poor turnout by British sympathizers assured that Oregon would be under American control. The meeting, near Salem, came to be known as the "Wolf Meeting."

LACKING THE PIONEER SPIRIT

In 1849, President Zachary Taylor asked Abraham Lincoln to serve as the governor of the Oregon Territory. Lincoln declined. Mrs. Lincoln, who reportedly did not want to move to the 'backwoods' of the Great West, exerted her influence in Abe's decision.

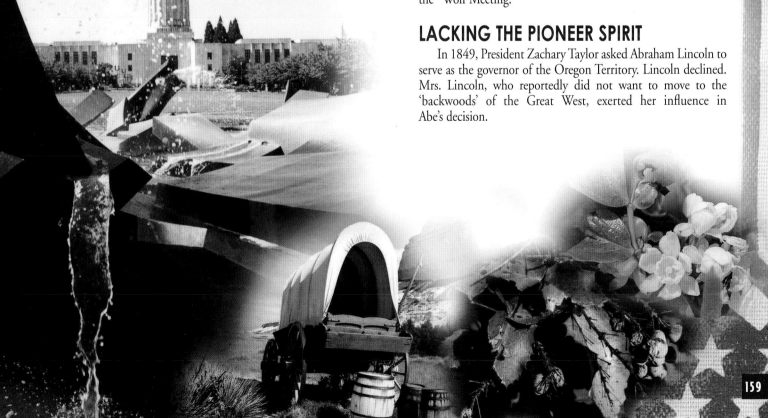

PENNSYLVANIA

Harrisburg

ART AND ARCHITECTURE MAKE A STATEMENT AT THE CAPITOL

From a mosaic tile floor to the green tiled dome, this capitol boasts majestic features.

"Virtue, liberty and independence"

Facts & Figures

Architectural style	Beaux Arts
Architect	Joseph M. Huston
Exterior material	Vermont granite
Dome surface	green-glazed tile
Building height (to tip of dome)	272'
Construction period	1902-06
First occupied	1906
Capital population (Census 2000)	48,950
Census estimate 2007	47,196
Direction capitol faces	West
Original cost (including furnishings)	$13,000,000

The Past Remembered

ROOTS

Pennsylvania traces its roots to William Penn, the first provincial governor in 1681. In the early years, the government met in temporary facilities until 1729 when land for a state house was purchased in Philadelphia. Shortly thereafter, Independence Hall was built, the site where the colonial legislature met and drafted the state constitution. Initially, Pennsylvania had a unicameral General Assembly. In 1790, a bicameral or two-house system was adopted. Pennsylvania is one of four states organized as a commonwealth, the other three being Kentucky, Virginia and Massachusetts. In 1799, the legislature moved to a courthouse in Lancaster.

SAVED BY THE CHURCH

The first state capitol was completed in Harrisburg in 1822. It served Pennsylvania for many years before being destroyed by fire in 1897. This prompted talk about relocating the capital to a different city. To prevent this from happening, Harrisburg residents acted quickly in securing a temporary meeting location in a Methodist Church.

A postcard shows a string of vintage automobiles parked along State Street leading to the capitol. Note the Methodist Church on the left, still standing today, where the legislature temporarily met.

MAKEOVER

With a budget of only $550,000, a new building, which was hastily built, proved to be a big disappointment. The Governor called it "repulsive to the eye." As a result, the building was never completed. In order to provide a more suitable capitol, a competition was held in which Joseph Huston was awarded the contract. Ironically, the foundation walls of the original inadequate building were used for the new capitol.

A DREAM COME TRUE

Prior to his being selected as architect and while living in Rome, Italy, Joseph Huston became intrigued with St. Peter's Cathedral at the Vatican. He would walk to St. Peter's on a daily basis and sketch this magnificent building. It became his dream to one day build a similar edifice. His dream was fulfilled when in 1902 he was commissioned as the architect for the Pennsylvania capitol. Two years and $13 million later, the capitol was ready for occupancy.

A DREAM BECOMES A NIGHTMARE

Shortly before the capitol was completed, the state treasurer discovered that contractors and the architect had defrauded the State. Huston was convicted of misusing public funds and served six months in prison.

MAGNIFICO

The grand staircase in the rotunda was modeled after a European architectural masterpiece, the Paris Opera House. The entire interior is lavishly adorned with spectacular artwork, lighting, stained glass, sculptures, clocks, marble and murals. The magnificence of the Pennsylvania capitol is difficult to describe. European designs from France, England and Italy are featured and styles of art and décor include Victorian, Roman and Greek. Magnificent it truly is!

FINISHING THE JOB

As with other capitols, inadequate space eventually became a problem. In 1922, plans were drawn calling for an addition to the capitol. The plans included additional office buildings and a court with sunken gardens modeled after the Versailles Terraces in France. Although the gardens were left out, a major addition completed in 1986 known as the East Wing, including a welcome center and underground parking, is both functional and complementary to the original building. Walkways, lined with landscaping and a fountain which spouts water in the shape of a dome provide the finishing touches in tying the buildings together.

The capitol dominates the cityscape with the Susquehanna River in the foreground. The reverse of the postcard is an advertisement for a jewelers' convention in 1913.

YOUR presence is requested at the Dedication of Pennsylvania's New Capitol. October 4th. 1906

Your Niece Lille Best

The Old and New Capitol Buildings Harrisburg, Pennsylvania

Old Capitol; Corner stone laid May 31, 1819, building destroyed by fire February 2, 1897 building to be dedicated October 4, 1906.

This postcard of the capitol dedication was mailed in 1906 to Mrs. Cornelius McClellan.

The Grand Staircase is modeled after the Paris Opera House.

A glass paperweight, c. 1910

A commemorative coin marks the 1906 dedication of the "new capitol." The reverse side shows the previous capitol, which burned in 1897.

Pearls of Wisdom

"There may be room there for such a holy experiment. For the nations want a precedent. And my God will make it the seed of a nation. That an example may be set up to the nations. That we may do the thing that is truly wise and just."

William Penn — August 26, 1681
Painted on a frieze around the base of the dome

Historical Happenings

1800

1900

1736	1787	1812	1822	1897
Independence Hall in Philadelphia serves as colonial capitol	Pennsylvania becomes second state to ratify Constitution	Harrisburg designated the capital	First capitol completed	Fire destroys first capitol

★ The Inside Story

A "PALACE OF ART"

The capitol is often referred to as a "Palace of Art." Four lunettes, set in recessed arches and circular panels, depict various scenes of early settlers. They were painted by artist Edwin Austin Abbey at a price of $50 per square foot. Other lunettes contain murals depicting religious groups, which had a part in settling Pennsylvania. In the corridor on the first floor are detailed plaster castings coated in gold leaf of persons representing various nationalities, including Native Americans.

GOLDEN GLOBES

The grand staircase in the rotunda is modeled after the Grand Opera House in Paris. Crafted from white Vermont marble, it rises twenty-five steps to a second landing before splitting to the right and to the left where it continues to a circular balcony above the rotunda. "Guarding" each side of the base of the staircase are two female "angels" which hold illuminated globes high above their heads.

The interior dome

JUSTICE IS DONE

The Pennsylvania "Supreme and Superior Court chamber," is truly unique. A domed ceiling of opalescent blue and green glass is in the center of the room.

Four chandeliers suspended from the ceiling, with a statuette at its center, represent small temples.

Each statuette represents one of the four law givers — Moses, Aristotle, King Solomon and Solon. Surrounding each statuette are lighted globes that glow an orange hue representing the Torch of Justice. The court traces its roots to 1722, predating the U.S. Supreme Court.

The House and Senate

Gold leaf-gilded images depict various citizens from nations that make up the Commonwealth.

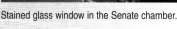

Stained glass window in the Senate chamber.

The Supreme Court chamber

1906   6418 ILL. 44   1986   1999   **2000**

Capitol completed

East Wing (legislative) completed

Renovation completed

★ Claim to Fame

ST. PETER'S LOOK ALIKE

Although many capitol domes may appear similar, Pennsylvania's dome was specifically modeled after the dome of St. Peter's Cathedral in Rome, also known as St. Peter's Basilica.

St. Peter's Basilica in Rome — note the resemblance to the Pennsylvania capitol.

The Vatican's dome design, originating from Michelangelo, was reconstructed in the year 1590. In essence, Huston had cloned the design of St. Peter's dome except that St. Peter's dome is crowned with a cross and is not green.

COLOR TILE

Unique among state capitols, the Pennsylvania capitol has a green-glazed tile dome. It is the only capitol with tile on its dome and the only dome with a bright, green color.

THE FLOOR SHOW

Described by artist Henry Mercer as "history written on the floor," the paved, red Moravian tile of the rotunda are interspersed with nearly 400 mosaic-theme tiles of animals including birds, as well as scenes depicting various occupations, travel and industries indicative of Pennsylvania life.

The mosaic tiles are placed in and around the rotunda and form a timeline from pre-historic Pennsylvania flora and fauna until the contemporary time of when the capitol was completed in 1906. The origin of the design is centuries old and has been traced to St. Mark's Square in Venice, Italy. When viewed from the upper floors, the pavement looks like a large Persian rug.

The green-glazed tile dome is unique among capitol domes. The dome weighs 52 million pounds.

★ For What it's Worth

PENNSYLVANIA PENNYPACKER

There were many distinguished guests present at the capitol dedication in 1906. Most noteworthy was President Theodore Roosevelt who remarked, "This is the handsomest State Capitol I ever saw." Also present was Pennsylvania's Governor Samuel Pennypacker — a name noteworthy in Pennsylvania history.

A PENN NAME

Atop the dome is a statue modeled after an allergorical figure of the Commonwealth of Pennsylvania. Although visitors and locals often nicknamed it "Miss Penn," attributing it to any particular person was simply a myth. Her official name is *"Commonwealth."* However, the name "Miss Penn" seems destined to last through the ages.

STATUES OF LIMITATIONS

Two prominent sets of marble statuary flank the sides of the main entrance. Although sculpted by George Gray Barnard in his studio in France, the marble is from quarries in Italy. When first unveiled in 1910, the nude figures were greeted with exuberance by Europeans, but evoked much criticism from U.S. citizens.

In response to the criticism, the sculptor added coverings to conceal what was thought to be too risqué.

RHODE ISLAND
Providence

INDEPENDENT THINKING LEADS TO TREND SETTING

Though a small state, Rhode Island was founded on principles of democracy and religious freedom that showed the way for others to follow.

STATE MOTTO

"Hope"

★ *Facts & Figures*

Architectural style	Neo-classical
Architect	McKim, Mead & White
Exterior material	White Georgia marble
Dome surface	White Georgia marble
Building height (to tip of dome)	235'
Construction period	1895-1904
First occupied	1900
Capital population (Census 2000)	173,618
Census estimate 2007	172,459
Direction capitol faces	South
Original cost (including furnishings)	$3,018,416

The Past Remembered

ON THE RIGHT RHODE

When the colony was founded by Roger Williams, an English clergyman, it was known as Providence Plantations. The settlers of Aquidneck Island, in Narragansett Bay, changed its name to Rhode Island. Later, the colony was united under the name "Rhode Island and Providence Plantations." The State of Rhode Island and Providence Plantations is the smallest state, with the longest name.

SHARED CAPITAL

In 1840, the legislature authorized the rotating of meeting locations between Bristol, East Greenwich, Newport and Providence with South Kingstown added later. From 1854 until 1900, the legislature met at the Old Capitol in Providence and on special occasions, at the Old Colony House in Newport. Both of these "retired capitols" as well as three others are still in existence.

RELIGIOUS LIBERTY

In founding Rhode Island, Roger Williams sought a place where he could enjoy religious freedom. Years later, his convictions were embodied in the first amendment of the Constitution in protecting the people from the government. When the U.S. Constitution was presented for acceptance, Rhode Island was the only state to reject it, arguing that "no particular religious sect or society ought to be favoured, or established by law in preference to others." Nearly three years later, Thomas Jefferson broke the stalemate by upholding the Rhode Island delegation. Jefferson asked "you have protected the government from the people, but what have you done to protect the people from the government?"

THE ISLAND CAPITOL

In 1850, one proposed design for the state house suggested the capitol be built on a man-made island located in Providence Cove. However, the idea was dismissed because it was considered impractical.

A SECOND ROUND SELECTION

After Smith Hill was selected for the capitol site, a two-phase or tiered design competition was begun in 1890. In the first phase, three Rhode Island architects were selected. These three architects advanced to the second round in which the competition was expanded to a national level. The committee charged with the selection process unanimously selected the design of Charles McKim of McKim, Mead and White of New York. Today, the capitol sits high atop Smith Hill surrounded by rolling hills of green grass.

PROTOTYPE

The Rhode Island capitol has been said to be a prototype for other states. Cass Gilbert, a former draftsman for McKim, Mead and White also designed the Minnesota, Arkansas and West Virginia capitols and used similar designs in all three. In the ensuing years, other state capitol architects adopted similar design features as well.

BABY DOMES

In addition to the massive marble dome at the center of the capitol, there are two saucer domes to each side that cover the legislative chambers. Around the perimeter of the center dome are four miniature domes which form a square around it. Each of these mini-domes is supported by a colonnade. These four little domes, mimicking the center dome, look as though the main dome "gave birth" to them.

The Old Colony House in Newport.

This postcard, postmarked 1906, included an additional decorative feature. Not only did the designer portray the white marble domes as green but he also laced the building with gold glitter.

"Pretty girls, pretty girls everywhere, But the Providence Belles are claimed most fair" exclaims a postcard by Tuck's.

A Litho-Chrome postcard sent in 1908 shows a ceremonial crowd of onlookers on Inauguration Day.

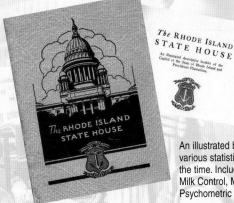

An illustrated booklet, distributed in 1936, lists various statistics and offices in the capitol at the time. Included are offices for Mother's Aid, Milk Control, Mosquito Control and a Psychometric Division.

Pearls of Wisdom

"To hold forth a lively experiment that a most flourishing civil state may stand and best be maintained with full liberty in religious concernments."

Roger Williams — 1636
(Inscribed on the south front of the State House)

Historical Happenings

1800

1663
King Charles II grants
Royal Charter to the Colony

1790
Thirteenth state to
ratify the Constitution

1891
Capitol design
chosen

1900

1899
Independent Man
mounted on dome

A view of the inner dome shows the four medallions.

The Senate chamber.

A replica of the state seal shows an anchor and the state motto, "Hope."

★ The Inside Story

TWO FOR THE PRICE OF ONE

A full-length portrait of George Washington, painted by Gilbert Stuart, hangs in the state reception room of the Governor's Office. Stuart, a Rhode Islander, was commissioned in 1801 to paint two identical portraits for $600. Its twin portrait hangs in the Colony House in Newport.

The Royal Charter.

STILL UNDER THE KING'S CONTROL?

The Royal Charter of 1663, which is made of parchment and is on display in a steel vault, was granted by King Charles II of England. Although statehood was achieved in 1790, the State continued to operate under this Royal Charter until the state constitution went into affect in 1843.

WALL TO WALL BOOKS

The State House Library.

The State House Library, uniquely designed and decorated, is worthy of note. The walls consist of three vertical tiers (sections) of bookshelves that rise from floor to ceiling, holding nearly fifty thousand books. The ceiling is covered with gold leaf and includes ornately carved seals from Renaissance printing houses. A skylight allows natural light to shine through.

The Library contains legislative and historical documents of Rhode Island, and also includes books and records related to the United States, as well as other states.

1904 Capitol completed

1924 Filibuster ends in chambers gassed – GOP relocates

1927 *Independent Man* struck by lightning

1947 Interior dome refurbished

1976 *Independent Man* returned to the dome

2000

★ *Claim to Fame*

THREE STRIKES AND YOU'RE OUT

In 1927, lightning struck the statue, the *Independent Man,* atop the dome. The damage was repaired by lacing copper stitches across the tear. Lightning struck again in 1951 causing damage. After being struck a third time in 1975, the statue was taken down for repairs and re-gilding. This time, after its restoration, it was displayed in the rotunda until the Bicentennial celebration in July of 1976. When the celebration ended, it was returned to its rightful place atop the dome.

A VIAL PLOT ENDS THE FILIBUSTER

In 1924, the senate was involved in a lengthy debate that lasted thirty hours. In an attempt to end the filibuster, Republicans perpetrated a scheme and hired some "thugs from Boston," as they were described, to come to the State House and end the proceeding. When signaled, one of the thugs threw a bag containing a test tube of bromine gas to the floor and stepped on it. Those remaining in the chamber, mostly Republicans, made a quick exit. Though some felt ill, no one sustained serious injury.

With accusations and threats being made, all but one of twenty-two Republican senators fled the state. They congregated in Connecticut and in the Boston area and rendezvoused in Rutland, Massachusetts. For six months, they remained at this temporary out of state location until order could be restored.

SMALL BUT MIGHTY

At 48 miles long and just 37 miles wide, Rhode Island is the smallest state in the U.S. But from the time its founder, Roger Williams, was "booted" out of the Massachusetts colony for his religious beliefs, Rhode Islanders have shown the way for others to follow. In 1772, it was Rhode Islanders who overtook and burned a British ship three years before the start of the Revolution. In 1776, prior to the Declaration of Independence, they were the first to declare an independent republic. Thus, it's no surprise that Rhode Island's motto is "Hope."

SIDEBURNS

Portraits of former governors are on display in the corridors. Among them is a portrait of former Civil War General, Governor, and US Senator Ambrose Burnside. The portrait depicts General Burnside standing in front of his horse. The general was known for his bushy side-whiskers — and that is how the term "sideburns" originated.

A close-up of the dome shows the *Independent Man* statue and two mini domes.

A red brick walkway leads to the State House.

★ *For What it's Worth*

THE STORY BEHIND THE STATUE

The bronze statue perched atop the dome, known as the *Independent Man,* holds a spear in one hand while resting the other on an anchor. The gilded bronze statue was made of metal from another statue — that of Simon Bolivar which had been displayed in New York. Originally, the design of the statue was to have been the likeness of Roger Williams, the state's founder. However, no artwork could be found from which to sculpt his likeness. Thus, the statue was simply named *Independent Man.*

19-GUN SALUTE

Every four years during the governor's inauguration, a ceremony is held in which the High Sheriff announces the election of governor. The announcement is followed by a 19-gun salute performed on the State House lawn. The Sheriff is decked out in formal attire including a frock coat with tails and a top hat.

SOUTH CAROLINA
Columbia

THE FIRST STATE TO SECEDE, THE PRIDE OF DIXIE

The ravages of war and changes in architects forced extensive delays in completing this State House. What began in 1855 was not finished until 1907.

"Prepared in mind and resources" and "While I breathe, I hope"

★ Facts & Figures

Architectural style	Roman Corinthian
Architect	Major John R. Niernsee
Exterior material	Granite
Dome surface	Copper
Building height (to tip of dome)	164'
Construction period	1855-1907
First occupied	1869
Capital population (2000 Census)	116,278
Census estimate 2007	124,818
Direction capitol faces	North
Original cost	$3,540,000

★ The Past Remembered

SHELL SHOCKED

The first State House, a wood-framed structure, was destroyed by fire during the siege of Columbia in 1865. Prior to this time and partially due to concern over a possible fire, construction of a new State House had already

begun in 1855. Work proceeded as scheduled until the onset of the Civil War. In November 1863, construction was halted as the State's resources were focused on the war effort. In 1865, six Union cannon shells struck the exterior of the uncompleted building and their damage is still visible today.

THE RAVAGES OF WAR

Although damage to the state house was minor, when the assessment of other damage was made, the destruction of construction materials was significant. This included granite Corinthian capitals, marble tiles, statues and architectural documents amounting to $700,000.

SETBACK AFTER SETBACK

Construction resumed in 1867 and legislators were allowed to occupy the State House two years later. However in 1876, a gubernatorial election dispute caused Federal troops to occupy the State House and construction was halted again.

By 1885, the State's treasury had recovered enough to rehire the original architect, John Niernsee, to finish the interior design. Another setback occurred later that year upon the architect's death. His partner, J. Crawford Neilson, replaced him. After he refused to relocate to South Carolina, Niernsee's son, Frank, was hired in 1888 to finish the job. But, he was not the last.

YOU'RE FIRED!

From 1900 to 1902, Frank P. Milburn directed the construction. Then, after some faulty work became apparent, he too was fired and replaced by Charles C. Wilson in 1904. Finally, Wilson was able to correct the problems, finish the stairs, and landscape the grounds to complete the building.

A sketch from Frank Leslie's 1861 *Illustrated Newspaper* shows the planned tower.

GREAT EXPECTATIONS

Shortly before the Civil War began, South Carolina was very prosperous and its people felt a showcase State House was in order.

Original plans called for a 180-foot tower that was architecturally in vogue at the time. In addition to the tower, plans included imported Italian marble to be used in the "grand marble hall" and other elaborate features. After the devastation of war, the original architect planned to use less expensive materials to finish the building. As late as 1900, the tower was still in the plans, but that was not to be.

Six tarnished bronze stars, bolted to the wall on the west side of the State House, mark the scars left by cannon shells making a hit. This occurred during General Sherman's assault on Columbia in 1865.

CHANGE IN PLANS

By the time Milburn took over the project, domes had become a symbol of government and were popular in other capitols being constructed. At Milburn's suggestion, the State agreed to change the plan from a tower to a dome.

THE RISE AND FALL OF FORTUNES

From the state house's original elegant design, through the war-torn era to the remarkable design of the interior representing the Victorian period, the dome represents the rise and fall of the fortunes of South Carolina and her citizens. Today, the State House stands as a reminder of what could have been and what came to be.

George Washington's statue was damaged (see arrow) by the Union Army during General Sherman's attack on Columbia.

A postcard with a 1918 postmark shows a celebration of pride in the old battle flag.

Historical Happenings

1788
Eighth state to ratify the Constitution

1855
Construction of State House begins

1860
South Carolina secedes from Union

1861
Carolina Confederates fire on Fort Sumter

1863
Work halted on the State House

The interior dome as restored in 1998.

A view from the lobby.

One side of the state seal is the focal point of this stained glass.

The dome before its 1998 restoration.

★ The Inside Story

BETTER THAN TIFFANY'S

Mosaic stained glass from Belcher Studios in Baltimore adorns the interior of the State House. A friend of the architect, known for his handiwork in glass, received the honor of fashioning these beautiful works of art. Notice the Palmetto tree that can be seen in the stained glass artwork. Reportedly, over 37,000 pieces of glass make up this mosaic.

EARLY FOOD COURT

Historical records indicate that when the building was first occupied during the 1870s, a sort-of mini-food court was housed inside the State House. It consisted of six eating places and a bar adjacent to the senate chamber. Apparently, some legislators preferred to "wine and dine" at work. As evidence of this period in the State House's history, the recent restoration process unearthed a number of liquor bottles, milk bottles and bones (indicating meals of pork, chicken and beef) found in excavations around the perimeter of the building.

SPRINGING A LEAK

The State House as planned had two domes: the exterior dome which is visible from the outside and the inner dome which is visible from the lobby. However, when the outer dome began to leak, a third dome was added between the two other domes in hopes that this would "catch" the water. Eventually, this third dome also began to leak. This time, plastic sheeting was used to stop the leakage. The problem was finally solved during the renovation when the copper was replaced on the exterior dome and the glass was restored in the inner dome.

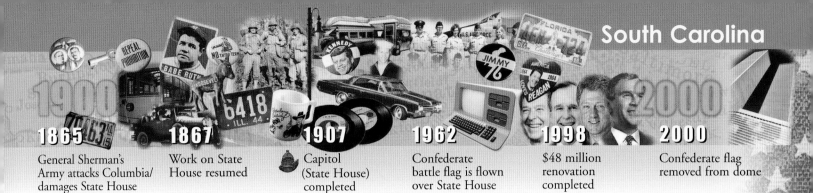

1865	1867	1907	1962	1998	2000
General Sherman's Army attacks Columbia/ damages State House	Work on State House resumed	Capitol (State House) completed	Confederate battle flag is flown over State House	$48 million renovation completed	Confederate flag removed from dome

★ Claim to Fame

RAISE THE FLAG

In 1962, the South Carolina General Assembly voted to resurrect the flying of the Confederate flag over the State House dome. Since that time, citizens of South Carolina and others have disputed the meaning and appropriateness of displaying the historic flag. To the Southern patriot, it is a symbol of bravery and honor for those who fought. But others insist that it conjures up feelings of bitterness and hatred, reminding them of slavery.

LOWER THE FLAG

In May of 2000, the legislature voted to take down the Confederate flag which flew over the dome. It is now memorialized on the grounds.

A SOUTHERN SALUTE

A recent monument added to the grounds is that of Senator Strom Thurmond. The late senator, who retired from office in 2002, was a living legend in South Carolina politics for over 50 years. Not only was he the oldest serving US Senator, but he was also the longest serving of any senator in U.S. history. Reportedly, when he took his first oath of office, a Civil War veteran was in the audience!

STROM THURMOND

The copper on the dome was replaced in 1998 allowing for a copper-colored appearance once again. Also shown is the oxidized green dome prior to its restoration. Experts claim it may take 15-20 years to oxidize to green again. Note the third flag, the controversial Confederate flag, which was taken down in 2000 shortly after this photo was taken.

★ For What it's Worth

GATOR TALES

In the early days, a pond was added to the State House's landscaping. In 1878, the pond was stocked with fish, turtles and two alligators. Newspaper accounts from the time period relate that one of the alligators took occasional land tours around the neighborhood. As might be expected, one of the neighbors was caught off guard by the alligator's unexpected visit and took matters into his own hands. The unwelcome alligator met an early demise.

PALMETTO FANS

The Palmetto tree, with its fan-like branches, is an important symbol because it represents the strength of a Palmetto log fort that survived repeated attacks by the British in the Revolutionary War. Battles fought in South Carolina during the Revolution turned the tide of the war in the south to the benefit of the Patriots. The Palmetto tree was central to the state seal designed in 1776 and was included in the state flag in 1861.

Live Palmetto trees can be found on the state house grounds. There is also a cast iron and copper Palmetto monument on the grounds dating from the 1850s representing the Palmetto Regiment that fought in the Mexican War (1846-1848).

SOUTH DAKOTA
Pierre

A SMALL TOWN CAPITOL WITH AN AESTHETIC SETTING

An artesian lake, migratory birds and trails lined with decorative trees provide a pleasing backdrop to the capitol.

"Under God the people rule"

Facts & Figures

Architectural style	Greek Ionic
Architect	C. E. Bell and M.S. Detweiler
Exterior material	Ortonville granite, Marquette raindrop sandstone and Bedford limestone
Dome surface	Solid copper
Building height (to tip of dome)	165'
Construction period	1905-10
First occupied	1910
Capital population (Census 2000)	13,876
Census estimate 2007	14,032
Direction capitol faces	South
Original cost	$951,000
Annex	$295,857

The Past Remembered

WASTING NO TIME

After statehood was achieved in 1889, South Dakota wasted no time in building its first capitol. By January of 1890, in less than two months time, the governor as well as other officers moved into a newly built, two-story wooden structure in Pierre. Located on the southwest corner of the present capitol grounds, the original structure was still standing after the present capitol was completed. Amazingly, this simple structure served as the capitol for nearly twenty years.

A 1913 photograph shows the capitol void of any landscaping.

THREEPEAT

After three special elections, Pierre was consistently the choice of the people for the state capital. The elections were held in 1889, 1890 and 1904. The town of Mitchell, located on the eastern part of the state, was a close contender.

COPYCAT CAPITOL

After the third election, officials wanted to solidify Pierre as the capital by constructing a more permanent capitol. The capitol committee visited the Montana capitol and decided to erect a similar building. The same Minneapolis architectural firm was selected to modify Montana's capitol design in keeping with Pierre's requirements. The site chosen for the new capitol was acquired from the Chicago Northwestern Railway in 1883. Until 1794, the Arikara Indians had occupied this site.

TRAIL MIX

Surrounding the capitol and throughout the grounds is a trail with nearly 60 different types of trees and shrubs. Because many believed that growing trees on the prairie was impossible, this effort encouraged many settlers in the area to plant their own trees. Over the years, many different species have been planted to demonstrate the different types of growth possible in this climate. Some of the many diverse trees that can be seen on the trail include the American Sycamore, Red Cedar, Sugar Maple, and Canada Red Cherry scattered throughout the trails.

The mural, *"The Peace that Passes Understanding,"* is 12 x 20 feet and is in the House chamber.

A 1977 photo shows a side view of the capitol.

This postcard sends a poetic message to a friend in Milwaukee in 1912. The capitol image was glued onto the card.

The rose is red;

The violet's blue;

This town's a hummer;

Let's hear from you

A pre-1907, hand-colored postcard shows an artist's early rendering, but not the final, of the capitol.

The button with a similar rendering has an 1899 patent date and was apparently circulated at a convention in Pierre.

Pearls of Wisdom

"… your building, both in its external appearance and especially in the interior finishings, will compare favorably with any of the capitols of the country …"

Edwin H. Blashfield, mural painter
June 30, 1910

Historical Happenings

1800

1861
Congress creates
Dakota Territory

1883
Bismarck selected
as territorial capital

1889
President Harrison
grants statehood

1900

Sunlight shines through the amber and ivory-colored stained-glass panels made of Victorian leaded glass.

A stenciled ceiling with unique artwork.

The mosaic tile floor glistens with light reflections.

The ceiling in the Senate is adorned with ornamental stained glass.

A view showing the Terrazzo floor, marble columns and a marble fountain.

★ The Inside Story

Four large murals, painted by artist Edward Simmons, encircle the rotunda dome. Each mural is said to represent a different mythical goddess — agriculture, livestock, mining, and love of family.

SET IN STONE — BLUE STONE THAT IS

Scattered throughout the Terrazzo tile floor are 66 blue-colored stone tiles. Why were these special tiles used? No one seems to know for sure. One possible explanation is that rather than the artist placing his initials or name on a tile, each of the Italian artisans used a blue stone to place as their "signature." Capitol staff can account for only 55 of reportedly 66 blue tiles. The remaining unlocated tiles are reportedly hidden by other work and remain a mystery.

A BROKEN HEART

Over the years, the building has settled causing many tiles to crack. During a restoration process, artisans were given a heart-shaped tile as a "signature stone." One of these tiles has a "cracked heart." Legend has it that this artisan was "broken hearted" over his woman and thus added special meaning to his "signature" by cracking the tile. Like an Easter egg hunt, it is not uncommon to see children as well as adults trying to account for all the blue and heart-shaped tiles.

ALL DOLLED UP

A popular attraction at the capitol is "The First Lady Gown Collection." The dolls, displayed in several glass cases, show replicas of each First Lady wearing the gown worn on the night of each governor's inauguration.

1904	1905	1910	1932	1964	2000 1989
Pierre selected as capital for a third time	Montana capitol selected as model for capitol	Capitol completed	Capitol Annex completed	Dome refurbished	Renovation completed

★ Claim to Fame

ICE BREAKER

Pierre is the only capitol served by an artesian lake. This man-made lake is considered as artesian because the water comes from deep wells that reach an aquifer, draining water from a higher surrounding area so the pressure forces a flow of water upward. As a result, the constant influx of water is warm and despite Pierre's northern climate, the lake never completely freezes over.

WINTER HAVEN

A beneficiary of this winter haven, besides the capitol staff and the people of Pierre, are hundreds of Canadian geese, mallards, wood ducks and other migratory birds. Were it not for this warm-water lake, the birds would be forced to migrate further south.

FOREVER GLOWING

The Flaming Fountain is a memorial to war veterans located on the northwest side of the Capitol Lake. Natural gas, with a high concentration of sulfur, surfaces from the artesian well and provides the fuel for this "eternal" fountain which glows every day of the year. Ignited in 1964, it burned continuously until it was temporarily extinguished for a restoration project in 2001.

Night or day, reflections appear on Capitol Lake. The capitol was first illuminated at night in 1964.

Note the spelling of the word "South." The "U" appearing as a "V" was formerly used interchangeably with a "V."

★ For What it's Worth

A GRAVE DISCOVERY

During the excavation for the capitol, several graves were discovered on the site. Initially, local residents were very upset over the idea of disturbing gravesites. Upon further research, it was learned that the site had served as a "Boot Hill"— a burial place for outlaws. Ultimately, the graves were relocated to a nearby cemetery.

WE NEVER CLOSE

Unlike other capitols, South Dakota's capitol is open to the public for extended hours. Although subject to change, it is open every day of the year and does not close until 10 p.m. Even more amazing — during the Centennial celebration — hours were extended to around the clock.

OVERPOPULATED

Although the 1890 census shows Pierre with a population of 3,235, the city directory reported a whopping 4,837 residents. History does not record the reason for the discrepancy.

FADE TO BLACK

Twenty tons of copper were required to cover the dome. Normally, the weathering process makes copper turn green as is seen in several other capitol domes. However, the South Dakota dome turned pitch black in color. Experts assert that this process occurred because of South Dakota's climate, a combination of altitude and warm temperatures. Locals say this is because of South Dakota's "pure" air. Despite the clean air, the elements have taken their toll on the dome. In 1964, it became necessary to strip the copper from the dome down to its steel structure and rebuild it with new concrete and copper facing.

TENNESSEE
Nashville

FINAL RESTING PLACE

The architect thought so highly of his "masterpiece" that he requested to be entombed in the capitol upon his death. His wish was granted as he now rests in the southeast corner of the building.

STATE MOTTO
"Agriculture and commerce"

★ Facts & Figures

Architectural style	Greek Ionic
Architect	William Strickland
Exterior material	Limestone (cut stone)
Dome surface	Limestone (cut stone)
Building height (to tip of dome)	207'
Construction period	1845-59
First occupied	1851
Capital population (Census 2000)	545,524
Census estimate 2007	590,807
Direction capitol faces	East
Original cost	$879,981

The Past Remembered

ACT IV

Nashville, known as "Music City USA," has been the scene for several melodramatic events at its capitol. From shots being fired in the capitol on two occasions, to being taken over by rival military forces, to the unveiling of the Andrew Jackson statue, to being the final resting place for four people, events taken place at the capitol are like acts from a theatrical performance.

CAMPBELL'S CAPITOL HILL

Tennessee's first capitol was located in Knoxville. The legislature also met in Murfreesboro and for only one day in Kingston before finally settling on Nashville in 1827. However, this location was not approved as the permanent seat of government until 1843. Two years later, an appropriation to begin construction of a capitol was approved. The selection of the capitol site was solidified when the mayor of Nashville offered a tract of land to the state, known as Campbell's Hill. The city had purchased the land, in anticipation of it becoming the capitol site, from Judge G.W. Campbell for $30,000.

FREE LABOR WAS NOT FREE

As is generally the case, the state did not have excess funds to commit to a new capitol. In considering various cost-saving measures, architect William Strickland suggested that the state could significantly reduce construction costs if prison labor was used. This decision was heavily criticized so the labor provided by prisoners was limited to work at the quarries. Records from 1846 show that the state also signed a contract "to supply 15 Negro men" to work on the capitol. It is noteworthy that although both the convicts and the slaves helped to lower the cost of construction, neither group was free at the time the capitol was constructed.

HOLD THE FORT

With the onset of the Civil War in 1861, the legislature offered their proud new capitol to be the capitol of the Confederacy. More than just symbolic, the capitol sat on a hill with a strategic view — especially with a two-tiered tower that made for a prime lookout over the surrounding countryside. Less than a year later, Union forces seized the capitol without a fight as Confederate forces fled Nashville. To enhance the fortress, the Yankees blocked the entrance steps with timbers, thus creating bunker-like effects. Records indicate that the Union Army used the building as a barracks, a hospital and as a stockade. The capitol became known as Fort Andrew Johnson.

CAUGHT IN A CROSSFIRE

In 1895, a fight broke out at the capitol. It all started when the prison warden, Andrew Vaughn, came to the capitol to talk with the Superintendent of Prisons, John Kirk. During his visit, he encountered O.B. Paxton, a guard at the prison. A fistfight broke out between Vaughn and Paxton. Vaughn pulled out his gun and fired several shots at J.T. Davis, a friend of Paxton's who had also become involved. Kirk, the prison superintendent, got caught in the crossfire and took a bullet in the head. He died a few days later.

THAT'S HOW THE COLUMN CRUMBLES

The capitol was built out of limestone in the 1850s so it is no surprise that the exterior columns were beginning to crumble after a century of deterioration. During a restoration project in 1956, the 28 columns were replaced. Instead of destroying them, it was decided to move the columns to the State Penitentiary. Then, in 1995 a few remnants were brought back to the capitol grounds as a fitting memorial to the past.

A one-pound, cardboard container of Capitol Brand Baking Powder, c. 1930, features the Tennessee capitol.

Postmarked 1909, this postcard was sent to a friend in Missouri. The sender was careful to tell the friend the location of the Andrew Jackson statue by marking an "x" on the postcard.

The artist created a special touch with this 1909 embossed postcard.

This building in Knoxville, though it doesn't resemble a capitol, served as Tennessee's first state capitol.

Remnants of columns which were removed and later returned to the capitol grounds reminds visitors that the capitol has been around for a long time.

A genuine Confederate $20 bill features the Tennessee capitol.

Historical Happenings

1800

1900

1784 — Attempt to be admitted as State of Franklin fails

1796 — President Washington grants statehood

1843 — Nashville selected as capital

1854 — Architect dies and is entombed in the capitol

1859 — Capitol completed

The spiral staircase in the State Library.

A gasolier lighting fixture, since converted to electricity.

Murals, stenciling and "Georgian" style woodwork decorate the governor's Reception Room.

The curvature of this vaulted ceiling creates a tunnel-like effect when looking down the corridor.

The House of Representatives

★ The Inside Story

STRONGER THAN YOU THINK

Shortly after the capitol was completed, bronze gasoliers were installed in the House and Senate chambers. In 1889, a report to the legislature stated the House gasoliers had "become dangerous and liable at any time to fall." In response, the legislature deemed it unsafe and ordered the lighting fixtures removed. The workers charged with the removal found that the gasoliers were so securely fastened that it took days for several men to complete the task!

THE REST OF THE STORY

As seen in this photo, this marble handrail has some chips taken out of it. Over the years, a story has been told over and over including printed versions, that a gunfight resulted in chips blasted out of the railing. The story goes something like this. In 1866, the Tennessee General Assembly was considering the ratification of the 14th Amendment, which would allow citizenship to African Americans. Members opposed to the amendment decided to leave the capitol to block a vote. They were met at the door by a posse hoping to persuade them to return. But this is where the truth ends. The rest of the story, though untrue, claims that guards fired warning shots at fleeing members wanting to avoid a vote — thus it makes a good story as to why there are chips in the railing. However, a chipped railing which predates the Civil War is not uncommon.

ARTS AND LITERATURE

One of the more interesting rooms in the capitol is the State Library. Although it has been restored, many of the features are original. An ornamental, cast iron spiral staircase is the focal point of the room. Bookshelves are also made of cast iron. A frescoed ceiling complements the spiral staircase. The balconies and the ceiling are lined with portrait medallions of notable Americans such as Washington, Jefferson and Franklin, but also of writers and other political figures. A gasolier lighting fixture, since converted to electricity, is the original from 1855.

1861
Serves as Capitol
of Confederacy

1862
Capitol occupied
by Union Army

1880
General Jackson
statue unveiled

1958
Exterior restoration
completed

1988
Interior restoration
completed

2000

Claim to Fame

TOMBSTONE, TENNESSEE

William Strickland, a celebrated architect from Philadelphia, relocated to Nashville to supervise the construction of the capitol. He considered the capitol to be his greatest achievement. Before the capitol was completed, Mr. Strickland died at age 66. He was so proud of his architectural masterpiece that he asked to be entombed in the capitol upon his death. His wish was granted and his remains were placed in a tomb he designed near the south entrance. However, the architect is not the only one buried on the capitol grounds. Samuel Morgan, the Chairman of the Building Commission died in 1880 and his body is also buried here. In the 1890s, the tomb of President and Mrs. Polk was moved to the capitol grounds as well. In all, four people are buried here.

SURPRISE!

The City of Nashville's Centennial celebration took place in 1880. As the highlight of the celebration, the Tennessee Historical Society purchased a statue of General Andrew Jackson to be unveiled on the capitol grounds. Thousands of citizens anxiously awaited its unveiling. Mounted on a stand, several men hid inside and pushed the covering away at the precise moment revealing the unique statue. Sculpted by Clark Mills as one of three identical statues he made, it was the first equestrian statue ever poised on the hind feet. Depicting the Battle of New Orleans in 1815, the horse is said to be ready for the next charge.

A statue of Sergeant Alvin C. York, sculpted by Felix De Weldon, was dedicated in 1968. Sergeant York, a Tennessee native and World War I hero, was awarded the Medal of Honor for his valor. Under much fire from the Germans, he led seven other surviving soldiers in overtaking a German regiment and forcing their surrender. The 132 Germans were taken prisoner and escorted to captivity. Later, he told his commander, "A higher power than man power guided and watched over me and told me what to do." In 1941, a movie, *Sergeant York* starring Gary Cooper, was made of his heroics.

For What it's Worth

A COW AND A CALF

In 1811, Judge George Washington Campbell sold a cow and a calf to a neighbor with payment to be made later. The judge soon learned that the neighbor planned to move but did not have money to pay. The neighbor, wanting to settle the debt, traded a long rifle, a leather jerkin and a piece of property that sat on a rocky hill referred to by the neighbor as "old Cedar Knob." The rest of the story is that this hill, thought to be worthless at the time, is the site on which the capitol was built.

A TENNESSEE WALTZ

On occasion, a legislature may pass a bill which future generations may wonder about. In 1870, the Tennessee General Assembly passed a resolution which stated in part, "Be it resolved ... that ... the Superintendent of the Capitol ... prohibit the use of Roller Skates in the Hall of the Capitol Building."

NO ROLLERBLADING
NO SKATEBOARDS
NO BIKES
**ON BRICK AND
STAIR SURFACES**

One of the more brilliantly lighted capitols, Nashville lives up to the glamour bestowed on it in being the country music capitol.

TEXAS
Austin

THE LONE STAR CAPITOL
With "miles and miles of Texas," the State traded some of its many miles of land for a capitol.

STATE MOTTO

"Friendship"

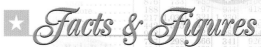

⭐ Facts & Figures

Architectural style	Renaissance Revival
Architect	Elijah E. Myers
Exterior material	Texas sunset red granite
Dome surface	Iron
Building height (to tip of dome)	303'
Construction period	1882-88
First occupied	1888
Capital population (Census 2000)	656,562
Census estimate 2007	743,074
Direction capitol faces	South
Original cost	$3,744,631

The Past Remembered

Texans pride themselves on how the people migrating to this region overcame adversity to become owners of this land. Accomplishing this required going to war to overthrow a tyrannical government and win its independence. Though various communities took their turn as capital, historic Austin's southern yet central location was chosen as the permanent site.

GETTING A PANHANDLE ON THINGS

An architectural design contest for the building concluded with the selection of Elijah Myers' design. Myers also designed the Colorado and Michigan capitols. After choosing the design based upon a Greek cross shape, the State's next step was to select a contractor. With an abundance of land stretching farther than the eye can see, the State recruited a contractor to build the capitol in exchange for land. The State accepted the low bid to trade 3,050,000 acres of land in exchange for the job. The rights to the land, originally designated as public domain, were assigned by the contractor to a third party and then later re-assigned. Eventually the tract of land, located in the Texas Panhandle, became known as the XIT Ranch.

TAKEN FOR GRANITE

Although Texas limestone was chosen to construct the capitol, plans changed once streaking problems developed. As an alternative, Indiana limestone was suggested. However, the idea of using non-native stone was not well received by the governor or other Texans. In response to this need, and as a gesture of goodwill, the owners of a Texas quarry called Granite Mountain donated the necessary granite. However, only the foundation was constructed of Texas limestone.

GETTING ON TRACK

The Granite Mountain quarry's location, however, proved to be a problem. It was about fifty miles from Austin so a railroad had to be built to haul the granite to the building site. Over 188,000 cubic feet of granite was shipped to the site which took approximately three thousand railroad carloads.

CAUGHT BETWEEN A ROCK AND A HARD PLACE

In an effort to further minimize the cost of construction, the State employed inmates to help cut and shape the marble blocks for the capitol. However, the union of granite cutters did not appreciate the state's use of convicts and invoked a boycott on the job. As a counter measure, the contractor enticed a group of cutters from Scotland to immigrate to the U.S. to work on the marble blocks. Enraged at this action, the union pursued the matter in court and prevailed. Despite the delays and fines levied, the capitol was eventually completed in 1888.

A postcard, postmarked 1913, shows the capitol surrounded by a cast-iron fence.

A salt and pepper shaker is a model of the capitol.

A ribbon badge, from a 1910 convention held in Austin, features the capitol.

Formerly the State Treasurer's Business Office, this room now holds the Capitol Information and Guide Service.

Pearls of Wisdom

"For any guy that can run Texas, running America ought to be a pipe cinch."

Will Rogers — November, 1927

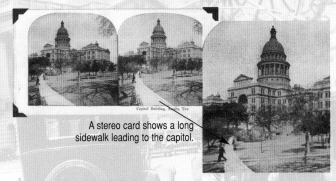

A stereo card shows a long sidewalk leading to the capitol.

Historical Happenings
1800 — 1900

1836
Texans and the volunteers
defeated at the Alamo

1836
Texans avenge the Alamo;
defeat Gen. Santa Anna;
declare independence;
becomes a republic

1839
Austin designated
as the capital by
Congress of The
Republic

1845
President Tyler
grants statehood

1861
Texas secedes
from the Union

The star in the dome is over 200 feet above the floor.

★ The Inside Story

THE UNDERGROUND CONNECTION

An underground capitol extension was completed in 1993. The addition has four levels, two for offices and two for parking, and connects to the historic capitol. Taking nearly three years to complete, it addressed the growing needs of the state and modernization of today's fast-paced government. Skylights, extending the length of the corridor known as "light courts," allow sunshine to penetrate the otherwise underground darkness, providing a sense of openness. Looking up through the skylights, the capitol dome is also in view.

SIX FLAGS OF TEXAS

The six flags that have flown over Texas are prominently displayed within the capitol. The national flags include Texas under Spain, France and Mexico, Texas as a Republic, Texas in the Confederacy and ultimately Texas in the U.S. The seals representing these countries are encased in the terrazzo tile floor in the center of the rotunda. Texas is most proud of the Republic of Texas flag. In 1836, after defeating General Santa Anna and his army at San Jacinto, Texas officially won its independence and became a republic. Although Texans voted in favor of annexation, a treaty of annexation was not ratified by both Congress and the Republic of Texas until 1845. Thereby, Texas existed as a sovereign nation for nearly ten years.

The ornately painted, cast-iron staircase
was imported from Belgium.

Chandeliers, shaped like a Texas star,
hang in the House of Representatives
and Senate chambers.

The Capitol Extension

A bronze hinge as seen on many of the doors.

Even some chair backs
feature the Texas star.

The six flags of Texas are embedded
in the terrazzo tile floor.

1888	1890	1936	1983	1993	1995	2000
Capitol completed	Ornamental iron fence added	Terrazzo tile floor completed	East Wing damaged by fire	Capitol Extension completed	$98 million restoration completed	

★ Claim to Fame

SUPER SIZED

Everything about Texas is big. Not only is it the largest of the contiguous states, it also has the largest state capitol in terms of floor space. At the time of completion, with the exception of the U.S. Capitol, it was said to be the largest public building in the United States. The original building footprint covers 1.8 acres of land while the floor space, including the Capitol Extension, occupies approximately 25 acres. At 302.64 feet tall, it stands taller than the U.S. Capitol.

What once was a copper penny is converted into a memento with the Texas capitol embossed on it at the Capitol Visitors Center.

The dome is taller than the U.S. capitol. The "Goddess of Liberty" holds a "Texas Lone Star."

FOR LAND'S SAKE

Texas is the only state that was allowed to keep its public lands rather than surrender them to the Federal government upon joining the Union. This became especially significant at the time the capitol was to be built as it allowed the state to barter using its most plentiful asset — land, in exchange for constructing its capitol.

MEETING THEIR WATERLOO

In 1839, President Mirabeau B. Lamar of the Republic of Texas chose a small community known as Waterloo to be the capital. Located on a bend in the Colorado River, the town was soon renamed Austin in honor of Stephen F. Austin who was known as the "Father of Anglo Texas."

★ For What it's Worth

STAR PERFORMANCE

Shortly after the capitol was completed, an ornamental iron fence was installed around the perimeter. Originally, it was painted black with gold stars symbolizing the "Lone Star State." Years later, it was painted green. It has since been restored to the original black with gold stars.

WELL VERSED

Since 1925, the incumbent governor has selected a passage of Scripture from the Bible and marked it for the incoming governor. The Bible, now worn with use over the years, is mostly kept in storage. Past selections have included the Ten Commandments, Proverbs 3:5-6, John 3:16 and II Timothy 2:15 which states: "Study to shew thyself approved unto God, a workman that needeth not to be ashamed, rightly dividing the word of truth." (KJV)

The cast-iron fence with the Texas stars.

183

UTAH
Salt Lake City

A LONG TIME IN COMING FOR THE BEEHIVE STATE

Stunningly landscaped grounds provide a scenic backdrop for the capitol overlooking the Great Salt Lake Valley.

STATE MOTTO

"Industry"

★ Facts & Figures

Architectural style	Classical Corinthian
Architect	Richard K. A. Kletting
Exterior material	Utah granite
Dome surface	Utah copper
Building height (to tip of dome)	286'
Construction period	1912-16
First occupied	1915
Capital population (Census 2000)	181,743
Census estimate 2007	180,651
Direction capitol faces	South
Original cost	$2,739,528

The Past Remembered

A STATE OF ITS OWN

Beginning in 1848 and continuing for nearly fifty years, citizens of this territory, predominantly Mormon, made several attempts to attain statehood. In 1849 they adopted a provisional government and constitution in naming their "State" Deseret. This term has its origin in the Book of Mormon and is said to mean honeybee — symbolizing work and industry. Although Deseret adopted the beehive symbol in 1848, it wasn't until 1959 that Utah formally adopted it as its state symbol. The self-proclaimed "State of Deseret" lasted for a year and a half (1849-51).

OCEAN FRONT PROPERTY

"Deseret" included parts of what are now nine states. Boundaries were arbitrarily drawn to include Utah, Nevada, most of Arizona, portions of Idaho, Colorado, Wyoming, New Mexico, Oregon and a section of the Southern California coast which included San Diego. A petition with a proposed constitution was drafted by the provisional government and submitted to Washington that included the newly drawn state. Around the time the petition was submitted, President Fillmore appointed Brigham Young as the first territorial governor. Although other factors such as the size of the territory and insufficient population played a role in Congress denying statehood, the Mormon stance on polygamy was also a factor. The majority of Congress, which strongly opposed this practice, voted against accepting "Deseret" as a state.

DOWNSIZING

In the ensuing years, the U.S. Congress took two actions. First, because it disapproved of the name, it was renamed as the Territory of Utah. Second, it downsized the territory by carving out various sections among which were created the territories and later states of Colorado, Nevada and Wyoming.

THE UTAH WAR

In 1857, the U.S. government appointed Albert Cumming, a non-Mormon, to preside as governor over the territory. In an effort to assure a peaceful transition, the Federal government sent 2,500 troops to the Utah Territory to accompany the newly appointed governor. Anticipating that the Federal government planned to forcibly remove the leadership and impose restrictions on the Mormon religion, Governor Brigham Young organized the Mormon militia to intercept the Federal troops. Young's forces burned the government supply wagons forcing them to camp for the winter. When President Buchanan strengthened his forces with another 3,000 troops, the Mormons evacuated Salt Lake City. Finally in 1858, a peaceful resolution was achieved in which Brigham Young surrendered the gubernatorial title and the new Governor Cumming was installed.

GOVERNMENT INTERFERES WITH CHURCH

Several later attempts at statehood also failed — primarily because of the Mormon Churches stance on polygamy. Finally in 1890, the Mormon Church officially abandoned the practice of polygamy and removed it from its doctrine. Shortly thereafter, Congress agreed to grant statehood. In 1896, President Cleveland signed a declaration admitting Utah as the 45th state.

Red berries add a splash of color to a dismal wintery day in 1974.

An 1851 boundary map shows the "State of Deseret" (outlined in red). Note the "ocean front" property.

A small cotton bag filled with salt from The Great Salt Lake is stitched to the reverse side of this postcard.

"Eagle Gate" frames the capitol. First erected in 1859, it was elevated in 1891 to allow trolley cars to pass under it. This early postcard shows an unpaved street. Compare this postcard mailed in 1915 with 1972 and 2002 photos taken from the same spot.

1972

2002

Pearls of Wisdom
"We expect this building to be one which will be a joy as long as it might stand, and we propose to build it so that it shall stand through all time."
Governor William Spry — December 26, 1912
At the Groundbreaking Ceremony

Historical Happenings

1800   **1900**

1847	**1849**	**1850**	**1855**	**1856**	**1857**
Mormon pioneers arrive in The Great Salt Lake Valley; Brigham Young declares "This is the place."	Provisional State of Deseret established	Congress "carves up" Deseret; Territory of Utah created	Fillmore serves as territorial capital	Salt Lake City designated capital	The Utah War (Mormons vs. U.S. Government)

★ *The Inside Story*

A three-ton brass chandelier is suspended 165 feet above the rotunda floor.

MORMON MURALS

Murals depicting events in the life of the Mormon settlers are displayed throughout the capitol including both Houses. Around the dome's interior are detailed murals that depict periods of Utah's history. A giant brass chandelier, suspended by a 95 foot chain from the center of the dome, weighs three tons. Painted into the dome are a field with clouds and seagulls. Seagulls were crucial to the settlers because they devoured countless numbers of crickets that were consuming the crops needed for daily survival in this arid climate and soil.

MATCHING MARBLE STAIRCASES

From the rotunda, one can look in opposite directions and see a grand marble staircase. The immense staircases create a grandiose setting for public events, including an occasional wedding. Although the interior is comprised primarily of Utah marble, Georgia marble was also used, particularily in the staircases.

THE GOLD STANDARD

The Gold Room, used as the Governor's reception room, has elaborate European furnishings and has a gold color scheme. Mirrors are trimmed with gold leaf while tapestries and green chairs are trimmed in 14 karat gold thread. The rug is from Scotland, the table from Russia and the chairs are from England. This ornately decorated and furnished private room is reserved for the governor and guests and generally is not open to the public.

One of the twin staircases

The "beehive state" proudly displays its symbol of work and industry throughout the capitol.

The Senate

The Gold Room

1890
Polygamy removed
from Mormon doctrine

1896
President Cleveland
grants statehood

1911
Windfall estate tax revenue
of $798,500 received

1916 **2000**
Capitol
completed

2008
Capitol restoration
completed

★ Claim to Fame

LATTER DAY LEGACY

Mormonism has had a significant impact in shaping Utah's history and destiny for which no other state can make such a claim. Since the time of the westward migration of the Mormons into the Great Salt Lake Valley in 1847, the development and progress of Utah has been dominated by the influence of the Mormon Church. Whether one believes

Overlooking the capitol and the Great Salt Lake Valley

founder Joseph Smith's claims that he received a revelation from an angel called Moroni, guardian of the golden plates, there is no denying the fact that Brigham Young and Joseph Smith have had a significant impact on the history and development of Utah.

THIS IS THE PLACE

On the arrival of the nearly 150 Mormon pioneers to the Great Salt Lake Valley, Brigham Young expressed his hallmark and legendary remark, "This is the place." In this case, his words were prophetic as the Mormons did establish their church at this location and today it is still the headquarters for the Mormon Church.

STREET SMART

When visiting Salt Lake City, the enormous width of its streets is immediately noticeable. Thinking toward the future, its founders appropriately planned for growth. After a visit in 1926, Will Rogers commented: "Salt Lake City is the only town in the world that saw far enough ahead and predicted the forthcoming traffic jam, and made wide streets."

The "Date Garden"

A stately statue of Brigham Young, who led the first Mormon settlers to the Great Salt Lake Valley, is located in the rotunda.

★ For What it's Worth

MAKING A DATE

A tradition practiced for years before the advent of day-date cameras and watches, the "Date Garden," as it is known, made it easy for visitors taking pictures to recall when they were at the capitol. Every day, gardeners carefully swap the flower trays to reflect the number(s) of the new day ahead.

FOCUSED ON FLOWERS

Utah's capitol grounds, 37 acres in all, are a photographer's delight. According to the land deed, the grounds are to be "maintained as a public park." Assorted flower beds line the walkways and pathways surrounding the capitol. It could aptly be named the "Flower Capitol." Each

section is meticulously manicured. From the walkway in front leading to the entrance, as well as the side and rear of the building, there are countless assortments of flowers. Many plants are annuals which require new plants each spring. The State spared no expense assuring that visitors depart with a lasting impression of this lavishly landscaped capitol.

VERMONT
Montpelier

CAPITOL IN THE COUNTRY
A small town atmosphere lends character to this quaint New England capitol.

STATE MOTTO
"Freedom and unity"

★ Facts & Figures

Architectural style...........Renaissance Revival

Architect.............................Thomas Silloway and Joseph Richards

Exterior material ....Barre granite

Dome surface.......................24 carat gold leaf

Building height (to tip of dome)..............135'

Construction period 1857-59

First occupied 1859

Capital population (Census 2000)......8,035
    Census estimate 2007 7,806

Direction capitol faces ....South

Original cost................................$150,000

⭐ The Past Remembered

LET'S MAKE A DEAL

In 1805, citizens of Montpelier struck a "deal" with state legislators to receive the right to be designated the permanent capital. They agreed to donate land and $8,000 toward the construction of a capitol, and promised that it would be completed by 1808. Vermont's first state capitol was completed on schedule. Worthy of note, much of the money pledged was actually fulfilled as barter in the form of materials, food and labor.

ON A COLD WINTER'S NIGHT

In 1836, after a larger building was completed, the first capitol was dismantled. This second capitol served Vermont for over twenty years.

On a cold winter's night in January 1857, workers were preparing the capitol for a Constitutional Convention meeting. In their haste, they covered cold-air intake vents. This careless mistake resulted in a devastating fire. After the smoke had cleared, all that remained standing were six columns of the portico and the outside walls of the building.

NOT WITHOUT A FIGHT

In the wake of the destruction, the fire destroyed not only the state house but also fueled the flames over relocating the capital. Accusations, insults and verbal abuse over temperance and prohibition were hurled back and forth between citizens of Montpelier and Burlington.

NEITHER FIRE NOR FLOOD

Other towns competing to be the state capital were Rutland and Middlebury. After much debate, the legislature voted for Montpelier and funding to rebuild the state house was then approved. While the new capitol was being built, representatives met in a nearby church while the Senate met in a courthouse. Tucked into the hillside, the third and present capitol was built on this same site as the previous. The Doric style of portico, left standing after the fire, was incorporated into this third capitol, but the walls were weakened by the fire and needed to be replaced. Both the second and third state house utilized granite from nearby Barre to construct the capitol. In addition to the fire, the site of the capitol also withstood a major flood in 1927.

NOT ALL THAT GLITTERS IS GOLD

The base material of the dome is wood. The original covering of the wooden dome was clad with copper but was painted a dark red. Toward the turn of the twentieth century, the national trend was to gild capitol domes. This became known as the "Gilded Age." In 1906, Vermont followed suit in gilding its dome.

An 1889 painting by James F. Gilman shows the original, dark-red color of the dome. This recently acquired painting is on display in the State House.

A photo reproduction shows the state capitol "all decked out" for the centennial celebration. The scene was illustrated in a monthly publication, *The Vermonter*, in 1905.

Etched on this tin ink blotter, c. 1910, are the words "State House Montpelier Vermont." [*sic*]

Mailed in 1913, the reverse of this postcard contains an advertisement for Lily White flour.

Pearls of Wisdom

"All who passionately love liberty revere the memory of Ethan Allen.... The record of his life will continue to inspire men who love liberty to dare greatly and fight courageously for the cause of human freedom."

Deane C. Davis (later Governor) — 1941
At the unveiling of the Ethan Allen monument

Historical Happenings

1800

1900

1791
President Washington grants statehood

1805
Montpelier chosen as permanent capital

1808
First State House on site completed

1836
Second State House completed

1857
Fire destroys second State House

1859
Capitol completed

The Battle of Cedar Creek nearly spans the length of the Governor's reception room.

The Senate chamber has an elliptical domed ceiling.

A large marble bust of Abraham Lincoln is in a first floor hallway. Sculpted by Larkin G. Mead c. 1870, it faces the front entrance.

The House of Representatives chamber.

A winding staircase provides a unique view.

★ The Inside Story

A CLEAN SLATE

In 1981, when a major restoration project began, an extensive search for the original fixtures and details of drapes, carpet, paint and other furnishings was undertaken to restore the State House to its 1859 appearance. In restoring original "look," slate blackboards were placed in committee rooms.

PIECING IT ALL TOGETHER

The search for original accessories produced gasolier light fixtures, chandeliers and stained glass skylights. The skylights, found in the attic, were in jagged and broken pieces. At first, putting all the pieces back together appeared hopeless. However, craftsmen were able to re-assemble essentially entire windows.

THE BATTLE OF CEDAR CREEK

The Governor's reception room, also known as the Cedar Creek Room, features a famous Civil War painting by Julian Scott. Scott completed the ten by twenty-foot painting in 1874, including the frame. It depicts *The Battle of Cedar Creek*, which took place in Virginia's Shenandoah Valley. In this battle, the "Old Vermont Brigade" reversed a Union retreat to lead the Union Army to victory. Remarkably, Julian Scott himself joined the Brigade at age 15 initially serving as the drummer boy, and lived to recreate Vermont's most important Civil War action in his famous painting. Scott painted another battle scene from his own memory which also hangs in the Governor's reception room.

A "CERES"IOUS MISTAKE

The original fourteen-foot statue atop the dome was sculpted by Larkin G. Mead in 1858. Since the statue, named *Agriculture*, was made of wood, it rotted over the years. In 1938, it was taken down and discarded except for a hand, which is in a museum. Not wanting the dome to be without a proper statue, the Sergeant-at-Arms volunteered to sculpt a replacement.

The replica still stands atop the dome. During the statue's history, it was commonly referred to as Ceres, the mythical goddess of agriculture. However, in the original communications between the State and the sculptor Larkin Mead, he never mentioned this name. Thus the correct name is *Agriculture*, not Ceres.

1906 Dome gilded

1941 Replacement statue *Agriculture* mounted on dome

1987 Building addition and cafeteria completed

2000 Major restoration completed

★ Claim to Fame

SMALL FRIES

According to the 2007 Census estimate, the population of Montpelier was 7,806, making it the smallest population of any state capital. But how small is it? Montpelier is the only state capital that does not have a McDonalds.

ON THE ROAD AGAIN

From the time of statehood in 1791 until 1805, Vermont's legislature met in 15 different towns during the fourteen-year period. In 1805, Montpelier was designated the seat of government and remains the capital today.

CAPITOL "D"

The House of Representatives chamber is shaped like the letter "D." Though built in 1859, both chambers have been well maintained and are considered to be in original condition, the oldest of any state capitol that can make this claim.

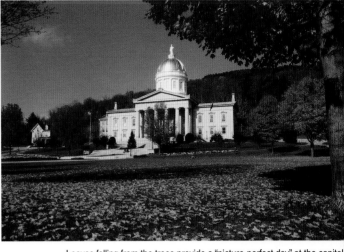

Leaves falling from the trees provide a "picture-perfect day" at the capitol.

★ For What it's Worth

STATE HOUSE OUT HOUSE

When the State House was completed in 1859, it did not have indoor plumbing. When the first restroom was installed, it was designated "for men only." Apparently, the building codes did not require restrooms for women. Finally, twenty years later — in 1906 — women were afforded the same privilege.

A "WHITTLE" TOO MUCH

Desks from the first State House, built in 1808, were constructed of pine. Back then, it was common practice for members of the legislature to whittle away at the soft wood of the benches with their jackknives. After about twenty years, the benches became unusable and were replaced. Apparently, they got a "whittle" carried away with their whittling.

"BARE" HILL?

Montpelier is a French word meaning "bare hill." Judging from its heavily forested surroundings today, one may wonder how it looked in the 1780's and what prompted the name.

A DAY TO REMEMBER

Until recently, Vermont was the only state that celebrated Memorial Day on the traditional May 30th. Thus Vermont's State House was open on the National Memorial Day but closed on the 30th of May. However, Vermont now celebrates the same as the rest of the nation.

From the mountain above, the State House looks as though it was built in the middle of a forest. The photo also illustrates why Vermont is known as the "Green Mountain State."

Said to be "calling for a surrender at Fort Ticonderoga," the Ethan Allen statue is located on the portico. This 1941 sculpture is a recreation of the 1861 statue. Ethan Allen is noted for leading the *Green Mountain Boys* in the first major victory over the British in 1775.

VIRGINIA
Richmond

A CAPITOL RICH IN HERITAGE

The scene of several historical events, Richmond is indeed rich in American heritage. Washington, Jefferson, Madison, Monroe and Jefferson Davis left their mark on this capitol.

STATE MOTTO

"Thus always to tyrants"

★ Facts & Figures

Architectural style	Neo-classical
Architect	Thomas Jefferson w/Charles-Louis Clérisseau
Exterior material	Stucco over handmade brick
Dome surface	None
Building height	82'
Construction period	1785-98
First occupied	1788
Capital population (Census 2000)	197,790
Census estimate 2007	200,123
Direction capitol faces	South
Original cost	(estimate) $140,000

★ The Past Remembered

TEMPLE FROM THE PAST

In 1785, Thomas Jefferson, who was asked to help design the Virginia capitol, was instructed to choose a design that would "unite economy with elegance and utility." The design chosen by Jefferson, a self-taught architect, was inspired by a Roman temple located in Nîmes, France known as La Maison Carrée. Jefferson employed the services of French draftsman Charles-Louis Clérisseau to draw the plans. The completed plans were sent from France in January 1786, though construction was already under way. A detailed plaster model, still at the capitol and also made in Paris in 1786, did not arrive until the following year.

Although steps are shown at the side of this model of the capitol, Virginia builders chose to construct larger and more elaborate steps than are shown on the model.

STEPPING OUT

Jefferson was in France working on the design as the beginning phases of construction began. Upon his return from France, he was surprised to see that there were no external front steps leading to the portico or main entrance. This was due to the location of the windows on the front of the building. The "cluster of steps" that led to each side entrance remained the subject of much criticism after completion. The building remained without portico steps for over 100 years until the two wings were added during 1904-06.

RELUCTANT REBEL OR CONFEDERATE YANKEE?

In this building, Robert E. Lee, a native Virginian, accepted command of the armed forces of the Commonwealth of Virginia in April 1861. A few days prior to this, he had been invited to Washington, D.C. and had been offered command of the Union army which he declined. Lee did not wish to take up arms against his native state of Virginia. Lee was given field command of Confederate troops from other southern states the following year. Jefferson Davis of Kentucky, who served as President of the Confederacy, was inaugurated on Capitol Square.

CAPITOL CALAMITY

In 1870, a Virginia Supreme Court hearing held on the third floor of the capitol drew so many spectators that the floor collapsed. The occupants fell thirty feet which tragically resulted in 62 deaths and 251 injuries.

THE EMPTY TOMB

The equestrian Washington monument on the Square includes a symbolic tomb that was designated for George Washington. However, he had chosen to be buried at his plantation home at Mount Vernon and his heirs declined to relocate him to Richmond. Thus, the tomb remains empty.

This 2002 photo shows the Roman temple after which Thomas Jefferson took his inspiration for the Virginia capitol. Located in Nîmes, France, the temple was built in about 3 to 5 A.D. for the sons of Augustus Caesar. The remarkable preservation of this ancient structure is said to be due to its continual use. The overlaying postcard, bearing a French postmark of 1907, shows an iron fence which has since been removed.

This likeness of George Washington is unequaled.

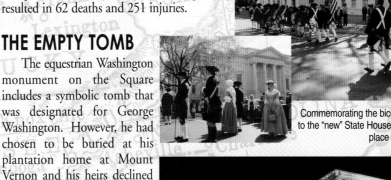

Commemorating the bicentennial of the move to the "new" State House, a re-enactment took place during October 1988.

A rare postcard showing the capitol prior to the addition of the wings being added in 1906.

Pearls of Wisdom

"It is perfectly plain on the top and rather flat. If a dome had been built on it, it would have given it a much grander appearance."

William T. Barry — March 27, 1804
Referring to the newly completed capitol

1780
Capital relocates from Williamsburg to Richmond

1785
Thomas Jefferson asked to help design capitol

1786
Architectural plans arrive from Paris

1788
Virginia becomes tenth state to ratify Constitution

1798
Capitol completed

1870
Third floor collapses – 62 people die

★ The Inside Story

FOSSIL FIND

White and black stone pavers are placed in a checkerboard pattern throughout the tile floors of the capitol. The black tiles encase fossils of various sea life from the Ordovician period, which according to archaeologists, dates to over 400 million years ago.

RESPECTING THE MACE

The mace

The Old Hall of the House of Delegates resembles a Roman courtyard. The coved ceiling simulates an outdoor appearance. On display in this room is Virginia's 20th century mace. The mace, symbolizing government authority, is an English tradition. Historically, the English monarchy used the mace as a club to protect royalty.

A TRUE LIKENESS, BY GEORGE

The rotunda features a life-size marble statue of George Washington sculpted by the world famous sculptor, Jean Antoine Houdon of France. It was completed in 1792 and has been on nearly continuous display since its delivery in 1796. Based on a plaster mold of Washington's face along with precise measurements of his body, it is said to be the closest likeness of Washington's features of any painting or other work of art. So real is the likeness that General Lafayette, who knew Washington well, remarked it was "A facsimile of Washington's person."

The interior dome

The rotunda features a checkerboard floor.

The coved ceiling and George Washington statue.

This rather large crinoid (snail) fossil is one of many clearly seen in the black tiles.

The Old Hall of the House of Delegates.

1900

1906

Two wings and portico steps added

1964

Renovation completed

1988

200 year celebration of capitol's first use

2000

2007

$105 million renovation/expansion completed

★ Claim to Fame

THE STEALTH DOME

Virginia was the first capitol to have an interior dome without also having an exterior dome. Although from inside the rotunda the dome appears to extend above the roof, it actually rests ten feet below the roofline.

THE RECORD HOLDER

Since the colonial days in 1619, the Virginia General Assembly holds the record of meeting, though not always in this building, longer than any state or colony. The capitol is also the first classical, temple-style building in the New World and the first American state house built after the Revolutionary War.

CONFEDERATE CAPITOL

During the Civil War, the Confederate States of America assembled in Richmond where it established its headquarters. The Virginia capitol served as both the Confederate National capitol and the Virginia State capitol from 1861 to 1865. Amazingly, the capitol was not damaged during the war.

During the Civil War, Confederate currency featured the Virginia capitol.

A statue of General Robert E. Lee stands proudly in the Old House of Delegates chamber.

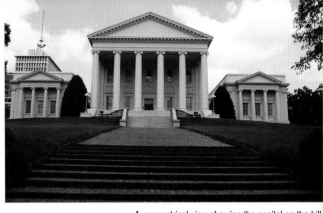

A symmetrical view showing the capitol on the hill.

★ For What it's Worth

HOW TIMES HAVE CHANGED

In the early years, the capitol served as both the state house and a meeting place for church services. Presbyterian and Episcopal congregations alternated services in the Old House chamber on a regular basis. During this period, many churches did not have sanctuaries of their own as few buildings were constructed to house large gatherings. Apparently, legislators did not consider the church meetings a threat to the "separation of church and state." The practice, normal for its day, presents an interesting juxtaposition with modern culture's obsession with separating religion from civic life, illustrating how differently our founding fathers viewed this issue.

PUTTING TEETH TO THE STORY

For many years, a myth was told that George Washington's dentures were made of wood. In 1973, this myth was dispelled. A dentist by the name of Reidar Sognnaes discovered that they were made of several materials including elephant ivory, hippopotamus tusk and even one of Washington's own teeth. In reality, Washington owned several sets of dentures, none of which were made of wood.

A COMMONWEALTH

Virginia is one of only four states organized and known as a Commonwealth. A commonwealth refers to the rule of law and political power given by consent of the people.

WASHINGTON
Olympia

THE CAPITOL GROUP

With sunken gardens providing a tranquil and striking setting, the Legislative Building is the focal point of a campus comprising the Capitol Group.

STATE MOTTO

"By and by"

★ Facts & Figures

Architectural style	Greek and Roman
Architect	Wilder and White
Exterior material	Wilkeson sandstone & index granite
Dome surface	Wilkeson sandstone
Building height (to tip of dome)	287'
Construction period	1922-28
First occupied	1927
Capital population (Census 2000)	42,514
Census estimate 2007	44,925
Direction capitol faces	North
Original cost (including furnishings)	$7,385,768

★ The Past Remembered

In 1853, Washington separated from the Oregon Territory to form the Washington Territory. Olympia was designated as the capital. Three years later, Olympia built its first capitol, a two-story frame building, on the present site.

A FALSE START

The State selected Ernest Flagg to design a new capitol. Although a foundation was laid in 1893, construction was halted when unforseen events put its completion in doubt. On the national scene, an economic depression caused hesitation. Then, a change of adminis-tration within the State resulted in a lack of support and funding as well as consid-eration to relocate the capital.

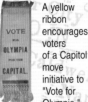

A yellow ribbon encourages voters of a Capitol move initiative to "Vote for Olympia."

In the interim, a court-house located in the downtown area was purchased and served as the capitol from 1905 until the present capitol was completed.

LUMBERING ALONG

Finally, in 1911, the construction was re-authorized. But this time, needs had grown and an entire complex was approved. A new design competition was held in which the firm of Wilder and White was selected. Funding for the complex was provided by converting excess timber in Federally donated lands, earmarked for a capitol, into cash which allowed the State to avoid going into debt altogether.

SAFE HARBOR

The Capitol Group is located at the southern tip of Puget Sound. The capitol, known as the Legislative Building, overlooks the harbor and is at the center of the six building campus which includes the governor's mansion. In 1949, a dam was constructed to separate the salt water of Puget Sound from the fresh water of Capitol Lake. Prior to the dam, ships were able to moor in the Capitol Lake harbor.

TWO SIDES TO EVERY STORY

A 71-foot story pole is located on the capitol grounds. Often mistaken for a totem pole, this pole tells a story. A story pole is said to teach children about values and responsibility whereas a totem pole is about family history. Carved in the 1930s by Chief Shelton at the request of the governor, the pole is from the Snohomish tribe of the Puget Sound area.

Although Chief Shelton died prior to its completion, other tribal members completed it. Over the years, it has been repainted and repaired several times. There are two sides to the pole; each side tells a different story.

A CASE OF THE SHAKES

The Olympia area is prone to earthquakes. Major quakes, in which the capitol has sustained damage, occurred in 1949, 1965 and 2001. During the 1949 quake, which registered 7.1 on the Richter scale, eight people were killed.

On February 28, 2001, a 6.8 earthquake caused shifting in pillars and stonework and other damage to the interior while the legis-lature was in session. Overall, the building withstood the quake quite well. Until the overall damage had been determined, the building remained closed for several days. Fortunately, the quake occurred more than 30 miles below the surface. If it had originated from the Seattle fault, experts theorize that the damage would have been more severe.

A different story is told on each side of the story pole.

This postcard, with vintage automobiles, c. 1940, shows an early view of the capitol.

In June 1933, the USS Constitution was moored in the Olympia harbor for over a week. Old Ironsides, as it is known, visited 90 ports during a national tour. The ship was towed from port to port by a minesweeper.

In 1957, a small carnival with a $500 budget, was held at Capitol Lake. The event soon became an annual tradition. The five-day festival is held in July and now has a $200,000 budget! Although events change from year to year, it has featured a street dance, a luau, a car show, arts and crafts, a volleyball tournament as well as other activities and culminates with a fireworks extravaganza.

Pearls of Wisdom

"I am through and damned glad of it.... May the gods preserve me from any other State work under the present administration."

A capitol architect — February 18, 1929

Historical Happenings

1800

1856
Territorial capitol constructed on site

1889
President Harrison grants statehood

1894
Construction on present capitol halted

1900

The inner dome

A replica of the state seal is embedded in the floor.

This statue of Marcus Whitman, a missionary pioneer and medical doctor holding a Bible and medical bags, is located in the entryway.

One of four bronze firepots.

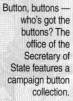

Button, buttons — who's got the buttons? The office of the Secretary of State features a campaign button collection.

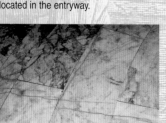

An 1965 earthquake reportedly caused this crack in the marble floor.

★ The Inside Story

A SOUND PERFORMANCE

After a chance discovery, a study by sound experts determined that the acoustics in the capitol rotunda was equivalent to the most renowned cathedrals. Once discovered, band performances, organ and choir recitals and other musical performances are held in the capitol to take advantage of these concert-like conditions. In addition to these audience-attended performances, a concert whistler came to the capitol to practice her music.

MERCY!

A five-ton chandelier, known as the "Angels of Mercy" is suspended from the rotunda dome. With over 200 lights, it is kept on reduced power continuously. Every ten years, the bulbs are changed — needed or not. It is said that a VW bug could fit inside the huge chandelier.

A FIRE IN EVERY POT

In each corner of the rotunda is a bronze firepot. Designed by Tiffany's of New York, they are replicas of firepots used by the Roman Senate. Historically, the Roman custom was to ignite the firepots whenever the Senate met. Now electrified, these firepots remain lit regardless of whether the legislature is in session.

George Washington, from which the State takes its name, is portrayed on door knobs.

1903	1911	1922	1928	2001	2000 2004
Legislature relocates to courthouse	New architects selected	Work on capitol resumes	Capitol completed	Capitol damaged by strong earthquake	Capitol rehabilitation completed

★ Claim to Fame

SOUNDS LIKE A PLAN

Washington was the first state to develop a plan to construct a group of related government buildings in a campus setting. It became known as the Capitol Group. In subsequent years, other states such as Delaware and West Virginia followed suit. The capitol, with its masonry dome, is the focal point of an overall master plan that includes a Conservatory, the Temple of Justice, administrative buildings and the Governor's Mansion.

BY GEORGE

Just as George Washington stands out among presidents, when all the flags of the states are displayed, the state of Washington also stands out. The Washington flag is the only green flag and the only flag with a portrait. Washington also stands out as the only state, currently, to be named after a U.S. President.

I'LL DRINK TO THAT

Not to be outdone, the city of Olympia is the only capital known to have a beer named after it with the same name as the city.

THE GREENHOUSE EFFECT

Since 1939, the Capitol Conservatory, a greenhouse, provided a variety of bedding plants which were used on the capitol grounds. Semi-tropical plants and cactus were also grown. However, it was closed in 2008 due to deterioration.

A replica of the Tivoli Fountain in Copenhagen.

A reflection in Capitol Lake provides an artistic fall scene.

★ For Whats it's Worth

SUNKEN GARDEN

The Washington state capitol is noted for well-planned and beautifully landscaped grounds. The Sunken Garden contains an assortment of colorful flowers and makes a gorgeous foreground to the capitol.

THEY DON'T GIVE A HOOT

Due to the damage from the 2001 quake, employees were relocated to other buildings. However the damage didn't seem to bother some owls that frequented the neighborhood. During the damage assessment process, three barn owls made the capitol their temporary new home via an open window.

A FACELIFT

Over the years, the Washington state seal has undergone many changes. Originally designed in 1889, a postage stamp with a picture of Washington was used as the design. Later, Washington's picture that appeared on a packing box for "coughs and colds" was substituted. In the ensuing years, other faces of Washington were used until 1967 when a Gilbert Stuart portrait of Washington was the final "facelift" used to create the state seal.

A view from Puget Sound harbor.

WEST VIRGINIA
Charleston

THE BYZANTINE GOLD DOME

With a dome that outshines other domes, the mountain state capitol overlooks the Kanawha River.

"Mountaineers are always free"

★ Facts & Figures

Architectural style	Italian Renaissance
Architect	Cass Gilbert
Exterior material	Indiana limestone
Dome surface	23 1/2 carat gold leaf over copper
Building height (to tip of dome)	292'
Construction period	1924-32
First occupied	1925
Capital population (Census 2000)	55,056
Census estimate 2007	50,478
Direction capitol faces	South
Original cost	$9,491,180

★ The Past Remembered

WHEELING AND DEALING

From 1863-70, West Virginia's capital was located in Wheeling. However, for the next five years, the legislature conducted business in Charleston. A group of businessmen in Wheeling, well aware of the benefits of being the capital city, refused to give up on the prestigious designation. In 1875, they offered the legislature a deal that was hard to refuse — the free use of a building in Wheeling. The offer was accepted and the legislators returned to Wheeling. Although the capital remained there for the next ten years, efforts by other communities to sway legislators continued. In 1877, a special election was scheduled to decide the capital's permanent location. Charleston, Clarksburg and Martinsburg were on the ballot. Oddly enough, Wheeling was not one of the choices.

CIRCUS ACT

Representatives from Charleston traveled across the state to drum up votes for the special election. While in Huntington and only ten days before the election, they heard a circus parade approaching. Thinking they could not compete with a circus, in their despair, they stopped at a bar. To their amazement, a man in the bar who happened to be with the circus offered to help their cause. The Charleston representatives were able to travel with the circus and were allotted five minutes before each circus performance to rally votes for Charleston. Their efforts were rewarded as Charleston received more votes than the other two communities combined.

KEEPING THE CAPITOL AFLOAT

When the capital was relocated from Wheeling to Charleston, the state records and archives were also transferred to the new capital. The Kanawha River runs through Charleston, making it the best way to ship materials. Thus, the records were shipped via river traffic to Charleston in three separate loads. One trip took nearly four months to complete. Steamers and barges, used to transport the records, were very slow and thus the capital was referred to as a "floating capital."

THE "PASTEBOARD CAPITOL"

In 1885, a new capitol was completed which served until 1921 when it was destroyed by fire. Shortly thereafter and as an interim measure, the State appropriated funds to construct a temporary capitol. Completed in just 42 working days, the building was constructed of wood and wallboard. Appropriately, it became known as the "pasteboard capitol." In 1927, this temporary capitol was also destroyed by a fire.

OUT WITH A BANG

In 1920, coal miners along with the owners of the coal mines clashed over labor issues. Fearing a civil war, the State police stored guns and ammunition on the top floor of the capitol. In 1921, a fire broke out which ultimately destroyed the capitol. As the fire spread and heated up, it rose to the top floor and ignited the "arsenal." The unexpected explosions sent surprised spectators heading for cover.

Looking more like a church with steeples, the previous capitol in Charleston is seen in this postcard mailed in 1908.

PIECE BY PIECE

Cass Gilbert, who also designed the capitols in Arkansas and Minnesota, was the architect for the West Virginia capitol. The capitol was completed in three phases. The west wing was completed first, followed by the east wing and lastly the center section. Together, the three buildings form a "U-shaped" complex. For each phase, a separate contract was signed and the building was completed before proceeding to the next phase. Theoretically, this approach resulted in a cost savings as each phase was completed under its appropriation. The open section has a circle with a fountain at its center. Originally, cars could park around the circle but now walkways crisscross the inner circle.

This 1986 photo shows the dome with a blue and gold, two-tone color. Originally, the panels were painted a brown-leather color while the rest was gold leaf.

A statue known as *Lincoln Walks at Midnight* is on the approach to the capitol.

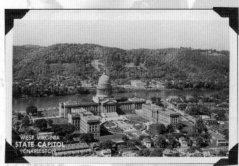

This postcard, c. 1940, shows an aerial view of the capitol.

Pearls of Wisdom

"Look at that color! That's Byzantine gold! Cass Gilbert would go crazy! He would absolutely adore it!"

**Emmanual Tsitsilianos — 1991
Contractor for re-gilding the dome**

Historical Happenings

1800

1863
President Lincoln grants statehood

1870
Capital relocates from Wheeling to Charleston

1875
Capital moves back to Wheeling

1877
Voters select Charleston as permanent capital

1900

1885
Capital relocates from Wheeling to Charleston for second time

The Senate

The House chandelier

The interior dome

The Rotunda

Rows of black and gold marble columns line each legislative corridor. Each column is topped with an Italian alabaster urn.

★ The Inside Story

CZECH MATES

The focal point of the rotunda dome is a huge chandelier suspended from the ceiling. Made from over 10,000 pieces of Czechoslovakian crystal, it weighs over 4,000 pounds. Identical, but smaller, versions are located in the Senate and House chambers.

UPPER AND LOWER

The two houses of the West Virginia legislature are known as the Senate or "Upper House" and the House of Delegates or "Lower House." Although the chambers are similar, the Senate has a domed ceiling.

GUNS AND AMMO

During the 1930s, there was continual strife between the miners and the legislators. Out of fear that the miners' anger would result in violence, and that they might attack the capitol, the government installed gun posts in the rotunda. Though never used, these gun posts are still visible today.

1921 Previous capitol destroyed by fire

1925 West wing completed

1932 Capitol completed

1991 Dome re-gilded

2005 Dome restored to architect's specifications

★ Claim to Fame

TWO-TONE

The architect, Cass Gilbert, designed the dome to be gilded with gold except for the flat panels, which were painted a brown-leather color. In just a few years, the paint and the gold deteriorated and thus, in 1946, the entire dome was painted. Over the years, it was repainted several times including a blue and gold two-tone color. West Virginia's capitol is unique in that it is the first and only capitol to have had a two-tone dome.

The dome was returned to all gold following a three-year re-gilding project which was completed in 1991. Then in 2005, West Virginians voted overwhelmingly to restore the dome to the architect's original color scheme of gold leaf and a grey color. The project was completed the same year.

OLD VIRGINIA

In 1861, when the State of Virginia voted to secede from the Union, most delegates from the western part of the state voted against the secession. These same delegates decided to split from "Old Virginia" and form a new government. As a result, the State of West Virginia was formed during the Civil War, the only state to hold the distinction of "breaking off" from another state during this time period.

★ For What it's Worth

TIME'S NOT UP

The previous capitol was a three-story brick and stone building with a clock tower. When the old capitol burned in 1921, the clock tower remained intact until the very end. Those watching the fire consume the building noted that the clock in the tower continued to chime until the building actually collapsed.

SQUIRRELED AWAY

Some years ago, an animal loving West Virginian surmised that squirrels on the capitol grounds could be better protected from the elements and could store their nuts if they had shelters. To accomplish this purpose, the Boy Scouts were recruited to do a "good deed" by building and placing squirrel houses in many of the trees on the capitol grounds. Although the little houses have been the subject of scorn and ridicule and attempts to remove them, they have survived to this day.

The dome as it appeared after being gilded with 23 1/2 karat Byzantine-gold leaf in 1991.

One of several squirrel houses on the grounds

SOLD! — TO THE HIGHEST BIDDER

It has been said that you can find anything on the Internet. In May of 2001, some of Cass Gilbert's original architectural drawings of the West Virginia capitol appeared on the internet in an e-Bay auction. The asking price was $2,000. The package was said to include over 50 original drawings as well as the 1921 signed contract between the architect and the governor. After receiving 19 bids, the auction ended with a sale price of $11,000!

WISCONSIN
Madison

WINGS OF WISCONSIN
With wings extending in each direction of the compass, the Wisconsin capitol forms the St. Andrew's cross.

STATE MOTTO

"Forward"

★ Facts & Figures

Architectural style	Beaux Arts
Architect	George B. Post & Sons
Exterior material	White Bethel granite
Dome surface	White Bethel granite
Building height (to tip of dome)	285'
Construction period	1906-17
First occupied	1909
Capital population (Census 2000)	208,054
Census estimate 2007	228,775
Direction capitol faces	Southeast
Original cost	$7,203,826

The Past Remembered

OSHKOSH BY GOSH

In 1836, the territorial legislature met in Belmont, near the town of Platteville. Meeting for only 46 days, they voted to locate the permanent capital in Madison. Once in Madison, other communities made efforts to lure the capital away from its present location.

After a fire in 1904 severely damaged the previous capitol, legislators and citizens of Milwaukee sought to relocate the capital to their city. Not to be outdone, the city of Oshkosh offered 40 acres of land as an enticement but the legislators would not be moved.

A BURNING DESIRE TO BUILD

The current capitol in Madison is the third structure built on the site. In 1903, one of the actions considered by the legislature was whether to expand or reconstruct the existing capitol. The legislators debated the question for months until the answer became obvious. During the night of February 27, 1904, a fire broke out which destroyed most of the capitol.

In response, bids and plans were solicited for a new capitol. The design submitted by the George B. Post & Sons architectural firm was selected. Construction of a new capitol began in 1906 and still stands today.

A postcard shows the previous capitol in flames in 1904. Although devastating, the fire provided the impetus to hasten the decision to build a new capitol.

COPY RIGHT OR COPY WRONG?

The postcard picture shown above with the previous capitol in flames was taken by a 15-year old boy who woke up during the night and had his Kodak camera handy. He sold copies for ten cents a piece though his father made him reduce the price to five cents. He raised enough money to buy a bicycle. A postcard printer purchased a copy and made reprints which he in turn sold. However, he did not share any of his profits with the boy.

ONE PIECE AT A TIME

The designers of the capitol utilized what could be salvaged from the old capitol. In fact, a portion of the old capitol was used during the construction of the new building which was completed in phases — one wing at a time. The west wing, which had suffered the most fire damage, was the first to be rebuilt and occupied. The entire building took nearly eleven years to complete.

NORTH BY NORTHWEST

Four equal wings of the capitol extend in four precise directions forming what is known as a St. Andrew's cross. Each wing points either due east, west, north or south — points of the compass. In between each wing are four main entrances to the capitol which face streets surrounding the capitol. They are labeled "Northwest," "Northeast," "Southwest," and "Southeast."

GOING GLOBAL

Forty-three different types of stone were used in building the capitol. Six countries and eight states supplied marble and granite selected to decorate the capitol. Stone was imported from the countries of France, Italy, Germany, Norway, Greece and Algeria. Other varieties were obtained from several different states.

DINING IN

During the 1920s, a restaurant known as the Capitol Café was located in the basement of the capitol. As it was also open on evenings and weekends, guests could order a complete Sunday dinner of fried chicken for just $1! Homemade pie was also served. The evenings featured live entertainment including celebrities such as Harry Houdini. The café became so popular that for several years the University of Wisconsin held its prom at the capitol. Finally in 1929, amidst charges of unfair competition, the café closed.

During the summer, Capitol Park is used extensively for activities and various celebrations. Events include the farmer's market, an art fair, summer concerts, and a dairy cow festival known as "Cows on the Concourse."

A 1917 photograph shows the newly completed capitol.

This postcard depicts "Wisconsin's New Capitol" with a gold dome. However, the dome has never been gold.

A plaster of Paris model of the capitol illustrates the four equal wings. It includes a label indicating it is a "Centennial model-1848-1948."

Pearls of Wisdom

"It is a style that won't live, that died, in fact, many years ago. But you can't put that much stone into one pile without creating some dignity and majesty. Anyway, there it is, and we should make the most of it."

Frank Lloyd Wright — 1941

Historical Happenings

1800

1836
Territorial legislature
meets in Belmont

1838
Capital relocates to
Madison

1848
President Polk grants
statehood

1900

1904
Previous capitol
damaged by fire

1914
Wisconsin statue
placed on dome

At the center of the inner dome is the *Resources of Wisconsin*.

The Senate features circular,
stained-glass artwork and
the mural, *The Marriage
of the Atlantic and Pacific*.

Pillars
frame the
Liberty Bell
replica.

Skylights and curved arches
highlight the majestic interior

★ The Inside Story

OVER THE EDGE

When first completed, a tour of the capitol included a trip to the upper reaches of the dome for those not bothered by heights. From a balcony that encircles the inner dome, the ceiling mural can be viewed at close range and is a spectacular sight. However, looking over the edge at the rotunda floor 200' below is also a breathtaking experience. Some people would "freeze up" when peering over the edge and had to be helped down. For safety reasons, the inner dome tour was discontinued in the 1940s.

BADGERS EVERYWHERE

The state animal of Wisconsin is the badger. Designers of the capitol made sure that badger images were plentiful and scattered throughout the capitol. They appear in murals and sculptures, are painted on ceilings, and to top it off, a badger sits on top of the helmet of the statue *Wisconsin* atop the dome.

TWO OCEANS WED

With a host of murals and sculptures located throughout the building, the capitol is a showpiece for many forms of art. On the ceiling of the rotunda dome is a mural entitled the *Resources of Wisconsin*. Painted by Edwin Blashfield, the mural represents the architectural style of the capitol known as Beaux Arts. The Senate chamber features a series of three murals known as *The Marriage of the Atlantic and Pacific*. These three separate paintings, collectively, symbolize the opening of the Panama Canal — with the Orient on the left and Europe on the right.

1917
Capitol
completed

1929
Capitol Cafe in
basement closes

1942
"W" is no longer
placed on dome

1965
Capitol
dedicated

2000

2002
Renovation
completed

★ *Claim to Fame*

ROCK OF AGES

Wisconsin has the only granite dome of the state capitols. The stone is from a granite quarry in Bethel, Vermont now known as the Rock of Ages Quarry.

RED LIGHT, GREEN LIGHT

In 1917, Wisconsin became the first state to install an electric voting system. Each desk in the Assembly was equipped with buttons that light up on a voting board on the wall. The legislator pushes a "no" or a "yes" button. Depending on how the legislator votes, either a red light or a green light appears.

WHAT'S AN ISTHMUS?

Madison is the only capitol located on an isthmus. A term unfamiliar to many people, an isthmus is a neck or stretch of land or cape. The capitol is situated on an isthmus bordered by two large lakes — Lake Mendota to the west and Lake Monona to the east.

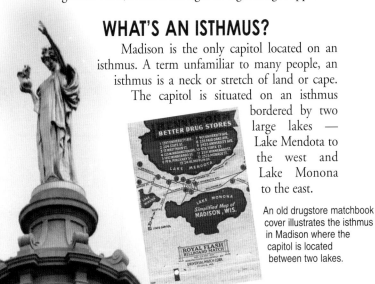

An old drugstore matchbook cover illustrates the isthmus in Madison where the capitol is located between two lakes.

Night or day, the huge granite dome is visible for miles.

★ *For What it's Worth*

GIVE ME A "W"

In 1937, the tradition of placing a lighted "W" sign on the capitol dome during football season began. The twelve by thirteen foot sign contained 250 red lights to spur the University of Wisconsin team on to victory. In 1942, the tradition of placing the "W" ceased.

A LOT OF HOT AIR

In 1933, *The Capital Times*, a Madison newspaper ran a front page story stating "Explosions Blow Dome Off State Capitol." Appearing in the April 1st edition with a picture of the toppled dome, the article described the destruction in great detail. Toward the end of the story, it mentioned the blast may have been caused by "weeks of verbose debate in the senate and assembly chambers...which had sent off excess quantities of hot air." The article ends with "April Fool!"

SUPER BOWL

The much acclaimed artist, Edwin Blashfield was commissioned to paint a mural in the rotunda dome. However, the ceiling in the rotunda was nearly 200 feet above the floor and thus it was difficult to gauge the right proportions. Although this presented a bit of a challenge for Blashfield, his solution was to make a 7-foot wooden bowl with the same curvature as the dome and use it as a model. He then used this model to transfer the mural to the oculus (inner dome surface) — 34 feet in diameter — and proceeded to paint his mural!

WYOMING
Cheyenne

RAILROAD TIES CAPITAL TO CHEYENNE
The route of the railroad and the wealth it generated greatly influenced the location of the capital.

"Equal rights"

⭐ *Facts & Figures*

Architectural style	Renaissance Revival
Architect	David W. Gibbs & Co.
Exterior material	Sandstone
Dome surface	24 carat gold leaf
Building height (to tip of dome)	146'
Construction period	1886-88
Offices	1888-90
Senate and House chambers	1917
First occupied	1888
Capital population (Census 2000)	53,011
Census estimate 2007	55,641
Direction capitol faces	South
Original cost	$131,275

The Past Remembered

THE REPLACEMENTS

Cheyenne was not the only Wyoming town interested in becoming the territorial capital. In 1873, a bill to relocate the capital to Casper was introduced. In order to get the majority to vote in favor of the move, sponsors of the bill crafted a scheme. Members absent at the time were declared as vacant seats. The "vacant seats" were then replaced by stand-ins that supported the move. However, the Governor recognized the ploy and refused to sign the bill. In so doing, Cheyenne was preserved as the capital.

A hand-painted commemorative plate, made in Germany and distributed by Adamsky Jewelry Store, Cheyenne, c. 1930s, reads an "Airplane view...."

RAILROAD TIES

The route of the Union Pacific Railroad ran through Cheyenne. Over the years the railroad became a dominant force in the area. In 1889, a rail contract with the city was a key factor in Cheyenne being chosen as the permanent capital. In addition to the Union Pacific, the lure of cowboy life and the open frontier helped to attract many easterners seeking work as well as an opportunity to own land and start a homestead.

ON THE BORDER

Unlike most states in which the capital is centrally located, Cheyenne is in the southeast corner of the state near the Colorado border. As other regions of Wyoming grew, interest in relocating the capital to Casper, a more central location, continued. However, the town of Cheyenne has prevailed.

CELEBRATING THE FRONTIER

Each July, Cheyenne hosts a celebration which attracts thousands of visitors. Cheyenne Frontier Days™ as it was coined, originated in 1897 and is noted as having the largest outdoor rodeo anywhere. A parade originates at the capitol and continues down Capitol Avenue. Cowboys, cowgirls and others having an appreciation for the "Old West" travel from all over the world to take part in this ten day festival. Festivities include parades, the "Daddy of 'em All" rodeos, pancake breakfasts and concerts.

An 1888 photo shows the capitol prior to the wings being added. (courtesy Wyoming State Archives)

A postcard shows Governor Brooks with Ezra Meeker at the capitol in 1910. Meeker with his covered wagon was about to embark on a trip to retrace the Oregon Trail.

Harvey Spoonhunter, also known as Three Bulls, poses during Cheyenne Frontier Days.™ His tribe, the Northern Arapaho, who now occupy the Wind River Reservation, once claimed Cheyenne as their home.

A postcard, postmarked 1929, shows a crowded street during the annual Frontier Days™ celebration. The sender writes "... stopping over for the Rodeo Show."

This undated postcard reads "Day before Frontier Carnival."

"Wyoming is the first place on God's green earth which could consistently claim to be the land of the Free."

Susan B. Anthony — 1871
(Regarding granting women suffrage
By the Wyoming Territory)

Historical Happenings

1800

1900

1867
First train of Union
Pacific Railroad arrives

1869
Women suffrage
granted in Territory

1888
Capitol
completed

1889
Union Pacific Railroad
contract signed

1890
President Harrison
grants statehood;
wings added

The repetition of the patterned floor and railings often causes a condition known as vertigo.

★ The Inside Story

VERTICAL VERTIGO

Tile floors in the capitol form a repeating, black-and-white marble, checkerboard pattern. Railings and banisters of the upper floors add to this repetitive pattern. The view is so striking from the upper floors that peering off the balcony sometimes causes vertigo — a visual over stimulation resulting in dizziness. An unsuspecting visitor may discover that he is rather disoriented from the view!

A TOUCH OF TIFFANY

Wyoming's capitol, compared to most, has a compact rotunda. Bright blue and green stained glass, surrounded by the state seal in four directions, accent the dome's interior. This hand-made, double-cut stained glass used in the rotunda was imported from England. The ceilings in the House and Senate chambers feature colorful displays of Tiffany stained glass.

NOBODY'S PERFECT

A lone spindle near the top of the cherrywood staircase is upside down. Unless a tour guide brings the spindle to the visitor's attention, it usually goes unnoticed. The staircase was built by Amish craftsmen. It was no accident that the craftsman, who assembled this baluster, endeavored to leave a lasting impression on Wyoming legislators and those who pass by. One spindle was placed upside down to symbolize humanity, reminding all who pass by it that no person or law is perfect.

The upside down spindle.

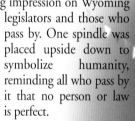

Encircling the stained glass in the dome are paintings of long-horned steers and bison — a Wyoming staple.

The state seal is at the center of this Tiffany, stained-glass ceiling in the House of Representatives.

Stained glass and a Tiffany chandelier decorate the Legislative Conference Room.

1897
First Cheyenne
Frontier Days™

1917
Senate and House
chambers added

1924
Wyoming elects first
female governor in U.S.

1980
Renovation completed

2000

★ *Claim to Fame*

The Esther Morris statue commemorating women's suffrage greets visitors to the capitol.

EQUALITY FOR ALL

Wyoming, known as the "Equality State," claims the distinction of being the first state — and known government — to allow women the right to vote. Near the front entrance is a bronze statue of Esther Morris commemorating her efforts to enact women's suffrage legislation which was approved by the Wyoming Territorial legislature in 1869. Upon achieving statehood in 1890, Wyoming also became the first state to approve women's suffrage legislation.

NO JOKE

Historical records suggest several possible reasons why Wyoming was leading the way in allowing women the right to vote. Across the nation, the women's suffrage movement was gaining momentum so Wyoming was not alone in considering it. Second, there was a very low ratio of women to men in the territory and legislators felt this change would encourage other women to move to the region. A third factor reported in the local newspaper at the time, though denied by many after the fact, was that some legislators passed the bill as a joke, expecting certain veto by the governor. If true, the joke was on them as it was not vetoed!

The Wyoming Cowboy monument features a cowboy with a lariat riding a bucking horse.

★ *For What it's Worth*

PROBLEM "A-DRESSED"

When Wyoming became a state, an official seal was proposed but not adopted. The seal included a picture of a naked woman. Until the next legislature met two years later, the state was without an official seal. The new version of the seal, which was adopted, also included a woman. However, the original complaint had been "a-dressed."

LOCO MOTIVE

Although the Cheyenne Frontier Days™ celebration began in 1897, Cheyenne held a celebration ten years prior to this event. In 1887, during the laying of the capitol cornerstone, a gala event was planned and included people from all over the territory. The Union Pacific route through Cheyenne and across Wyoming made this possible by providing transportation for visitors from across the region. The event included a parade, barbeque and a festive celebration honoring the future capitol.

Fall colors surround the golden dome.

Retired Capitols

"The remembrance of a nation's glory in the past stimulates to national greatness in the future."

National Society of the Colonial Dames of America
(Preamble) 1917

ARIZONA
PRESCOTT
1864-1867

★ Served as Territorial Capitol and
  Governor's Mansion
★ Currently the Governor's Mansion/
  Sharlot Hall Museum

ARKANSAS
LITTLE ROCK
1836-1911

★ Served as Territorial and State Capitol
★ Currently the Old State House Museum

★ Postcard unidentified, postmarked 1909

CALIFORNIA
MONTEREY
1846-1849

★ Served as site of Constitutional Convention
★ Known as Colton Hall
★ Currently a State Historic Site
★ Postmarked 1930
★ Postcard by Detroit Photographic Company,
  postmarked 1906

BENICIA
1853-1854

★ Currently a State Historic Park
★ Restored in 1958

★ Postcard by Frank J. Stumm Publisher

COLORADO
COLORADO CITY
1862

★ Served as a Territorial Capitol for only a few days
★ Currently restored and relocated to Bancroft Park (Colorado Springs)
★ Photo, c. 1905

GOLDEN
1866-1867

★ Served as a Territorial Capitol
★ Known as the Loveland Block
★ Currently a restaurant (Old Capitol Grill) and offices
★ Damaged by fire, November 2005

CONNECTICUT
HARTFORD
1796-1878

★ Served as State Capitol
★ Currently the Old State House Museum and National Historic Site

★ Postcard by The Hartford News Company, postmarked 1914

★ The Connecticut Supreme Court was formerly known as the Supreme Court of Errors and is located in the old capitol

NEW HAVEN
1830-1874

★ Served as State Capitol
★ Razed in 1887
★ Postcard by The Rotograph Co., postmarked 1909

DELAWARE
NEW CASTLE
1732-1777

★ Colonial Assembly and first state assembly met here
★ Currently a state museum known as the New Castle Court House

★ Postcard Dexter Press

DOVER
1792-1933

★ Currently Delaware State House Museum

★ Postcard by C.E. Wheelock & Co.

GEORGIA
MILLEDGEVILLE
1807-1868

★ Currently the main facility at the Georgia Military College
★ Engraving from Frank Leslie's *"The Soldier in Our Civil War,"* 1893

★ Postcard by Culver & Kidd, postmarked 1909

HAWAII
HONOLULU
1882-1969

★ Served as the Capitol of the Republic, Territorial and State Capitol
★ Currently known as Iolani Palace

★ Postcard by The Island Curio Co., c. 1915

IDAHO
BOISE
1886-1912

★ Served as Territorial and State Capitol
★ Razed in 1919

ILLINOIS

KASKASKIA
1818-1820

★ A rented facility
★ From a page in *Guide to Illinois Capitol*, dated 1938
★ Destroyed by encroachment of Mississippi River in 1898

VANDALIA
1837-1839

★ Currently a State Historic Site

SPRINGFIELD
1840-1876

★ Abraham Lincoln practiced law and delivered "House Divided" speech here
★ Dismantled and rebuilt from 1966-1969
★ Currently Old State Capitol Historic Site

INDIANA

VINCENNES
1811-1812

★ Built 1805
★ Rented as capitol of Indiana Territory
★ Known as the "Red House"
★ Building relocated and currently a State Historic Site

★ Postcard by I.M. Ottenheimer

CORYDON
1816-1825

★ Served as Indiana Territorial and State Capitol
★ Currently a State Historic Site

★ Postcard by Souvenir Post Card Mfg. Co., postmarked 1912

INDIANAPOLIS
1835-1877

★ Served as State Capitol
★ Razed in 1877
★ Postcard by Souvenir Post Card Mfg. Co.

First State House, Erected 1836, Indianapolis, Indiana

IOWA
IOWA CITY
1842-1857

★ Served as Territorial and State Capitol
★ Fire destroyed dome and damaged interior in 2001
★ Currently administrative offices for
  The University of Iowa
★ Known as the Old Capitol Museum

★ Postcard by The Acmegraph Co.

KANSAS
PAWNEE (FT. RILEY)
1855

★ Territorial legislature met only for a few days
★ Restored by the Union Pacific Railroad in 1928
★ Currently a State Historic Site and Museum

★ Postcard by R.O. Thomen, postmarked 1909

SHAWNEE INDIAN
MISSION (FAIRWAY)
1855

★ First Territorial legislature met for six weeks
★ Currently a State Historic Site

LECOMPTON
1857-1858

★ Served as Territorial Capitol
★ Currently a State Historic Site
★ Known as Constitution Hall

★ Painting by unknown artist

KENTUCKY
FRANKFORT
1830-1910

★ In 1900, Governor Goebel was assassinated
  in front of building (see postcard)
★ Only capitol captured by Confederate forces (1862)
★ Currently occupied by the Kentucky
  Historical Society

★ Postcard by Ill. Post Card Co., postmarked 1905
★ Handwritten note refers to "spot"(the X) where
  the governor was shot

LOUISIANA
BATON ROUGE
1852-1862; 1882-1932

★ Captured and used by Union Army in 1862
★ Known as the "Old Gray Castle"
★ Reconstructed in 1882
★ Currently the Musuem of Political History

★ Postcard unidentified

MARYLAND
ST. MARY'S CITY
1676-1694

★ Razed in 1829
★ Replica built in 1934
★ From an original drawing
  by Harold Wrenn, Esq. 1674

MASSACHUSETTS
BOSTON
1713-1798

★ Currently the Old State House

★ Postcard unidentified

MINNESOTA
ST. PAUL
1882-1904

★ Sketch from a geology report dated 1882
★ Razed in 1937-38

★ Postcard by V.O. Hammon Pub. Co.

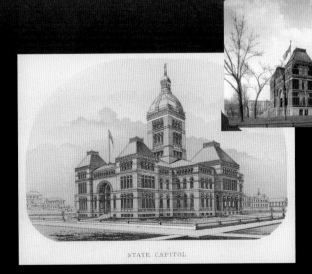

STATE CAPITOL

219

MISSISSIPPI
JACKSON
1839-1903

★ Currently the Old Capitol Museum
★ Restored during the 1950s
★ Suffered major damage from Hurricanes
  Katrina and Rita
★ $14 million restoration completed in late 2008

★ From a book, *The Higher Officials of the United
  States, and Buildings Where All Laws Are Made*
  dated 1893.

MISSOURI
ST. CHARLES
1821-1826

★ Legislature met on second floor of building
  with archways
★ Currently a State Historic Site

JEFFERSON CITY
1840-1911

★ Wings added in 1888
★ Destroyed by fire in 1911
★ Postcard by The South-West
  News Company, postmarked 1908
★ Black and white photo postcard, unidentified

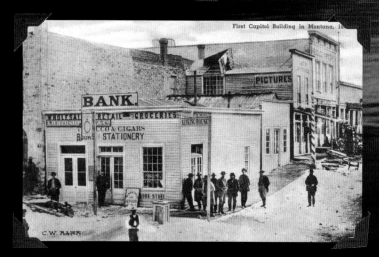

MONTANA
VIRGINIA CITY
1865-1875

★ Served as Territorial Capitol
★ Legislators met on second floor
  of masonry building (left of bank)
★ Currently a National Historic Site known
  as Stonewall Hall

NEBRASKA
LINCOLN
1886-1925

★ Razed to make room for the current
  capitol in 1925
★ Photo postcard c.1910

NEW MEXICO
SANTA FE
1610-1886; 1892-1900

★ Served as Capitol for Kingdom of New Mexico
  and Territorial Capitol
★ Currently a state museum known as
  "The Palace of the Governors"

★ Postcard by Jesse L. Nusbaum, postmarked 1915

1901-1950

★ Served as Territorial and State Capitol
★ Renovated in 1950 and dome removed
★ Currently part of Bataan Memorial Building

★ Postcard unidentified, postmarked 1909

1950-1966

★ Currently the Bataan Memorial Building
★ Postcard by Curteich

NEW YORK
KINGSTON
1777-1806

★ First Senate met here
★ Currently the Senate House State Historic Site
★ Postcard by Weltpostverein, postmarked 1910

ALBANY
1797-1807

★ Razed in 1883
★ Postcard by A. deBlaey, New York
★ Demolished in 1836

1807-1879

★ Razed in 1883
★ Postcard by Albany Historic Post Card Series

NORTH DAKOTA
BISMARCK
1883-1930

★ Territorial and State Capitol
★ Destroyed by fire in 1930
★ Postcard unidentified

★ Photo postcard by Hoskins-Meyer

OHIO
CHILLICOTHE
1802-1809, 1812-1817

★ Razed in 1852
★ Postcard by Scholl Printing Co.,
  postmarked 1928

OKLAHOMA
GUTHRIE
1907-1910

★ Served as Territorial Capitol
★ Currently a county courthouse

★ Postcard unidentified, postmarked 1909

OREGON
SALEM
1876-1935

★ Destroyed by fire in 1935
★ Postcard unidentified

1935

★ Senate met here temporarily due to the capitol fire
★ Known as the Marion Hotel
★ Destroyed by fire in 1971
★ Postcard by Genuine Curteich

PENNSYLVANIA
PHILADELPHIA
1736-1799

★ Served as Colonial Capitol for the Assembly
★ Served as National Capitol for three periods
  from 1775 to 1783
★ Currently Independence Hall

★ Stereocard by American Scenery

HARRISBURG
1821-1897

★ Destroyed by fire in 1897
★ Postcard by Ferriday, postmarked 1908
★ Black and white postcard, unidentified

RHODE ISLAND
NEWPORT
1739-1901

★ Served as Colonial and State Capitol
★ Served as U.S. Capitol for a few days
★ Currently the Newport Colony House and a National Historic Landmark

★ Postcard unidentified

PROVIDENCE
1762-1900 (intermittently)

★ Known as the Old State House
★ Currently the Rhode Island Historical Preservation and Heritage Commission
★ Postcard by The Rotograph Co., postmarked 1906

SOUTH DAKOTA
PIERRE
1890-1910

★ Sold to school district in 1910, then razed
★ Postcard unidentified, postmarked 1906

★ Postcard by C.E. Wheelock & Co, postmarked 1908

TENNESSEE
KNOXVILLE
1796

★ Postcard by Detroit Photographic Co. 1903

TEXAS
COLUMBIA ON THE BRAZOS
1836-1837

★ Served as the Capitol of the Republic of Texas
★ Destroyed in a 1900 storm, razed in 1906
★ Building has been reconstructed
★ Postcard by Freeport Pharmacy

HOUSTON
1837-1839

★ An engraving from a drawing
★ Currently the Old Capitol Hotel

UTAH
FILLMORE
1855

★ Currently the Territorial Statehouse Museum

SALT LAKE CITY
1866-1895

★ Currently the Utah Travel Council and Zion Natural History Association Book store

1896-1916

★ Currently the Salt Lake City and County Building

★ Postcard by C.E. Wheelock & Co, postmarked 1908

VERMONT
BENNINGTON
1770-1777

★ Provisional government met here sporadically
★ Known as Old Catamount Tavern
★ Destroyed by fire in 1871
★ Postcard by Griswold

RUTLAND
1784-1786

★ State legislature met here
★ Razed during the 1900s
★ Postcard by Hugh C. Leighton Co., postmarked 1908

VIRGINIA
WILLIAMSBURG
1705-1747

★ Served as colonial capitol
★ Burned in 1747, rebuilt in the 1930s
★ A similar, second capitol served from 1753 to 1780 and burned in 1832

★ Postcard by the Albertype Co., undated

WASHINGTON
OLYMPIA
1856-1902

★ Served as Territorial and State Capitol
★ Postcard by Fred W. Convery
★ Razed in 1911

1903-1928

★ Served as temporary State Capitol
★ Currently houses Office of Superintendent
   of Public Instruction and known as
   The Old Capitol

★ Postcard unidentified

WEST VIRGINIA
WHEELING
1863-1870

★ Served as Territorial and State Capitol
★ Known as the Linsly Institute Building
★ Page from 1908 West Virginia
   Second Biennial Report of Department
   of Archives and History

1875-1885

★ Postcard by J.C. McCrorey & Co,
   postmarked 1910

CHARLESTON
1885-1921

★ Destroyed by fire in 1921
★ Postcard by Hugh C. Leighton Co

WISCONSIN
BELMONT (LESLIE)
1836

★ Postcard by H. J. Youmans Pub,
   postmarked 1913

MADISON
1869-1904

★ Destroyed by fire in 1904
★ Postcard by Detroit Photographic Co,
   postmarked 1904

★ Black and white postcard, Alberttype Co.

Governors' Mansions

"...for the authorities are God's servants, who give their full time to governing. Give everyone what you owe him: If you owe taxes, pay taxes; if revenue, then revenue; if respect, then respect; if honor, then honor."

Romans 13:6,7
New International Version

In colonial days, the official residence of the chief executive of the colony was often known as a "Governor's Palace." Today, the states commonly refer to them as the "Governors' Mansions." However, some states adopted other names to denote the governor's residence including "Executive Mansion," "Executive Residence," "Governor's House," "Governor's Residence" and "Government House." Five states — Arizona, California, Massachusetts, Rhode Island and Vermont do not currently provide an official residence for their governor. This is always subject to change. Although New Hampshire has a Governor's Mansion, the governor does not reside there. Some states did not build a new house but rather acquired an historic home that may have belonged to distinguished citizens over the years. Some of these homes have retained the name of their former owner or an historic name such as the Blaine House in Maine, Terrace Hill in Iowa and Drumthwacket in New Jersey. Some states, California for example, have retired their executive mansion due to security reasons, location or the need for a more modern residence. The State of California elected to retain ownership of their former governor's mansion but maintain it as an historic site and museum. Ronald Reagan was the last to occupy this mansion. In the pages that follow, the governors' mansions are illustrated with photos and/or older postcards.

NOTE: At press time, Idaho recently acquired a governor's mansion and is in the process of getting the residence ready for occupancy and thus is not shown.

Governor's

ALABAMA

★ Built: 1907
★ Governor's Mansion since 1950

ALASKA

★ Built: 1912

ARKANSAS

★ Built: 1950
★ Featured in TV series

COLORADO

★ Built: 1908
★ Governor's Mansion since 1959

CALIFORNIA

★ Built: 1877
★ Governor's Mansion from 1903-67

side view

Mansions

CONNECTICUT

★ Built: 1909
★ Governor's Mansion since 1945

DELAWARE

★ Built: 1790
★ Governor's Mansion since 1966
★ Known as Woodburn

FLORIDA

★ Built: 1957
★ Postcard by Scenic South Card Co.

Governor's Mansion

HAWAII

★ Built: 1846
★ Governor's Mansion since 1922
★ Known as Washington Place
★ Postcard by The Island Curio Company

GEORGIA

★ Built: 1968

Governors'

ILLINOIS
★ Built: 1855

★ Postcard by State Register HDQTRS, 1906

INDIANA
★ Built: 1928
★ Governor's Mansion since 1975

IOWA
★ Built: 1869
★ Governor's Mansion since 1976
★ Known as Terrace Hill

KENTUCKY
★ Built: 1914
★ Known as the Executive Mansion
★ Postcard by W.M. Cline Co.

KANSAS
★ Built: 1928
★ Governor's Mansion since 1962
★ Known as Cedar Crest

Mansions

LOUISIANA

★ Built: 1963

MARYLAND

★ Built: 1870
★ Known as The Government House

Augusta, Maine. The Blaine Mansion. Pub. by COMFORT, Augusta, Maine, the big magazine at 10 cents a year.

MAINE

★ Built: 1833
★ Governor's Mansion since 1919
★ Known as The Blaine House

★ Postcard by W.H. Gannett, postmarked 1907

MINNESOTA

★ Built: 1912
★ Governor Mansion since 1965

MICHIGAN

★ Built: 1902
★ Governor's Mansion since 1945
★ Summer residence on Mackinac Island

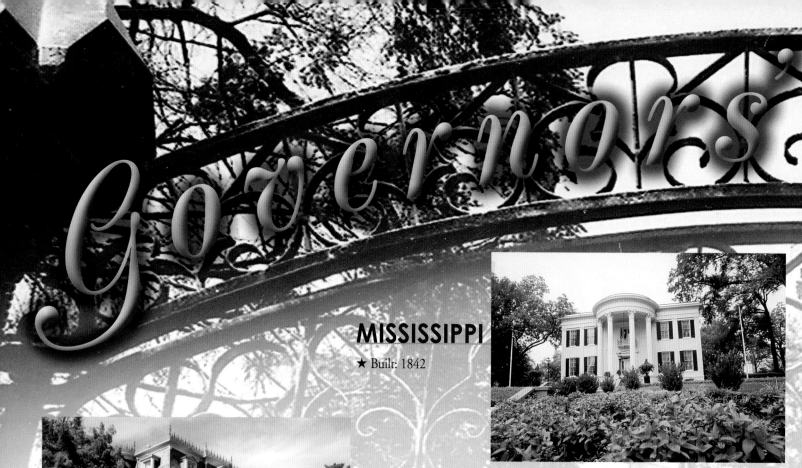

Governors'

MISSISSIPPI
★ Built: 1842

MONTANA
★ Built: 1959

MISSOURI
★ Built: 1871

NEBRASKA
★ Built: 1957

NEVADA
★ Built: 1909
★ Postcard by unidentified publisher

Mansions

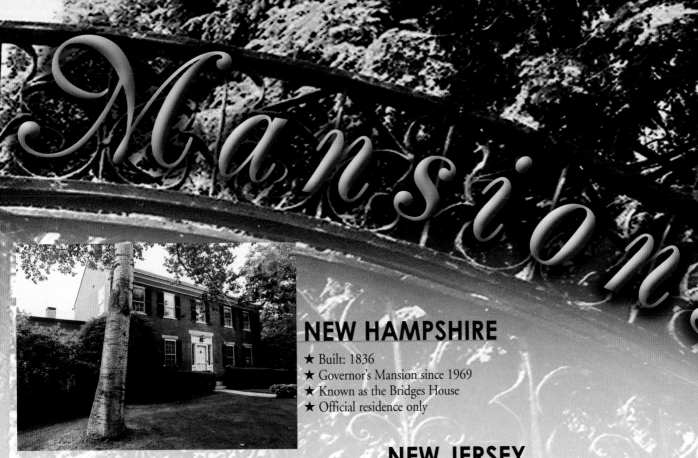

NEW HAMPSHIRE

★ Built: 1836
★ Governor's Mansion since 1969
★ Known as the Bridges House
★ Official residence only

NEW JERSEY

★ Built: 1835
★ Governor's Mansion since 1982
★ aka Drumthwacket
★ Located in Princeton

NEW MEXICO

★ Built: 1955

NEW YORK

★ Built: 1856
★ Governor's Mansion since 1875

★ Postcard by Hugh C. Leighton Co.,
   Postmarked 1906

NORTH CAROLINA

★ Built: 1891
★ Postcard by C.T. American Art Colored,
   Postmarked 1936

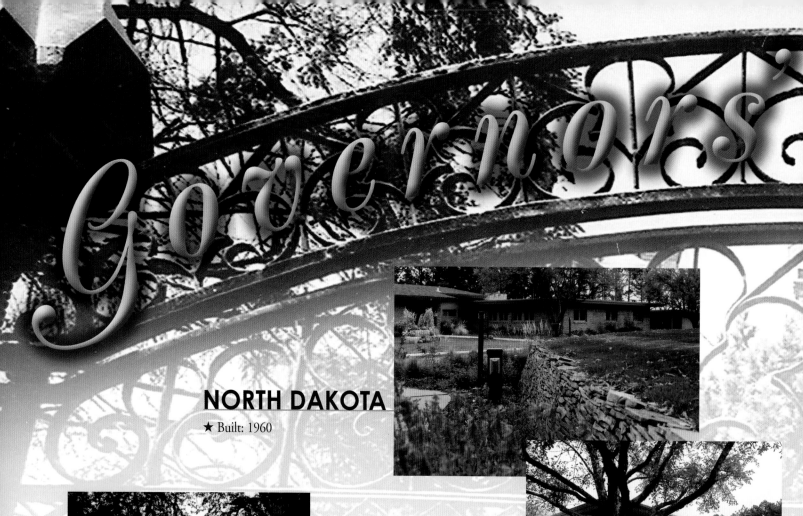

Governors'

NORTH DAKOTA

★ Built: 1960

OHIO

★ Built: 1925
★ Governor's Mansion since 1957
★ Located in Bexley

OKLAHOMA

★ Built: 1928

★ Postcard by Dexter Press

OREGON

★ Built: 1924
★ Governor's Mansion since 1988
★ Known as Mahonia Hall

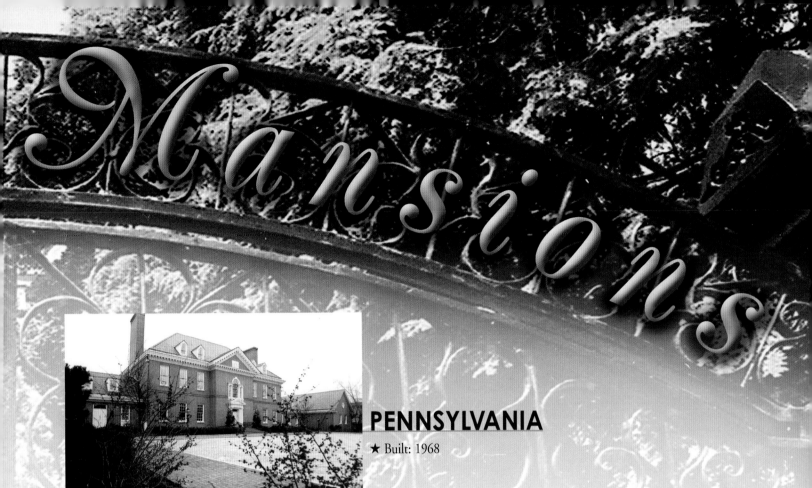

Mansions

PENNSYLVANIA

★ Built: 1968

View from back

SOUTH DAKOTA

★ Built: 1937

★ Postcard by F.J. Freytag

SOUTH CAROLINA

★ Built: 1855
★ Governor's Mansion since 1868

★ Postcard by Rotograph Co., Postmarked 1907

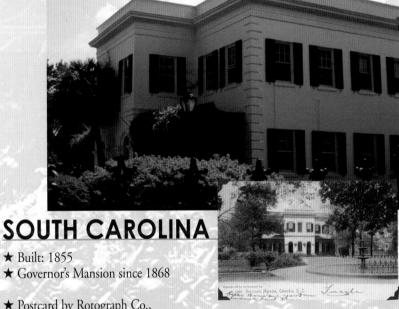

TENNESSEE

★ Built: 1929
★ Governor's Mansion since 1949
★ Known as Far Hills
★ Photo by State of Tennessee Photo Services

TEXAS

★ Built: 1856
★ Fire causes major damage,
  June 8, 2008

★ Postcard by Natural
  Color Postcard

UTAH

★ Built: 1902
★ Governor's Mansion
  1937-57;1980-Present

VIRGINIA

★ Built: 1813

★ Postcard by unknown
  publisher, Postmarked
  1911

Mansions

WASHINGTON
★ Built: 1908

★ Postcard c. 1910 Winstanley
  & Blankenship

WEST VIRGINIA
★ Built: 1925

WISCONSIN
★ Built: 1927
★ Governor's Mansion since 1949

WYOMING
★ Built: 1976

Capitol Domes

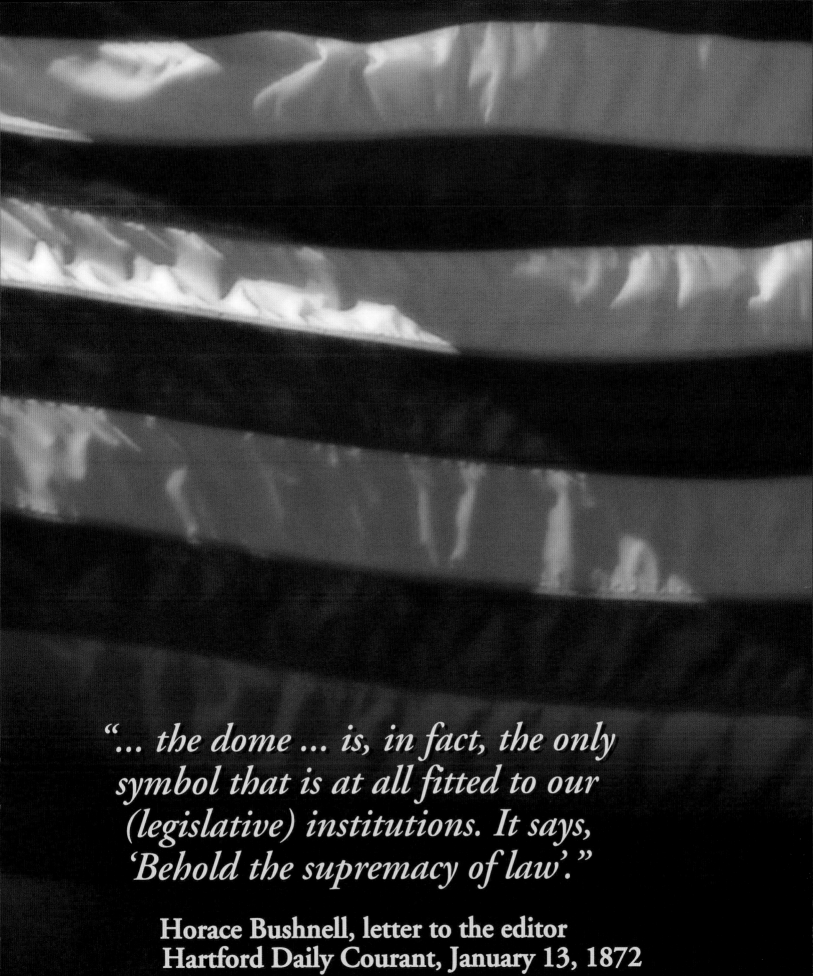

"... the dome ... is, in fact, the only symbol that is at all fitted to our (legislative) institutions. It says, 'Behold the supremacy of law'."

Horace Bushnell, letter to the editor
Hartford Daily Courant, January 13, 1872

ALABAMA

ARIZONA

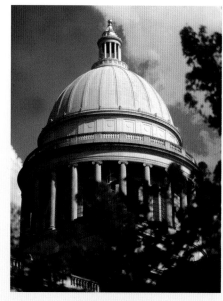

ARKANSAS

CALIFORNIA

COLORADO

CONNECTICUT

DELAWARE

FLORIDA

GEORGIA

HAWAII (OPEN DOME)

IDAHO

ILLINOIS

INDIANA

IOWA

KANSAS

KENTUCKY

LOUISIANA

MAINE

MARYLAND

MASSACHUSETTS

MICHIGAN

MINNESOTA

MISSISSIPPI

MISSOURI

MONTANA

NEBRASKA

NEVADA

NEW HAMPSHIRE

NEW JERSEY

NORTH CAROLINA

OHIO

OKLAHOMA

OREGON

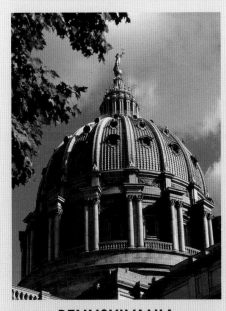

PENNSYLVANIA

RHODE ISLAND

SOUTH CAROLINA

SOUTH DAKOTA

TENNESSEE

TEXAS

UTAH

VERMONT

WASHINGTON

WEST VIRGINIA

WISCONSIN

WYOMING

Multi-Domes

IOWA

NEVADA

RHODE ISLAND

"I often think that the night is more alive and more richly colored than the day."

Vincent van Gogh

Colorado

Nebraska

Iowa

Michigan

Mississippi

Minnesota

North Dakota

South Dakota

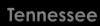
Tennessee

Texas

Utah

Washington

2002 Oklahoma Dome Celebration

251

Capitol Improvements

"*Look not mournfully into the past, it comes not back again. Wisely improve the present, it is thine. Go forth to meet the shadowy future, without fear and with a manly heart.*"

Henry Wadsworth Longfellow

Over the years, architects, building commissions and artisans have sought to perpetuate the capitols that eventually do wear down. Some capitols have stood the test of time better than others due to the choice of materials or a location that has a more forgiving climate. But one thing is inevitable; they all eventually succumb to the elements and/or become technologically obsolete.

Whether the building was completed in 1819, such as the New Hampshire capitol or whether it was completed in 1966, as the New Mexico capitol, there comes a time when the capitol is in need of renovation. This may involve the physical plant, facing materials, floors and walls or even murals may need refurbishing. No matter if built with brick and mortar or sandstone, whether the dome is made of wood or steel, the weather and the elements will eventually take its toll and repairs are inevitable. Whether the dome is gilded with gold or whether covered with tile, "weather and moth will corrupt."

Restoring a capitol can be rather costly. Work performed ranges from cleaning and painting to sandblasting the stone or in some cases, it may require that the building be "gutted" leaving primarily a shell. In many situations, it may cost more to restore a capitol than the cost of original construction. At a minimum, a restoration requires that a capitol be sectioned off for a few months and on some occasions, it may be closed to the public for more than a year. For example, the State of Texas undertook a major restoration, which included an annex connected by a tunnel and the addition of underground parking. Legislators were given a choice of completely shutting down the capitol and setting up temporary offices in nearby buildings versus keeping the building open which would require construction crews to work around the business of government. To close the building, the project could be completed in less than two years. The additional time for contractors to work around the ongoing business of state would have extended the project completion date many more years. The decision was made to close the building and, as a result, they were able to move back into the capitol much sooner.

SIDEWALK CLOSED

CONNECTICUT - 1981

IOWA - 1997

CAUTION CAUTION

ILLINOIS - 2000

Gold leaf fallen to the floor.

MISSOURI - 2000

Gold stenciling in the process of being reapplied.

MONTANA - 2000

255

NEBRASKA - 2001

NEW JERSEY - 1998

NEW MEXICO - 1991

NORTH CAROLINA - 1991

256

PENNSYLVANIA - 1998

UTAH - 2002

WYOMING - 1988

257

Liberty Bells

Let Freedom Ring

The original Liberty Bell, shown here, is on display near Independence Hall in Philadelphia. In 1950, 54 Liberty Bell replicas were cast in France and one was given to each state and territory as part of a savings bond campaign. As shown here, most states have chosen to display their bell at their capitol.

"Yes there's a lady that stands in a harbor for what we believe.
And there's a bell that still echoes the price that it cost to be free."
Aaron Tippin — "Where the Stars And Stripes And Eagles Fly"

ALASKA

ARIZONA

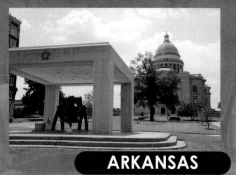

ARKANSAS

COLORADO

DELAWARE

IDAHO

IOWA

MINNESOTA

MISSOURI

NEW HAMPSHIRE

OREGON

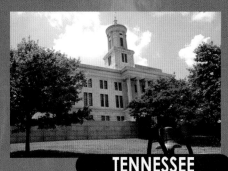

TENNESSEE

UTAH

WISCONSIN

WYOMING

PHYSICAL FEATURES

State	Principal Exterior Material	Height of Dome/ Building	Gold Dome	No Exterior Dome	Sculpture Atop Dome	Name of Sculpture	Architectural Style
AL	brick covered with stucco	120'					Greek Revival
AK	brick and limestone	97'		X			Modern
AZ - old¹	Tufa stone, granite, Malapai rock	92'			X	Winged Victory	Neo-classical
- new	pre-cast concrete panels	136'		X			High-rise
AR	Batesville limestone & Arkansas granite	213'					Neo-classical
CA	granite with plaster on brick	242'					Renaissance Revival
CO	gray granite	272'	X				Corinthian
CT	New England marble & granite	257'	X		X	6 Aspects of Humanity	High Victorian Gothic
DE	handmade bricks	125'					Georgian
FL - old¹	stucco over brick	161'					Greek Revival
- new	concrete	307'		X			New Classicism
GA	Indiana limestone	271'	X		X	Miss Freedom	Classical Renaissance
HI	concrete	100'		X			Modern
ID	sandstone & Vermont granite	208'			X	Eagle	Neoclassical
IL	Bedford limestone & granite	361'					Neo-classical with French influence
IN	Indiana limestone	235'					Renaissance Revival
IA	granite, limestone & sandstone	275'	X				Neo-classical & Palladian
KS	Kansas limestone	306'			X	Ad Astra	French Renaissance (predominantly)
KY	Indiana limestone	212'					Beaux Arts
LA	Alabama limestone	450'					Art Deco
ME	Hallowell white granite	185'			X	Wisdom	Classical Revival
MD	red brick	179'					Georgian
MA	red brick	155'	X		X	Pine Cone	Neo-classical Federal
MI	Ohio sandstone & Illinois limestone	267'					Renaissance Revival
MN	Georgia marble & gray granite	223'			X	The Progress of the State	Italian Renaissance
MS	Georgia granite & Bedford limestone	180'			X	Eagle	Beaux Arts
MO	Carthage & Phenix marble	262'			X	Ceres	Roman Renaissance
MT	Columbus sandstone & Montana granite	165'			X	Montana	American Renaissance
NE	Indiana limestone	400'	X		X	The Sower	Art Deco
NV	sandstone	120'					Italianate/Neo-classical
NH	Concord granite	150'	X		X	"Peace" Eagle	Eclectic
NJ	Indiana limestone	145'	X				Eclectic
NM	stucco	60'		X			Pueblo Indian Adobe
NY	Maine gray granite	221'		X			Eclectic²
NC	gneiss	98'			X	Anthemion Crown	Greek Revival
ND	Indiana limestone	242'		X			Art Deco
OH	brick & Columbus limestone	158'					Greek Revival
OK	Indiana limestone	243'			X	The Guardian	Greco-Roman
OR	Vermont white marble	168'			X	Oregon Pioneer	Modern Greek
PA	Vermont granite	272'			X	Commonwealth	Beaux Arts
RI	white Georgia marble	235'			X	The Independent Man	Neo-classical
SC	granite	164'					Roman Corinthian
SD	granite, sandstone & limestone	165'					Greek Ionic
TN	limestone (cut stone)	207'					Greek Ionic
TX	Texas sunset red granite	303'			X	Goddess of Liberty	Renaissance Revival
UT	Utah granite	286'					Classical Corinthian
VT	Barre granite	135'	X		X	Agriculture	Renaissance Revival
VA	stucco over handmade brick	82'		X			Neo-classical
WA	Granite & Wilkeson sandstone	287'					Greek & Roman
WV	Indiana limestone	292'	X		X	Eagle	Italian Renaissance
WI	White Vermont granite	285'			X	Wisconsin	Beaux Arts
WY	sandstone	146'	X				Renaissance Revival

¹ Although Arizona and Florida now have high rise capitols, the old capitols which are still on the grounds are included for comparative purposes.
² Romanesque, Gothic, Italian Renaissance and French Renaissance

State	Architects	Unique Features
AL	Daniel Pratt	Twin spiral staircases, clock
AK	James A. Wetmore w/U.S. Treasury Dept.	Only accessible by sea or by air
AZ - old	James R. Gordon	Copper dome, cactus garden
- new	Varney, Sexton, Sydnor & Assoc.	
AR	George R. Mann/Cass Gilbert	Tiffany bronze doors, gold leaf on cupola finial
CA	R. Clark, G. Cummings & A. Bennett	40 acre site w/park, mosaic tile
CO	Elijah E. Myers	Rose onyx, one mile high
CT	Richard M. Upjohn	12 statues on dome, castle appearance
DE	E. William Martin	Colonial architecture
FL - old	Cary Butt & Frank Milburn	Red and white striped awnings
- new	Edward Stone	
GA	Edbrooke and Burnham	Largest gold dome in U.S.
HI	Belt, Lemmon & Lo & Warnecke & Associates	Open dome, reflecting pools
ID	J.E. Tourtellotte & Chas. Hummel (remodel)	Geothermally heated
IL	John Cochrane & Alfred Piquenard	Tallest domed capitol
IN	Edwin May & Adolph Scherrer	Octagonal interior dome
IA	John Cochrane & Alfred Piquenard	Gold dome plus four copper domes
KS	E. Townsend Mix & John G. Haskell	Cage-type elevator in use
KY	Frank M. Andrews	Floral clock, nave
LA	Seiferth, Weiss and Dreyfous	Tallest capitol, Huey Long assassination
ME	Charles Bulfinch/G. Henri Desmond	Dome rebuilt
MD	Joseph H. Anderson	Oldest capitol in continuous legislative use, largest and oldest wooden dome
MA	Charles Bulfinch	Bulfinch dome
MI	Elijah E. Myers	Elongated dome, glass floor
MN	Cass Gilbert	Charioteer on dome
MS	Theodore C. Link	4750 interior lights
MO	Swartwout & Tracy	Thomas Hart Benton murals
MT	Charles Bell, John Kent, Frank Andrews, Charles Haire, John Link	Charles Russell mural
NE	Bertram G. Goodhue	Unicameral legislature, tower with a gold dome, Nebraskan Indian doors
NV	Joseph Gosling	Multi-domes painted silver
NH	Stuart J. Park	Largest legislature and longest to continually meet in original chambers
NJ	Jonathan Doane (original only)	Multiple additions and architectural styles
NM	W.C. Kruger	Circular building
NY	Thomas Fuller, Henry H. Richardson[3]	Million Dollar staircase, stone carvings
NC	Ithiel Town, Alexander Jackson Davis & David Paton	Crown atop dome, cantilevered rotunda gallery, all interiors are original
ND	Holabird & Root	19 story building, monkey wood
OH	Henry Walters, Nathan Kelly, William West & Is. Rogers	Burgee flag, drum in lieu of dome
OK	Wemyss Smith & S.A. Layton	Oil wells on grounds, 2002 dome addition
OR	Francis Keally	Tower with 15' gold statue
PA	Joseph M. Huston	Green tiled dome
RI	McKim, Mead & White	Original charter by King Charles II
SC	Major John Niernsee	Cannon shell marks from Civil War (General Sherman's Army)
SD	C.E. Bell & M.S. Detweiler	Marble floor with blue signature tiles
TN	William Strickland	Tower type of dome
TX	Elijah E. Myers	Texas stars throughout the capitol
UT	Richard K.A. Kletting	Matching marble staircases, Mormon murals, Gold Room
VT	Thomas Silloway & Joseph Richards	Ethan Allen statue, "D" shaped House of Representatives
VA	Thomas Jefferson with Charles Louis Clérisseau	George Washington statue
WA	Wilder & White	Sunken Garden, has withstood several earthquakes, Roman firepots
WV	Cass Gilbert	Byzantine gold dome
WI	George B. Post & Sons	Latin cross, largest dome by volume, only granite dome, located on isthmus
WY	David W. Gibbs & Co.	Vertigo sensation, upside down spindle

[3] For New York, other architects include Leopold Eidlitz, Isaac Perry, Frederick L. Olmsted

TOUR INFORMATION

State	Capitol	Direction Capitol Faces	Gift Shop in Capitol	Chapel	Guided Tours	Weekend Hours	Nickname/aka
AL	Montgomery	west	X		X	X	Goat Hill
AK	Juneau	south			summer		
AZ -old	Phoenix	east	X		X		
-new		west					Executive Tower
AR	Little Rock	east	X		X	X	
CA	Sacramento	west			X	X	Capitol Hill/The Heart of California
CO	Denver	west			X		Mile High capitol
CT	Hartford	north			X	X	
DE	Dover	west			X		Legislative Hall
FL -old	Tallahassee	east	X		X	X	Capitol Center
-new		west	X	X	X	X	
GA	Atlanta	west			X		
HI	Honolulu	northeast		X	X	X	
ID	Boise	south	X		X		
IL	Springfield	east		X	X	X	State House
IN	Indianapolis	south		X	X		
IA	Des Moines	west			X	X	
KS	Topeka	north	X		X	X	Capitol Square
KY	Frankfort	north	X	X	X	X	
LA	Baton Rouge	south	X	X	X	X	River capitol
ME	Augusta	east			X		
MD	Annapolis	east			X	X	State House
MA	Boston	south	X		X		Bulfinch State House
MI	Lansing	east			X		Capitol Square
MN	St. Paul	south			X	X	
MS	Jackson	south			X		New Capitol
MO	Jefferson City	south			X	X	
MT	Helena	north			summer		
NE	Lincoln	north	X		X	X	Tower on the Plains
NV	Carson City	west	X[1]		X[2]	X	
NH	Concord	east	X		X[2]		State House Park
NJ	Trenton	north			X	X	State House
NM	Santa Fe	east			X	X	Roundhouse
NY	Albany	east			X	X	Capitol Hill
NC	Raleigh	east			X	X	Union Square
ND	Bismarck	south			X	summer	Capitol Park
OH	Columbus	west	X		X	X	Capitol Square
OK	Oklahoma City	south	Kiosk		X	X	
OR	Salem	north	X		X	X	Capitol Mall
PA	Harrisburg	west			X	X	Capitol Hill
RI	Providence	south	X		X		Capitol Hill
SC	Columbia	north	X		X	X	State House
SD	Pierre	south			X	X	
TN	Nashville	east			X	X	Capitol Hill
TX	Austin	south	X		X	X	
UT	Salt Lake City	south	X		X	X	Capitol Hill
VT	Montpelier	south	X		X	X	State House
VA	Richmond	south	X		X	X	Capitol Square
WA	Olympia	north	X		X	X	Capitol Group/Legislative Building
WV	Charleston	south			X	X	
WI	Madison	southeast			X	X	Capitol Park
WY	Cheyenne	south			X		

[1] Located in legislative building
[2] By reservation only

NOTE: Tours and weekend availability are subject to change from time to time and thus it is advisable to check with the capitol.

of July 1. ...esult of an official state census taken in 1925 is indicated by *. For states which s... ...in population between 1910 and 1920, the popula...1920 is given; thess...

FACTS AND FIGURES

State	Capital	Completed Year	After 1920	Years to Finish	Original Cost	Population (Census Estimate 2007)	Previous State Capital Locations	Most Recent Building Restoration
AL	Montgomery	1851		2	$64,000	204,086	Cahawba, Tuscaloosa	1985-1992
AK	Juneau	1931	X	3	1,000,000	30,690	none	1984
AZ -old	Phoenix	1900		2	135,774	1,552,259	none	1998-2002
-new	Exec Tower	1974	X	2	18,250,221	1,552,259		
AR	Little Rock	1915		16	2,205,779	187,452	different site in city	2002-2003
CA	Sacramento	1874		14	2,972,925	460,242	San Jose, Vallejo	1975-1982
CO	Denver	1908		22	2,704,900	588,349	Colorado City, Golden	
CT	Hartford	1879		7	2,532,524	124,563	New Haven and Old State House	1979-1989
DE	Dover	1933	X	2	749,306	35,811	different site in city	1994
FL -old	Tallahassee	1845		6	55,000		same site	1982
-new		1977	X	4	43,070,700	168,979		
GA	Atlanta	1889		5	999,882	519,145	five other towns	2000
HI	Honolulu	1969	X	4	24,576,900	375,571	none	1991-1995
ID	Boise	1920		15	2,098,955	202,832	none	
IL	Springfield	1888		20	4,315,591	117,090	Kaskaskia, Vandalia & different site	2007
IN	Indianapolis	1888		10	1,980,969	795,458	Corydon, Vincennes	1988
IA	Des Moines	1886		15	2,873,295	196,998	Iowa City	1986-2001
KS	Topeka	1903		37	3,200,589	122,642	none	1998-2010
KY	Frankfort	1910		5	1,820,000	27,098	different site	c. 1955, 1980
LA	Baton Rouge	1932	X	1	5,000,000	227,071	different site in city & New Orleans	1998
ME	Augusta	1832		3	138,991	18,367	Portland	1994-1998
MD	Annapolis	1779		7	£7,500	36,603	none	2009
MA	Boston	1798		4	133,333	599,351	different site in city	2000-2002
MI	Lansing	1878		6	1,427,739	114,947	different sites in city	1989-1992
MN	St. Paul	1905		9	4,500,000	277,251	different sites in city	1999
MS	Jackson	1903		2	1,093,641	175,710	different sites in city	1979-1982
MO	Jefferson City	1918		5	4,044,153	40,564	St. Louis, St. Charles	2001
MT	Helena	1902		4	540,000	28,726	none	1999-2001
NE	Lincoln	1932		10	9,800,440	248,744	same location	1999-2007
NV	Carson City	1871		1	169,831	54,939	none	1977-1981
NH	Concord	1819		3	82,000	42,392	Portsmouth	1975
NJ	Trenton	1792		2	£4,242	82,804	several locations	1985-
NM	Santa Fe	1966	X	2	4,676,860	73,199	same site	1992
NY	Albany	1899		32	25,000,000	94,172	Kingston and Albany	1978-
NC	Raleigh	1840		7	532,682	375,806	same location	1990-2000
ND	Bismarck	1934	X	2	1,977,000	59,503	same location	minor only
OH	Columbus	1861		22	1,359,121	747,755	Chillicothe, Zanesville	1996
OK	Oklahoma City	1917		3	1,515,000	547,274	Guthrie	2002
OR	Salem	1938	X	3	2,500,000	151,913	same site	1977
PA	Harrisburg	1906		5	13,000,000	47,196	Philadelphia, Lancaster	
RI	Providence	1904		9	3,018,416	172,459	different site in city and Newport	
SC	Columbia	1907		52	3,540,000	124,818	Charleston	1995-1998
SD	Pierre	1910		5	951,000	14,032	none	1989
TN	Nashville	1859		15	879,981	590,807	Knoxville, Kingston and Murfreesboro	1984-1988
TX	Austin	1888		6	3,744,631	743,074	none	1991-1995
UT	Salt Lake City	1916		4	2,739,528	180,651	different sites in city	2004-2008
VT	Montpelier	1859		2	150,000	7,806	none	1981-2000
VA	Richmond	1798		13	140,000	200,123	Williamsburg	2004-2007
WA	Olympia	1928	X	6	7,385,168	44,925	six different buildings in Olympia	2000-2004
WV	Charleston	1932	X	8	9,491,180	50,478	site in Charleston and Wheeling	1995
WI	Madison	1917		11	7,203,826	228,775	same site	1988-2002
WY	Cheyenne	1888		4	$131,275	55,641	none	1971-1980

Capitol Charts (5)

YEARS TO COMPLETE

State	Capital	Construction Period (Rounded)
LA	Baton Rouge	1
NV	Carson City	1
AL	Montgomery	2
AZ	Phoenix (new)	2
DE	Dover	2
MS	Jackson	2
NJ	Trenton	2
NM	Santa Fe	2
ND	Bismarck	2
VT	Montpelier	2
AK	Juneau	3
AZ	Phoenix (old)	3
ME	Augusta	3
NH	Concord	3
OK	Oklahoma City	3
OR	Salem	3
FL	Tallahassee (new)	4
HI	Honolulu	4
MA	Boston	4
MT	Helena	4
UT	Salt Lake City	4
WY	Cheyenne	4
SD	Pierre	5
GA	Atlanta	5
KY	Frankfort	5
MO	Jefferson City	5
PA	Harrisburg	5
FL	Tallahassee (old)	6
MI	Lansing	6
TX	Austin	6
WA	Olympia	6
CT	Hartford	7
MY	Annapolis	7
NC	Raleigh	7
WV	Charleston	8
MN	St. Paul	9
RI	Providence	9
IN	Indianapolis	10
NE	Lincoln	10
WI	Madison	11
VA	Richmond	13
CA	Sacramento	14
ID	Boise	15
IA	Des Moines	15
TN	Nashville	15
AR	Little Rock	16
IL	Springfield	20
CO	Denver	22
OH	Columbus	22
NY	Albany	32
KS	Topeka	37
SC	Columbia	52

YEAR COMPLETED

State	Capital	Year Completed	
MD	Annapolis	1779	
NJ	Trenton	1792	
MA	Boston	1798	
VA	Richmond	1798	<1800
NH	Concord	1819	
ME	Augusta	1832	
NC	Raleigh	1840	
FL	Tallahassee (old)	1845	
AL	Montgomery	1851	
TN	Nashville	1859	
VT	Montpelier	1859	
OH	Columbus	1861	
NV	Carson City	1871	
CA	Sacramento	1874	
MI	Lansing	1878	
CT	Hartford	1879	
IA	Des Moines	1886	<1880
IL	Springfield	1888	
TX	Austin	1888	
WY	Cheyenne	1888	
IN	Indianapolis	1888	
GA	Atlanta	1889	
NY	Albany	1899	
AZ	Phoenix (old)	1901	<1900
MT	Helena	1902	
KS	Topeka	1903	
MS	Jackson	1903	
RI	Providence	1904	
MN	St. Paul	1905	
PA	Harrisburg	1906	
SC	Columbia	1907	
CO	Denver	1908	
KY	Frankfort	1909	
SD	Pierre	1910	<1910
AR	Little Rock	1915	
UT	Salt Lake City	1916	
OK	Oklahoma City	1917	
WI	Madison	1917	
MO	Jefferson City	1918	
ID	Boise	1920	
WA	Olympia	1928	<1925
AK	Juneau	1931	
LA	Baton Rouge	1932	
NE	Lincoln	1932	
WV	Charleston	1932	
DE	Dover	1933	
ND	Bismarck	1934	
OR	Salem	1938	
NM	Santa Fe	1966	<1950
HI	Honolulu	1969	
AZ	Phoenix (new)	1974	
FL	Tallahassee (new)	1977	

CAPITAL POPULATION

State	Capital	Census 2000	Census Estimate 2007
AL	Montgomery	201,568	204,086
AK	Juneau	30,711	30,690
AZ	Phoenix	1,321,045	1,552,259
AR	Little Rock	183,133	187,452
CA	Sacramento	407,018	460,242
CO	Denver	554,636	588,349
CT	Hartford	121,578	124,563
DE	Dover	32,135	35,811
FL	Tallahassee	150,624	168,979
GA	Atlanta	416,474	519,145
HI	Honolulu	371,657	375,571
ID	Boise	185,787	202,832
IL	Springfield	111,454	117,090
IN	Indianapolis	781,870	795,458
IA	Des Moines	198,682	196,998
KS	Topeka	122,377	122,642
KY	Frankfort	27,741	27,098
LA	Baton Rouge	227,818	227,071
ME	Augusta	18,560	18,367
MD	Annapolis	35,838	36,603
MA	Boston	589,141	599,351
MI	Lansing	119,128	114,947
MN	St. Paul	287,151	277,251
MS	Jackson	184,256	175,710
MO	Jefferson City	39,636	40,564
MT	Helena	25,780	28,726
NE	Lincoln	225,581	248,744
NV	Carson City	52,457	54,939
NH	Concord	40,687	42,392
NJ	Trenton	85,403	82,804
NM	Santa Fe	62,203	73,199
NY	Albany	95,658	94,172
NC	Raleigh	276,093	375,806
ND	Bismarck	55,532	59,503
OH	Columbus	711,470	747,755
OK	Oklahoma City	506,132	547,274
OR	Salem	136,924	151,913
PA	Harrisburg	48,950	47,196
RI	Providence	173,618	172,459
SC	Columbia	116,278	124,818
SD	Pierre	13,876	14,032
TN	Nashville	545,524	590,807
TX	Austin	656,562	743,074
UT	Salt Lake City	181,743	180,651
VT	Montpelier	8,035	7,806
VA	Richmond	197,790	200,123
WA	Olympia	42,514	44,925
WV	Charleston	53,421	50,478
WI	Madison	208,054	228,775
WY	Cheyenne	53,011	55,641

ORIGINAL COST

State	Capital	Orignal Cost (Rounded)
NJ	Trenton	£4,200
MY	Annapolis	£7,500
FL	Tallahassee (old)	$55,000
AL	Montgomery	64,000
NH	Concord	82,000
WY	Cheyenne	131,300
MA	Boston	133,300
AZ	Phoenix (old)	135,800
ME	Augusta	139,000
VA	Richmond	140,000
VT	Montpelier	150,000
NV	Carson City	169,800
NC	Raleigh	532,700
MT	Helena	540,000
DE	Dover	749,000
TN	Nashville	880,000
GA	Atlanta	1,000,000
AK	Juneau	1,000,000
SD	Pierre	1,000,000
MS	Jackson	1,093,600
OH	Columbus	1,359,100
MI	Lansing	1,427,739
OK	Oklahoma City	1,515,000
KY	Frankfort	1,820,000
ND	Bismarck	1,977,000
IN	Indianapolis	1,981,000
ID	Boise	2,098,500
AR	Little Rock	2,205,800
OR	Salem	2,500,000
CT	Hartford	2,532,500
CO	Denver	2,704,900
UT	Salt Lake City	2,739,500
IA	Des Moines	2,874,000
CA	Sacramento	2,972,900
RI	Providence	3,018,400
KS	Topeka	3,200,600
SC	Columbia	3,540,000
TX	Austin	3,744,600
MO	Jefferson City	4,044,200
IL	Springfield	4,315,600
MN	St. Paul	4,500,000
NM	Santa Fe	4,676,900
LA	Baton Rouge	5,000,000
WI	Madison	7,203,800
WA	Olympia	7,385,800
WV	Charleston	9,491,200
NE	Lincoln	9,800,400
PA	Harrisburg	13,000,000
AZ	Phoenix (new)	18,250,200
HI	Honolulu	24,576,900
NY	Albany	25,000,000
FL	Tallahassee (new)	43,070,700

Capitol Trivia

1. What is the difference between capitol and capital?

2. Which four capitals are home to major league baseball?

3. Which is the only state that has never had a foreign flag fly over it?

4. Which is the only state with a flag that has a shape other than rectangular?

5. Which capital was named after a former Kansas governor?

6. Which state capitol also served as the nation's capitol for a period of time?

7. Which state located its capital in fourteen different cities after becoming a state?

8. Which current capitol was the first constructed?

9. Which state capital is the oldest known seat of government of the state capitals?

10. Which capital does not have a McDonalds?

11. Which capital has the largest population?
    A. Phoenix
    B. Atlanta
    C. Boston
    D. Denver

12. Which capital has the smallest population?
    A. Juneau, AK
    B. Pierre, SD
    C. Montpelier, VT
    D. Helena, MT

13. Which capital has a beer that shares its name?

14. Which capitol is the tallest?

15. Which capitol has the tallest dome?

16. Which capitol has the most people buried on its grounds and/or entombed in the building?

17. How many capitols have gilded domes?

18. How many capitols do not have exterior domes?

19. How many states do not have governors' mansions? Name them.

20. How many states are known as "commonwealths" instead of states? Name them.

21. Which state was the first to have an official state cookie?

22. How did "two oceans wed" in the eyes of the artist in the Wisconsin capitol?

23. Which capitols do not have any steps leading to their front entrance?

24. Why does the Arkansas flag have a diamond in it?

25. Name three major sporting events that take place at capitals in the spring?

26. Which previous capitol had its dome removed but retained the building for its capitol?

27. Which capitol is surrounded by water?

28. Which state paid for its capitol in a trade for land?

29. Which two capitals have the shortest distance between them?

30. Which capitals are named after presidents?

31. Which architect designed the most capitols and how many did he design?

32. Which capital has the highest elevation?
    A. Denver
    B. Boise
    C. Helena
    D. Santa Fe

Answers

1. A capitol refers to the building in which the business of government is conducted. A capital refers to the city in which government is located.
2. Four; Atlanta, Boston, Denver and Phoenix
3. Idaho
4. Ohio
5. Denver
6. Annapolis, 1783-84
7. Vermont
8. Annapolis, 1772
9. Santa Fe
10. Montpelier
11. Phoenix
12. Montpelier
13. Olympia
14. Baton Rouge
15. Springfield
16. Nashville (4 people)
17. Eleven: Colorado, Connecticut, Georgia, Iowa, Massachusetts, Nebraska, New Hampshire, New Jersey, Vermont, West Virginia, Wyoming
18. Seven: Alaska, Hawaii, Louisiana, New Mexico, New York, North Dakota, and Virginia (Nine if you only count current capitols. Arizona and Florida have high-rise capitols but also maintain their historic capitols as museums on the grounds)
19. Five: Arizona, California, Massachusetts, Rhode Island and Vermont — Idaho acquired a governor's mansion in 2004 and was preparing it for occupancy.
20. Four: Massachusetts, Kentucky, Virginia and Pennsylvania.
21. New Mexico
22. Three side-by-side paintings depict the opening of the Panama Canal. They symbolize "The marriage of the Atlantic and the Pacific."
23. Arizona (both the Capitol Museum and the Executive Tower do not have steps) and Hawaii.
24. Arkansas is the only diamond producing state in the U.S.
25. The Indy 500, Boston Marathon and Atlanta 500
26. Santa Fe in 1950
27. Honolulu
28. Texas
29. Boston and Providence are less than 50 miles apart
30. Lincoln, Madison and Jefferson City.
31. Elijah Myers designed four: Colorado, Michigan, Texas and the former Idaho capitol.
32. Santa Fe at 7199'.

Key to Domes

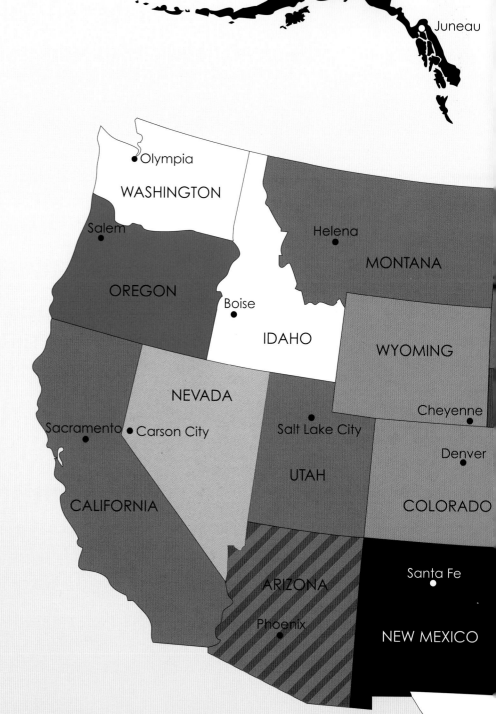

ALASKA

Juneau

Olympia
WASHINGTON

Salem

Helena

MONTANA

OREGON

Boise

IDAHO

WYOMING

Cheyenne

NEVADA

Sacramento • Carson City

Salt Lake City

Denver

UTAH

CALIFORNIA

COLORADO

Santa Fe

ARIZONA

Phoenix

NEW MEXICO

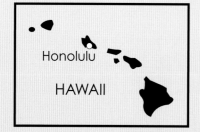

Honolulu

HAWAII

Note: The current and historic capitols for Arizona and Florida are portrayed.

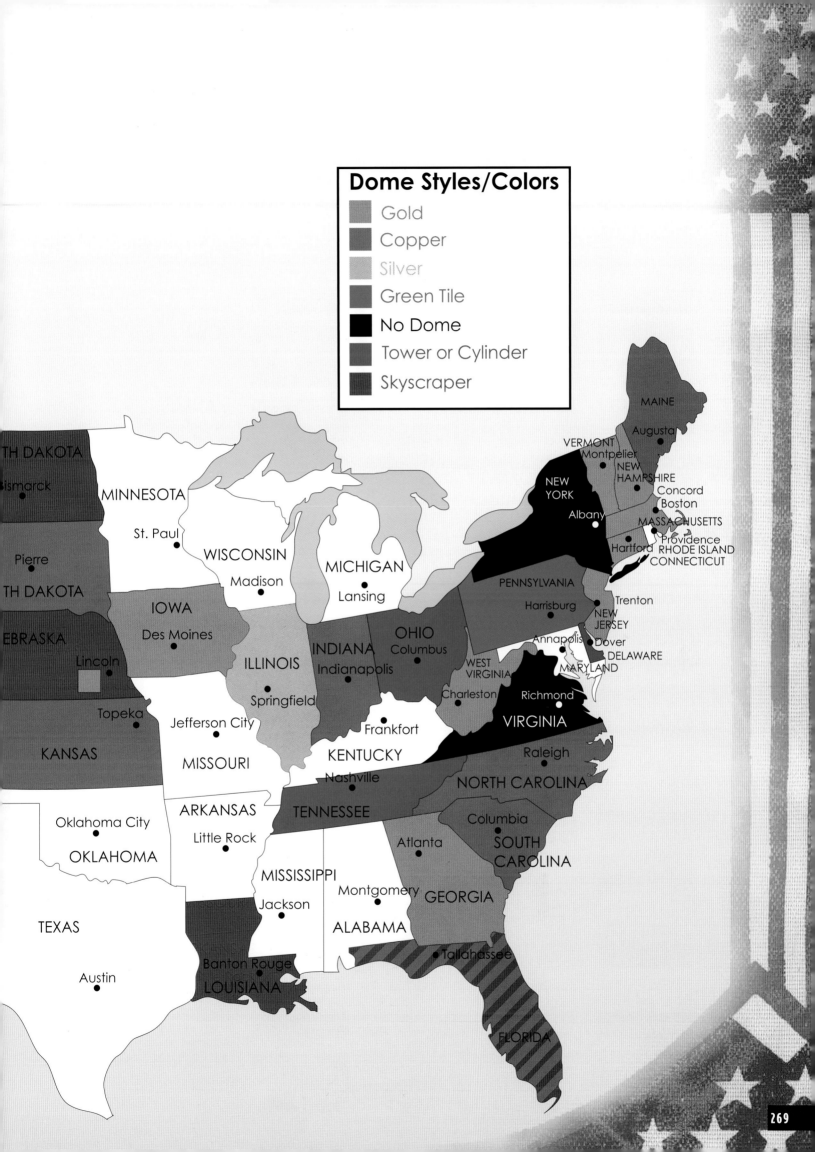

Dome Styles/Colors

- Gold
- Copper
- Silver
- Green Tile
- No Dome
- Tower or Cylinder
- Skyscraper

MAINE

Augusta

VERMONT
Montpelier
NEW
HAMPSHIRE

NEW
YORK
Concord
Boston

Albany
MASSACHUSETTS

Providence
Hartford RHODE ISLAND
CONNECTICUT

PENNSYLVANIA

Trenton
Harrisburg
NEW
JERSEY

Annapolis Dover
WEST
VIRGINIA DELAWARE
Charleston MARYLAND

Richmond

VIRGINIA

TH DAKOTA
Bismarck

MINNESOTA

St. Paul

WISCONSIN

MICHIGAN

Lansing

Pierre

TH DAKOTA

IOWA

Des Moines

OHIO
Columbus

EBRASKA

Lincoln

ILLINOIS

INDIANA

Indianapolis

Springfield

Topeka

Jefferson City

Frankfort

KANSAS

MISSOURI

KENTUCKY

Raleigh

Nashville

NORTH CAROLINA

ARKANSAS

TENNESSEE

Oklahoma City

Little Rock

Columbia

OKLAHOMA

Atlanta

SOUTH
CAROLINA

MISSISSIPPI

Montgomery GEORGIA

TEXAS

Jackson

ALABAMA

Banton Rouge

Tallahassee

Austin

LOUISIANA

FLORIDA

Capitol Checklist

ALABAMA
Montgomery

Date:___/___/_____

ALASKA
Juneau

Date:___/___/_____

ARIZONA
Phoenix

Date:___/___/_____

ARKANSAS
Little Rock

Date:___/___/_____

CALIFORNIA
Sacramento

Date:___/___/_____

COLORADO
Denver

Date:___/___/_____

CONNECTICUT
Hartford

Date:___/___/_____

DELAWARE
Dover

Date:___/___/_____

FLORIDA
Tallahassee

Date:___/___/_____

GEORGIA
Atlanta

Date:___/___/_____

HAWAII
Honolulu

Date:___/___/_____

IDAHO
Boise

Date:___/___/_____

ILLINOIS
Springfield

Date:___/___/_____

INDIANA
Indianapolis

Date:___/___/_____

IOWA
Des Moines

Date:___/___/_____

KANSAS
Topeka

Date:___/___/_____

KENTUCKY
Frankfort

Date:___/___/_____

LOUISIANA
Baton Rouge

Date:___/___/_____

MAINE
Augusta

Date:___/___/_____

MARYLAND
Annapolis

Date:___/___/_____

MASSACHUSETTS
Boston

Date:___/___/_____

MICHIGAN
Lansing

Date:___/___/_____

MINNESOTA
St. Paul

Date:___/___/_____

MISSISSIPPI
Jackson

Date:___/___/_____

MISSOURI
Jefferson City

Date:___/___/_____

Capitol Checklist

MONTANA
Helena

Date:___/___/_____

NEBRASKA
Lincoln

Date:___/___/_____

NEVADA
Carson City

Date:___/___/_____

NEW HAMPSHIRE
Concord

Date:___/___/_____

NEW JERSEY
Trenton

Date:___/___/_____

NEW MEXICO
Santa Fe

Date:___/___/_____

NEW YORK
Albany

Date:___/___/_____

NORTH CAROLINA
Raleigh

Date:___/___/_____

NORTH DAKOTA
Bismarck

Date:___/___/_____

OHIO
Columbus

Date:___/___/_____

OKLAHOMA
Oklahoma City

Date:___/___/_____

OREGON
Salem

Date:___/___/_____

PENNSYLVANIA
Harrisburg

Date:___/___/_____

RHODE ISLAND
Providence

Date:___/___/_____

SOUTH CAROLINA
Columbia

Date:___/___/_____

SOUTH DAKOTA
Pierre

Date:___/___/_____

TENNESSEE
Nashville

Date:___/___/_____

TEXAS
Austin

Date:___/___/_____

UTAH
Salt Lake City

Date:___/___/_____

VERMONT
Montpelier

Date:___/___/_____

VIRGINIA
Richmond

Date:___/___/_____

WASHINGTON
Olympia

Date:___/___/_____

WEST VIRGINIA
Charleston

Date:___/___/_____

WISCONSIN
Madison

Date:___/___/_____

WYOMING
Cheyenne